Successful
Biotech Investing

Successful
Biotech Investing

Every Investor's
Complete Guide

JOE DUARTE, M.D.

PRIMA MONEY
A Division of Prima Publishing
3000 Lava Ridge Court • Roseville, California 95661
(800) 632-8676 • www.primalifestyles.com

Library of Congress Cataloging-in-Publication Data

Duarte, Joe.
    Successful biotech investing : every investor's complete guide / Joe Duarte.
        p.   cm.
    Includes index.
    ISBN 0-7615-3301-X
    1. Biotechnology industries—Finance. 2. Investments. 3. Stocks. I. Title.
HD9999.B442 D8 2001
332.63'22—dc21   2001021319

01 02 03 04 05 06 HH 10 9 8 7 6 5 4 3 2 1
Printed in the United States of America

How to Order

Single copies may be ordered from Prima Publishing, 3000 Lava Ridge Court, Roseville, CA 95661; telephone (800) 632-8676. Quantity discounts are also available. On your letterhead, include information concerning the intended use of the books and the number of copies you wish to purchase.

Visit us online at www.primalifestyles.com

Contents

1

The Dawn of a New Era

This book is designed to teach investors how to think when they analyze the barrage of information about the latest drugs that are meant to save mankind. It is designed to teach you the road to winning stock picks but also to be able to know when not to believe the hype. And it is designed to provide a balanced, systematic, lifelong philosophy about investing in any sector, for many of the techniques presented here are easily adaptable. But perhaps the intangible bonus of the information contained here is the message of hope that this technology can help bring about.

Biotechnology, in a global sense, may provide humanity with multiple ways to correct errors in its own genetic code. Lives may be saved, and diseases may be prevented and even eradicated. Thus, the dawn of a new era has risen where it is suddenly plausible to expect that errors and frailty in human heredity, at least in the context of diseases both caused by genetic defect and environmentally transmitted, may be little more than an occasional inconvenience. The human race is on the verge of an unprecedented era, with both wonderful and daunting prospects. While life may be prolonged indefinitely and disease and suffering may be significantly decreased, the choices of who lives and who dies and the criteria used for making those ultimate decisions are beginning to creep into the subconscious minds of independent thinkers.

Again biotechnology may come to the rescue, as improved methods of producing foods and fuels and cleaning up the environment may emerge to balance the potential problems of overcrowding and increased life spans.

Despite today's easily available information on the Internet and through constant media scrutiny, the amount and complexity of data is often beyond the capacity of the average investor to understand. Usually, this is not because of a lack of intellect but more because of the pressures of day-to-day living that have increased with the advent of new technologies. These new technologies have increased productivity but have also increased the workday and shortened deadlines. Thus the average individual spends more time doing more work and less time taking care of daily living, even though more is often getting accomplished from a business standpoint.

It is the basic premise of this book that this paradigm of increased productivity but less time in which to enjoy it has created a vacuum of useful information available in an easy-to-learn and easy-to-follow format for investors. In my prior book, *After-Hours Trading Made Easy,* a great deal of effort was spent listing, synthesizing, and condensing information so that an individual with limited time could have access to that information and make rapid use of it profitably. It is on this basic principle that this book is built, making the often difficult-to-understand principles of science easier to interpret and apply to investing.

Like all philosophies that are of any subsequent use, the methods discussed here will be equipped with the ability to evolve as the game changes since the ability to build on previously learned concepts is central to success in investing. Thus, to paraphrase the Bible, the goal of this book is to teach you to fish instead of giving you a fish to eat. In a world where technology is advancing faster than the ability of the population and the government to keep up, a manual such as this is more than a bedside table adornment. It is a survival guide.

In the introduction to *Visions,* physicist Michio Kaku discusses the three pillars of science: matter, life, and the mind. He continues by describing the splitting of the atom, the decoding of the nucleus of the cell, and the development of computers as the crowning achievements of the 20th century. Thus, humanity is indeed at a crossroads in its history, for now that we have developed the tools and have obtained a great deal of knowledge, the task of the next generation, and the next obvious step, is the implementation phase, or the use of technology for the improvement of conditions on the planet, whether curing disease, producing food, or cleaning up the environment.

On the one hand, the decoding of the human genome, the Internet, and the continuous progression toward smaller microchips that can do more computations per second can lead only to an explosion in technology. Thus, the increasing pressures on governments to provide entitlements such as health care for the elderly and free medical care for the indigent and to foster the development of the telecommunications infrastructure have led to an impressive set of dynamics that have in and of themselves led to a rapid increase in the development of new technologies, with the built-in and potentially conflicting expectations of high profit and low cost.

Although Dr. Kaku's vision of the future—one with which more and more people are becoming familiar and one in which the potential for good and evil is often at odds—is not necessarily the same vision being espoused by scientists, the potential for endeavors, light and dark, can be found in the rapid dissemination of knowledge. The unscrupulous use of information is one of the oldest professions in the world. One of the central themes of *Visions* is that in the occasional review by the mainstream media of what the future holds, very few scientists are ever consulted. Instead, the opinions of journalists, politicians, and other non-science scholars are sought.

While there is merit to Dr. Kaku's argument, much of the blame is in the hands of the science community, which fails to communicate the message of beauty, which is what science is all about. For example, the perfect symmetry of a DNA molecule is usually described in abstract terms, such as "double helix." This is a very elegant description that is also highly accurate. However, to the casual observer, who happens to be someone whose basic being is encoded in DNA, this word often puts a glazed look in one's eyes. My point is that science is much too often shrouded in mysterious and highly descriptive scientific terms that often are cumbersome to the general public.

A perfect example is a television show that used to air on public television: *Bill Nye: The Science Guy*. This was a great attempt at simplifying science for children. Unfortunately, as often happens with science, the ratings were low, and the show was replaced with something much softer with an even simpler message, but one not likely to help anyone understand the world around them.

Therefore, my goal is to make this book as balanced and as easy to understand for a nonscientific audience as possible. By blending scientific fact with trained observation, I'll describe key science concepts as they apply to biotechnology, with the final purpose of teaching you how to apply the concepts to making money by owning biotechnology stocks.

The real purpose of this book is to bring stock picking and science together. As a physician and an investment adviser and financial journalist, I have brought the two disciplines together in my columns and my managed accounts. Now, through this book, my goal is to do the same for as many people as possible, as scientists and financiers have too long cloaked themselves in jargon and esoterica. Although such jargon is important in scientific circles, the public often suffers since much of the "high brow" tone of the discussion leads to glazed eyes. But few authors tackle the central problem of dogma: the deciphering of it.

As I grow older and look around me, I have learned that no matter how the scientific community feels, life and science fiction are blurring. History repeats itself, and those who fail to acknowledge that basic fact and learn to use it to predict, plan, and profit from the future are doomed to repeat the mistakes of the past.

Humanity is on the verge of a true liberation—from political oppression, from the shackles of censorship, and eventually from the gravity of the planet Earth, as space exploration continues to move ahead. Thus change is inevitable in life and in science— the paradox that the more things change, the more they stay the same, is the constant conceptual companion of the inevitability of change. Investors who fail to grasp the key concepts of what I believe will be the major investment theme of the next 20 years will be left behind. It is in that same vein that I can comfortably say that biotechnology will be a guiding light in the next 20 years and that this book will contribute in its own way to that progress by providing information and guidance to investors who wish to profit from the tidal wave of discovery and implementation that is about to be unleashed. I say this because, although China and South America still have dictatorships, oppression and tyranny are finished, and a new era of progress has dawned, even as some of the old villains remain in power, cowering about their prospects.

By the same token, and as I'll discuss in detail in a later chapter, power is continually being transferred from the hands of governments to the hands of the people and, more important from an investor's standpoint, to the hands of central banks. A poignant example is a quote in a news interview from the person who makes the inaugural ball gowns worn by First Ladies of the United States.

As the 2000 U.S. presidential election was being contested in the new American fashion of blow-by-blow news coverage, this hard-working craftswoman was asked for her thoughts on the subject. Her answer was remarkable, and I paraphrase: "This will all blow over. We'll have a president. And not much will change, as long as that guy that works the money is all right." Of course "that guy" is Alan Greenspan, the chairman of the Federal Reserve.

It is crucial to understand the subtle rhythm of the dance between central banks and markets, for a disturbance in that relationship can lead to a disturbance in the flow of money to research companies, especially those in biotechnology, which are solely dependent on outside capital for many years as they develop products. Once again citing the importance of the Federal Reserve during the 2000 election drama, the markets continued to fall after the Fed made it clear that it would not get involved in the political drama. Even the markets were holding out hopes that the Fed would lower interest rates in order to prevent market volatility, as it did in 1998 during the Asian crisis. Knowledge is indeed power, and power that is balanced by wisdom can be the key to success in both life and investing.

As I mentioned earlier, science and science fiction are increasingly close cousins. A recent news release touted scientists who have created a robot that can repair itself and create other robots that are better than itself at performing their tasks. We note that in *2001: A Space Odyssey*, a self-aware computer, Hal, was a little bit too human, and its agenda was not always the same as the crew's. Scientists continue to clone animals and have received the approval from the British government to clone human embryos, a practice that was deplored a few years earlier when it was successfully attempted in the United States, although the embryos were allowed to live for only a few days. Australian scientists are taking a page out of *Jurassic Park* by attempting to clone a Tasmanian tiger, extinct since 1936, whose DNA has been found. Diseases such as multiple sclerosis and Parkinson's disease are commonly alleviated with biotechnologically derived medications, and bacteria can be tricked into producing human hormones, such as insulin, which is used to treat diabetes.

The dark side is the vision of biotechnology explored in the movie *Blade Runner*, where Harrison Ford plays a futuristic policeman whose job is to hunt "replicants," or biotechnologically derived human beings bred by large corporations to perform hard labor usually impossible for nonreplicants. True *Blade Runner* fans know that in the director's cut, the hero turns out to be a replicant himself.

I don't want to come off as someone who focuses on the negative but rather as a bringer of balance. Too many authors present an unbalanced picture of a topic in order to sell books. This is a serious business, and it would be irresponsible to produce a work of this magnitude without making sure that you are aware of the potential risk involved in investing in a single sector of industry. This book is not intended to be a rote exercise in memorizing stock charts or fundamental analysis. Instead, it is designed to incorporate chart, market, and fundamental analyses of stocks to a field that is evolving so rapidly that you must become familiar, at least in a conversational sense, with seemingly remote terminology, such as protein synthesis and monoclonal antibodies.

When we look at biotechnology, we must examine the science and the response to that science. Scientists will search for truth and often see the beauty of the discovery without fully exploring the consequences of their actions. Governments, politicians, and entrepreneurs will err on the side of profit and control. Investors must learn to analyze the three sides in order to make the right decisions. Thus, the three contingencies—science, government, and entrepreneurs—which at face value may seem to be at odds, in reality work toward a common goal: that of producing things that help humanity, meet stringent regulations for the common good of society, and make a lot of money for investors. The interplay among the three contingencies raises the bar for companies to produce better goods faster, more efficiently, and more affordably.

Political agendas will greatly influence the process. A perfect example occurred in March 2000, when U.S. President Bill Clinton and British Prime Minister Tony Blair caused a biotechnology stock minipanic by suggesting that research performed in the private sector that had been funded by government money and led to the unraveling of the human genome should be part of the public domain and not a for-profit property.

The biotechnology sector had been in a very bullish advance and was ripe for a fall. Thus, Clinton and Blair likely accelerated a set of events that would have happened on their own. However, when issues of this magnitude become increasingly debated, there are many external forces that will cause short- and intermediate-term trend swings.

Yet, even as President Clinton and Prime Minister Blair caused a short-term problem, the biotechnology sector rebounded and reached new highs by the late summer of 2000. This is the dynamic that we will explore: how an industry group finally achieves critical mass and hits the sweet spot that will lead investors to the potential of the promised land.

The interaction among science, government, and entrepreneurs doesn't always work well, as is evident with managed care, where the government mandated the creation of health maintenance organizations (HMOs) to deliver privately funded health care to a larger percentage of the population. In principle, it was a beautiful concept. The government would save money since there would be fewer people on welfare and Medicare, the doctors could build a large practice and improve their earnings with the increased volume and guaranteed income and incentives, the patients would always receive excellent care at a lower cost, and the insurers would derive large profits from increased participation of the population in health care coverage.

The truth has been diametrically the opposite. No one has liked managed care. Insurers have closed plans, especially for the elderly; doctors are quitting their practices because they can't stand the scrutiny and the slow payments of the system; the government wants to impose more control on the health care system; and patients have had less access to medical care in many cases.

This is the reason why this book goes to great lengths to look at both sides of the issues. I am personally aware of how the managed care situation developed and resulted in an unfortunate outcome for all parties involved. Where I think biotechnology differs is that while medical care is an important aspect of most people's lives, it is not as appealing a subject as that of living until they are a century and a half old and in good health. That is the promise of biotechnology and why learning to analyze this sector in detail is important to those who want to profit from it.

Another reason why biotechnology is a different issue than managed care is that while patients and physicians are poorly organized and have no really effective lobby in Washington, the pharmaceutical and biotechnology companies are well represented and well funded. Thus, while physicians may have had a difficult time shaping the outcome of the managed care debate, biotechnology companies, on their own (or, more likely, with the aid of their powerful allies, the drug companies), are in a much better position to lobby lawmakers effectively. This is not a suggestion of illegal or unethical practices. Physicians are a highly individual group of people in largely underfunded and nonmilitant organizations. Drug companies have a constant presence in Washington and are well funded and well versed in how to get things done.

A perfect example of effective lobbying was the turnaround in the remarks made by President Clinton and Prime Minister Blair. A few weeks after the two world leaders uttered their ill-timed and ill-thought-out remarks, both cautiously and almost nonchalantly retraced their steps carefully. This came as a combination of public and private lobbying, as a backlash from the investment community, which has become an indirect lobby for the everyday person, whose retirement plans depend on the performance of the markets. Thus, in this case, the investor is the big winner since the checks and balances built in to the political system are in better working order in this setting.

When one places these dynamics in the context of a planet that has increasing wealth disparity, dwindling natural resources, and a rising population, only one conclusion can be reached: We are headed for the stars. It isn't just a natural progression; it's a natural necessity if humanity is to survive, for we are running out of room and resources on this planet. Biotechnology is a key component of interplanetary expansion, as animals, bacteria, and even cloned humans and perhaps cyborg beings that will combine both biological and mechanical parts can be programmed into performing tasks by the manipulation of the basic building block of life, DNA. Thus, despite all the money that technology has produced for investors, the biggest gains appear to still lie ahead, as the exploration of space provides a nearly limitless potential for the application and development of new technologies.

Humanity has the potential to discover the secret to immortality, and once the train leaves the station, there will be no stopping it. The repercussions will infinitely reach the lives of all living organisms on the face of the earth and on other worlds that we may visit and attempt to conquer.

The prolongation of life through technically enhanced methods, both mechanical and biological, are within a decade of reaching their maximal initial growth phase. By the year 2010, the first mission to Mars may have been launched and completed, and the world as we know it will never be the same again. Those investors who learn to analyze the patterns that lead to winning investment decisions will have the potential for great financial gains.

I do not want to be misunderstood here or be mistaken for a huckster. My educated opinion is that the biotechnology sector will be the most profitable of all in the first decade of the 21st century. But this prediction is not infallible, and it is subject to revision. This is also not a disclaimer, and it is not a hedge. History has shown that even brilliant thinkers, certainly with greater intellect and insight than myself, have been wrong or at least partially wrong.

I base my assumptions on the fact that the potential for real products with real impact and real earnings has increased logarithmically for the biotechnology industry as a result of the unraveling of the human genome. It is a similar dynamic to that experienced in the early 1980s, when companies like Intel developed microprocessors that allowed computers to perform increasing numbers of highly complex operations at a higher rate of speed. Thus, it makes sense that if we now have the key to new drug developments and cures for diseases, companies that can execute their business strategies will be highly profitable. But predictions and analysis must be carefully dissected and scrutinized.

A perfect example of how analyzing a prediction carefully can yield better understanding than just taking something at face value comes from looking at the work of Dr. Ravi Batra, a professor of economics at Southern Methodist University. Dr. Batra's most famous work, *The Great Depression of 1990,* was mauled by critics when his prediction apparently didn't come true. After all, the United States did not collapse under the weight of huge budget deficits and the increasing disparity in wealth, which are Batra's main arguments for the collapse of societies.

But careful scrutiny proves that he was correct in predicting a depression, and he was correct in more than one instance. His mistake was in assuming that the depression would occur in America. Instead, the depression hit Japan and lasted until 1999 by most accounts. His analysis was also correct in a previous work, *The Downfall of Capitalism and Communism,* where Dr. Batra predicted that the two major ideologies in the world would falter. In this case, he was half right, as Communism has been nearly eradicated from the earth.

My point is that biotechnology is the wave of the future. The road may not be smooth all the time. The quest for immortality may not be in our lifetime. But the quest for the profits that the revolution is spawning and how you can take part in this begins today.

What Is Biotechnology?

There are many complex definitions of biotechnology, but an all-encompassing one is that biotechnology is the integrated use of biochemistry, microbiology, molecular biology, and engineering to study, isolate, and mass-produce, if possible, compounds that can then be used to alter the world around us. I will add here that biotechnology involves taking every bit of science ever learned and then applying it to life's problems. It is as if Biology 101 were given a turbo engine and turned loose.

Biotechnology includes the disciplines of genetics, biochemistry, chemistry, microbiology, electronics, biochemical engineering, chemical engineering, mechanical engineering, food technology engineering, and food science. While most of the concepts in these disciplines seem difficult to interpret for the average person, I would like to demystify some of the science early in this book in order to get you in the right frame of mind. Biotechnology is as simple as making beer, and the making of alcoholic beverages is the most common use of biotechnology, followed by cheese manufacturing and the production of antibiotics. The first man-made biotechnological process may have come as early as 6000 B.C., when the Sumerians and the Babylonians made beer. Thus, despite the complexities of the modern arena, the origins of the science are quite humble. The big change came when the concept of sterility, or the manufacturing of products in a germ-free environment, was introduced and the biotechnological sciences were turned onto the world of medicine. When penicillin was discovered and successfully used as an antibiotic, the world of biotechnology changed dramatically and has never stopped.

The spectrum of biotechnology products and their uses is equally broad and involves both diagnostic and therapeutic uses in medicine. But more interesting, and receiving less recognition, is the use of biotechnological processes in agriculture, food, environment, and chemical intermediates. An often overlooked aspect of biotechnology is the effect that the need to find answers has had on the development of scientific equipment.

Thus, biotechnology is a part of all our lives in more ways than we could imagine. Everything, from the water we drink to the bread we eat to the clothes we wear, has been either influenced by or directly produced as a result of a biotechnological process.

The History of Biotechnology

Despite humanity's long-term involvement with the science, biotechnology truly began when the first bubble closed around amino acids and primitive sugars in the first world that was ever created. But the most widely accepted beginning of biotechnology, as we know it in our world, has been credited to Herbert Moyer of the University of California, San Francisco, in 1977. Dr. Moyer constructed a synthetic version of the human insulin gene and inserted it into a bacterium, and the chase began. Soon thereafter, the grand dame of biotechnology companies, Genentech (NYSE:DNA), programmed bacteria into producing human growth hormone inhibiting factor, a protein known as somatostatin.

The government immediately saw the need to get involved, so 16 bills were introduced in Congress to prevent the development of microorganisms that could escape the laboratory. None passed.

In 1978, once again Genentech and the City of Hope Medical Center produced human insulin by using recombinant DNA technology. Yes, here is your first real opportunity to glaze your eyes. The word "recombinant DNA" is nearly guaranteed to get non-science types to turn the sound off the TV or close the book.

But don't let the language turn you off here. This is all really important stuff. If you don't have even a single idea as to what recombinant DNA means, you won't understand the explanations of monoclonal antibodies or proteomics or the information from which decisions that will mean the difference between big money or big losses will be made.

It's not that difficult a concept. Recombinant DNA just means that DNA from two different species is put together into one single piece of DNA and placed into an organism with the hope that the organism can be tricked into producing something that we can use. I like to think of recombinant DNA as similar to putting cream in coffee. You take something dark and bitter and add something light, rich, and creamy to make it taste better. Recombinant DNA is a similar concept: taking two parts of different organisms and having them compromise to make something useful.

The gene for human insulin was successfully placed into bacteria, which then were able to produce the hormone, and diabetics have had it better ever since. This was a crucial development from which was spawned the now common interaction, cooperation, and business relationships between traditional pharmaceutical companies and biotechnology companies. As we progress in this book, we will note that the distinction between the two continues to blur and likely will disappear within the next 10 to 20 years as biotechnology replaces most other methods of drug discovery.

In 1979, John Braxten cloned the gene for human growth hormone. This advance led to improvements and increased interest in the controversial branch of biotechnology.

By 1980, the battle between industry, science, and entrepreneurs had reached the U.S. Supreme Court. A landmark decision was handed down that allowed for the development of genetically engineered life forms. The victory was followed by Exxon's patent of oil-eating bacteria, and the door to commercial exploitation was opened.

In the same year, Kary Mullis and others at Cetus Corporation were able to multiply DNA sequences in test tubes by a proprietary technique dubbed polymerase chain reaction (PCR). This was the most revolutionary new technique in molecular biology in the 1980s, as it allowed for sufficient quantities of special DNA fragments to be produced more rapidly and efficiently, allowing for more effective and faster study. Cetus patented the technique and, in what could be a seminal, tradition-setting move, sold the patent to drug giant Hoffman-La Roche for $300 million. By now, the traditional pharmaceutical industry's interest in biotechnology was evident and an important validation of how far the new science had come in just 14 years. Mullis won the Nobel Prize in Chemistry in 1993 for inventing PCR.

The year 1981 was a watershed one, as Genentech cloned interferon gamma. There are three kinds of interferon, which was discovered in 1957 by Scottish virologist Alick Isaacs. Interferon is a protein produced by cells in the human body in response to a viral infection and is part of the normal immune response, or defense mechanism, against disease like cancer. Type I interferons are divided into alpha, beta, tau, and omega and are involved directly in improving a cell's ability to fight infection. Gamma interferon is also known as type II and functions in the maintenance of the overall immune system. Alpha interferon is a protein that is produced by specialized cells in the body and is a useful defense against cancer. Interferon beta 1B is used to treat multiple sclerosis, a disease of the nervous system in which antibodies destroy nerve cells and lead to generalized weakness. What's important here is to remember that interferon was an important protein at the beginning of the biotechnology revolution. As I'll discuss later, it still is important because it is still a leading area of research, especially in cancer, diseases of the nervous system, and liver disease. Thus, there is a good chance that you'll be investing in stocks that will release some kind of news about their interferon research at some point. The stock will move, and you may have to make a decision. It would be nice to have an idea about what interferon is and what it does when thousands of dollars may be on the line.

Other advances in 1981 included the creation of animals that had genes from others successfully transplanted in them. The gene for insulin was completely mapped, setting the stage for the ability to map whole genomes in a test tube.

Once again, the pharmaceuticals industry came into the picture as Hoechst AG, a German chemical company, gave Harvard's Massachusetts General Hospital $70 million to build a new Department of Molecular Biology in exchange for exclusive rights to patents that emerged from research at the institution. Congressman Al Gore held hearings on the effect of large sums of money from corporations and their influence on the academic environment.

In 1982, Genentech received Food and Drug Administration (FDA) approval to market genetically engineered human insulin. Advances were also made in the application of biotechnology to animal and plant science, and issues regarding the use of biotechnology in biological weapons were raised.

The year 1983 saw Eli Lilly (NYSE:LLY), a huge pharmaceuticals company, receive a license to make human insulin, marketed as Humulin. Eli Lilly has continued in its pursuit of biotechnology, having purchased the biotechnology company Centocor in the 1990s. Centocor's main business had been derived from a biotechnologically created clot-dissolving drug called Rheopro, used to break up blood clots associated with heart attacks. Most recently, Lilly also announced that it had made great progress in finding a potential cure for sepsis, a condition that amounts to infection of the entire body, which is usually deadly. Thus, the tradition of biotechnology leading the pharmaceuticals industry continues.

In 1983, the University of San Francisco and the Pasteur Institute in Paris isolated the AIDS virus.

In 1984, a gene associated with the control of blood pressure was isolated, while Chiron (NASDAQ:CHIR) cloned and sequenced the genome of the AIDS virus. Alec Jeffreys introduced DNA fingerprinting to identify individuals. A year later, genetic fingerprinting entered the courtroom.

In 1985, the National Institutes of Health approved guidelines for performing experiments involving gene therapy on humans. This was a major watershed event, as all the animal theory and experimentation could now be taken to the next step. The possibilities for cures, capital gains, and controversy all grew logarithmically as a result of this development.

By 1986, antibodies and enzymes were combined. The resulting molecule, called an abzyme, would allow a more rapid creation of drugs. The FDA also granted Chiron the license for the first recombinant vaccine for hepatitis, while the Environmental Protection Agency (EPA) approved the release of the first genetically engineered crop, tobacco—an interesting choice, to say the least.

In 1987, Calgene received a patent for an enzyme that extends the shelf life of fruit. Centocor's ovarian cancer tumor marker test was approved by the FDA. This set the stage for an increasing cure rate of ovarian cancer, which was among the deadliest of cancers as near as a generation earlier.

The year 1988 proved to be a landmark one for animal experiments, as a patent was awarded for mice susceptible to breast cancer and for AIDS research. These animal models, as we will see later, are crucial in the early stages of experimentation. The balance between science and profit was once again endorsed, giving private industry and science a leg up against government. This has often been useful for investors, as government agendas continue to be beaten back on the basis of precedent.

Again the partnership between Hoffman-La Roche and Cetus Corporation became evident as the two companies negotiated a licensing agreement for two cancer drugs. This agreement has become a prototype for similar agreements in the industry.

In 1989, a vaccine was developed to fight a virus that had killed millions of cattle in developing countries. Perhaps the most important development in modern history was initiated in 1989 with the creation of the National Center for Human Genome Research, headed by James Watson, of Watson and Crick fame, who discovered the double-helix structure of DNA. The center's mission was to map the human genome by 2005. The budget for the entire project was $3 billion. The human genome was deciphered in 2000, once again showing that scientific advances are occurring at the speed of light.

In 1990, Mary Claire King, at the University of California, Berkeley, discovered the gene linked to breast cancer in families with a high degree of incidence before age 45. This discovery was followed in 1991 by King's finding that a gene on chromosome 17 causes the inherited form of breast cancer and predisposes one to ovarian cancer.

Michael Crichton's *Jurassic Park* was published in 1990. The novel explores what can go wrong with genetic experiments. This is a similar situation to the cloning of the Tasmanian tiger that I discussed earlier in this chapter. The Human Genome Project, an international effort to map the human genome at a projected cost of $13 billion, was launched.

In 1993, scientists at George Washington University cloned human embryos and nourished them in a petri dish for several days. Great controversy was sparked, but, as noted earlier, the British government has now approved human cloning. A rough map of human chromosomes was produced. Genentech funded and launched Access Excellence, a communications network program to give high school biology teachers access to their peers and experts. (The organization's Web site, *www.accessexcellence.org*, was a crucial research tool in compiling this history and in the preparation of this book. My sincere thanks.)

The Flavr-Savr tomato, the first genetically engineered food product, was approved by the FDA. Genentech's Nutropin, a treatment for growth hormone deficiency, was approved by the FDA, some 17 years after the hormone was produced by bacteria. Breast cancer genes in inherited cancer were also identified in noninherited cancers.

Illness-related gene discovery exploded in 1994, as genes for obesity, aging, cell differentiation, and reproduction of the AIDS virus were identified. Genes associated with cataracts, bipolar disorder (manic depressive illness), melanoma, hearing loss, dyslexia, thyroid cancer, prostate cancer, and dwarfism were identified in 1994.

In the same year, advances were made in the treatment of cystic fibrosis, a condition in which a genetically inherited defect leads to the buildup of protein in the lungs of the affected, making it nearly impossible to breathe. The first crude map of the human genome appeared in the scientific literature.

In 1995, organ transplants were made across different species. O. J. Simpson's criminal trial was decided on DNA evidence. STS gene mapping, which would speed up the work on the Human Genome Project, was created. Animal models for Alzheimer's disease were biotechnologically derived, and gene therapy, immune system modulation, and genetically engineered antibodies were used against cancer.

In 1996, Biogen's Avonex (interferon beta-1a) drug was approved for treatment of multiple sclerosis. Scientists sequenced the whole genome of baker's yeast, the largest genome sequenced until then. It is mind-boggling that the science of sequencing went from baker's yeast to the human genome in five years. A gene associated with Parkinson's disease was isolated in 1996. A survey indicated that the public regarded research into the human genome with fear and mistrust, once again highlighting the delicate balance among science, government, and the private sector.

The year 1997 was the year of the clone. Dolly and Polly, two cloned sheep, appeared. Polly had the distinction of carrying human genes. The implications with the latter were tremendous, as human-compatible organs could be grown in animals and then, theoretically, farmed for their transplantability. The gene responsible for the circadian rhythm, or the innate 24-hour cycle of mammalian rest and activity, was discovered and called Clock.

In 1999, the largest animal genome was sequenced, belonging to a worm. This was a prelude to the announcement that the human genome had been unraveled.

The Pharmaceuticals Market

Before we move into a discussion of drug approval proceedings, it is important to note that pharmaceuticals truly are an international market, with Europe, Japan, and the United States being the major players. In a prescient paper published by the Academy of Managed Care Pharmacy *(www.amcp.org)*, authors Ines M. Vilas-Boas and C. Patrick Tharp provided a useful appraisal of the market and of the key differences that separate these marketplaces.

Traditionally, the FDA was the "gold standard" for drug evaluations. But the creation of the European Medicines Evaluation

Agency (EMEA) in 1995, a prelude to the European Union, created a serious competitor to the FDA because of the larger size of the European market. The creation of a serious competitor to the FDA has led to an increased need for uniform drug evaluation standards around the world.

How an Idea Becomes a Drug

The pharmaceuticals industry is often portrayed by politicians as a greedy group who prey on the elderly and the infirm for unjust profits. While that may be true in some cases, it is most certainly not true in most cases. Among other things, many drug companies provide medication free of charge to those who qualify through special programs created for this purpose. Many patients in my own practice have benefited from such programs. Both I and the patients are eternally grateful.

An equally important issue is that of the time and cost required to develop a new drug. The following sections will deal first with the organization of the FDA, the EMEA, and the Kosheisho, the Japan Ministry of Health and Welfare.

We will look at the basic steps that a drug company takes in order to attain FDA approval and see important differences between the FDA and its counterparts in Asia and Europe. The main purpose of including these sections is to help you make better sense of news reports about clinical trials and the different stages of new drug approval. In the biotechnology sector, almost nothing creates more volatility than news of an FDA approval or rejection. The situation can, in principle, be extrapolated to the other two agencies as well.

A perfect illustration of the sensitivity of the biotechnology industry to news reports and action from the FDA is Cephalon (NASDAQ:CEPH). The company's flagship drug, Provigil, is the world's leading treatment against narcolepsy, a central nervous system disorder that causes the sufferer to fall asleep during the daytime. The prior treatment method included a class of drugs called amphetamines, which are controlled substances, meaning that they are abusable and potentially addicting. Thus regulations have to be followed by physicians and pharmacists, and the whole situation is quite cumbersome. Provigil is not a controlled substance and thus has gained wide acceptance, not just because it works well but also because it is easier to prescribe.

A common strategy for drug companies is to leverage the use of drugs. This means that if they can expand the number of uses for the same drug, they can make it more profitable for the seven years in which they are forgiven from competition from generic drugs. Cephalon's strategy for Provigil was to expand its use into a condition known as sleep apnea, in which patients have spells during their sleep in which they stop breathing. This often translates itself into daytime sleepiness, but if it goes on uncontrolled, it can lead to long-term heart and lung problems. From a financial standpoint, the intended population for sleep apnea is much greater than that of narcolepsy, which is a fairly rare disorder.

But when the FDA rejected the application for the expanded use of Provigil to include sleep apnea, Cephalon stock, as figure 1.1 indicates, fell hard and fast. The figure also shows that the stock slowly recovered. Both patterns are quite common in the biotechnology arena and will be areas of further discussion in later chapters. For now, you should store the knowledge that biotechnology is a volatile, news-sensitive sector that requires a great deal of patience and knowledge in order to successfully navigate. This book is intended to provide the knowledge that will foster patience and understanding, for the rewards could greatly exceed the short-term volatility.

The Food and Drug Administration

The FDA *(www.fda.gov)* is one of America's oldest consumer protection agencies, regulating over $1 trillion worth of products per year. It houses nearly 9,000 employees whose function is to monitor the manufacture, import, transport, storage, labeling, and sale

Figure 1.1. *Cephalon and its bad news day. Note the huge gap in July 2000, when the Provigil indication for sleep apnea was not approved by the FDA. Also note that the stock recovered significantly and had more than doubled compared to its October 1999 low.*

of medicines, medical devices, radiation-emitting products, animal food, and cosmetics.

The agency, in its own description, is "first and foremost" a public health agency that enforces the Federal Drug, Food, and Cosmetic Act and related laws. Its 1,100 investigators and inspectors are found in district and local offices in 157 U.S. cities. The investigators visit more than 15,000 facilities per year and are responsible for the regulation of 95,000 businesses. The agency has the power to bring sanctions, including going to court and seeking criminal penalties when companies fail to meet regulations.

The FDA finds an average of 3,000 products every year that are unfit for consumers and detains an average of 30,000 import shipments per year at the port of entry if the goods appear to be unacceptable.

Twenty-one hundred scientists, including 900 chemists and 300 microbiologists, work in the FDA's 40 nationwide laboratories. Their function is to evaluate field samples as well as new compounds submitted for approval. The FDA also operates the National Center for Toxicological Research and the Engineering and Analytical Center, which tests medical devices as well as radiation-emitting compounds and equipment.

The FDA's main function is to assess the risk/benefit ratio presented by the products in the categories it regulates by ensuring that they meet certain standards. The FDA does not do its own drug research. Instead, it examines the results of the evidence presented by the drug manufacturer that is seeking approval. The agency also protects the food and blood supply as well as "biological," which are medications derived from living organisms, such as the bacteria-produced Humulin (insulin).

Finally, the surveillance and scrutiny does not end with approval for marketing. The FDA continues to monitor the products it allows to be sold to the public by reviewing and analyzing adverse reports.

The New Drug Development and Approval Process

While biotechnology encompasses many areas of academic activity, including life sciences, the focus of this book is on the effect of the biotechnology revolution and its impact on the pharmaceuticals industry—an impact that is so profound that there is almost a symbiosis between the formerly distant industries. The pharmaceuticals industry can no longer afford to ignore the start-up, research-stage, venture-capital-funded biotechnology companies, and the biotechnology companies cannot afford to do without the initial financing and the latter distribution and marketing infrastructure that the large pharmaceutical companies have in place. Thus, it is in this increasingly entangled web that a scientist either discovers or endeavors to find a new compound that he or she hopes will be a solution to a disease or condition ailing humanity.

It is important to understand that the most valuable quality of both a biotechnology investor and a researcher is patience. Not only is the new drug approval process lengthy and cumbersome, it is almost always preceded by an equally time-consuming, costly, and constantly revised research effort. Thousands of chemical compounds must be made and tested prior to finding one that is worth pursuing. This is the main reason for the nearly constant cash drain exhibited by biotechnology stocks.

This reality of life for the sector makes it difficult to analyze stocks on the basis of traditional earnings and valuation criteria, which is the reason why this book goes to great lengths to prepare you to do a reasonable amount of research and be duly diligent before investing in the hottest new biotech stock. The truth is that the road is littered with great-sounding start-up companies that weren't able to make the grade. For every Amgen (NASDAQ: AMGN), there are numerous other companies that never become profitable and that are never fortunate enough to be bought by a larger company in order to continue their work.

Therein lies a basic tenet of this book. Even large biotechnology companies may not have products on the market for years after going public and achieving wide acceptance on Wall Street. Thus my goal is to teach you how to make an educated decision as to whether the company's technology is good enough to make it attractive to both venture capitalists and/or larger biotechnology or pharmaceutical companies so that money can continue to be raised until the product cycle arrives. A perfect example of longevity, which should be used as a benchmark, is Genentech, which took over a decade to produce its first licensing revenue from Eli Lilly for Humulin. Throughout the period, Genentech was financed by outside sources. Very little has changed in this aspect of the sector. The lifeline of biotechnology is still research money.

The New Drug Application

The road to drug approval ends with the new drug application (NDA), which is a thorough, lengthy, and expensive-to-compile proposal that the drug company or sponsor presents to the FDA. The NDA is a request for the authorization to sell a new drug in the United States. In the NDA, the company must summarize the results of its nonclinical (animal) and clinical (human) test data as well as all the available information on the drug and the manufacturing procedures. The NDA must satisfy the FDA's requirements for safety, risk/benefit ratio, effectiveness, and labeling.

It is important to note that biomechanical devices must also go through a rigorous preapproval process.

Preclinical Research

The first step in creating a new drug prior to seeking approval for marketing is called preclinical research. Here scientists perform traditional laboratory experiments, literature searches, and computer simulations in order to come up with ideas and working models. The FDA estimates that it takes an average of eight and a half years to study and test a new drug before it can be approved for the general public, including early laboratory and animal testing. It often takes hundreds to thousands of test tube experiments to find and screen compounds worthy of moving on to the next step. Cell cultures, enzymes, and other reagents must be in ample supply for this labor-intensive trial-and-error process.

This stage also includes animal testing, both short and long term. The goal of preclinical testing is to produce data that show that the drug is reasonably safe to be used in small-scale clinical trials involving people. Tests to evaluate the potential for genetic damage to subjects, as well as any toxic effects of the drug and any breakdown products, are produced. The minimum requirements here are a profile of the drug's effects, including the duration of effect and the toxic effects in two species of animals, which can range from weeks to years.

Often a news item on a biotechnology company will be released that states that laboratory data were encouraging about compound XYZ, intended to cure ABC cancer. The stock, if it is publicly traded, may make a substantial move on the news. But the fact remains that these are preliminary data and that it could be several years before the company knows whether the data are useful in humans. This is another example of the advantage of having a working knowledge of the basics of biotechnology, both in the scientific sense (to be discussed later) and on the procedural end.

At first glance, the data in the news release may be encouraging. But by the next day, when the analysts and the fund managers have had a chance to sift through the data, they may discover that another company has better research and is further ahead. As a result, the stock could lose its gains and may even fall below the point where it rallied in response to the news. As a rule, the smaller the stock, the greater the chance for a big move that may be undone.

This kind of event is a perfect opportunity for investors to draw on their knowledge of technical analysis (to be discussed later) in order to make decisions about the conviction of Wall Street in putting its money into the company. As we will discuss later, there are tried-and-true characteristics in stock movements with a high degree of correlation and predictive accuracy with which to gauge winners.

Clinical Studies

Once the laboratory research has been conducted, the next step is clinical studies. Clinical studies must be approved by institutional review boards (IRBs), which are private organizations at research centers and hospitals. Institutional review boards are composed of experts and laypeople. Their main function is to provide study participants with full disclosure and to approve of and monitor the safety of the study design. In turn, IRBs are monitored by the FDA.

Clinical studies are performed on people and are conducted in three phases.

Phase 1: Clinical Trials

Phase 1 studies are closely monitored and are usually conducted on healthy volunteers. The goal is to study the actions and breakdown of the medication in humans and to establish safety and side-effect profiles. A successful phase 1 trial provides enough information to either kill the project or go to phase 2.

Often news reports will discuss "experimental evidence" on humans, and a stock will rise. It is important to pinpoint at what level the experimental evidence was obtained. A drug that causes no significant harm to healthy volunteers in controlled circumstances may well be deadly to the target population it is meant to aid. Thus, investors should be cautious before acting on reports of experimental evidence, unless the drug is clearly something that is the best possible alternative to death from the targeted illness. In these cases, the clinical trials may be stopped early or the FDA may give "fast track" status to the drug. Both are go-ahead signs.

Phase 2: Clinical Trials

Phase 2 trials expand phase 1 trials. Again, the studies are well controlled and may involve a relatively small number of patients. Where a phase 1 trial may be conducted in fewer than 100 patients, a phase 2 trial is likely to include several hundred. Short-term side-effect and risk profiles of the drug are emphasized.

Phase 3: Clinical Trials

Phase 3 trials are expanded and are both controlled and uncontrolled. In scientific terms, "controlled" means that the drug under study is compared to placebo, or a substance known to have no effect. Phase 3 trials are designed to expand the knowledge obtained in phase 2 and are the basis for extrapolating results into the general population. Phase 3 studies usually include several hundred to several thousand people. If the FDA stops a phase 3 trial, it can often be disastrous to the company.

Thus, when investing in biotechnology stocks, it is important to keep an eye on the company's Web site since information about clinical trials and drug pipelines is usually updated there. Another great source of information is to join the company's e-mail list if available.

A visit to Cephalon's Web site *(www.cephalon.com)* was quite revealing and illustrative of the knowledge that is available to investors online. Under the Product Development Pipeline link, it was noted that phase 2 trials were under way for Provigil for use in depression, Alzheimer's disease, Parkinson's disease, multiple sclerosis, and cancer. Phase 3 work was under way for use in sleep apnea, shift work, and attention deficit hyperactivity disorder in both adults and children. This is the reason that the stock had a setback but also made its way back. The company is likely to find another significant indication for Provigil and is working hard on many fronts to expand the revenue stream. More important was the information on other drugs for Alzheimer's and Parkinson's, which were in phase 1, development, and research phases. In addition, phase 1 and phase 2 trials were under way with drugs to treat prostate and pancreatic cancers.

Cephalon's Web site was also full of information about narcolepsy and sleep apnea. Details of the design and results of the clinical trials were provided, as was the company's affiliation and licensing information. Investor data such as earnings reports and the company's outlook were also listed. It should be noted that although most companies are truthful about their prospects and follow the rules, investors should always double-check information at other sources and look at the action in the stock. Stock characteristics are discussed in detail in later chapters.

At this point, the investor should understand that company Web sites can offer snapshots of what the future holds and can help an investor with a long-term horizon to decide whether a stock is worth taking a chance on. For those who do their homework, a big setback, like the one described with Cephalon, often will present a long-term buying opportunity.

Accelerated Review

A drug that is given "fast track," or accelerated, review status should make investors take special notice of the company. Accelerated review is not commonly granted and suggests either that the need for anything to treat the condition targeted is dire or that the drug has more than met expectations in a shorter time than usual.

Accelerated review will usually mean either that the drug is fantastic or that it can be used with a great deal of restrictions. Investors want to own a company whose accelerated review comes as a result of fantastic results, not because a high level of restriction will be imposed. Companies must continue to test the drug after approval is given, or the FDA can withdraw the approval more easily than usual.

The European Medicines Evaluation Agency

Established in 1995, the EMEA *(www.eudra.org)* follows two procedures for granting drug approval: the centralized procedure and the non-centralized procedure.

The centralized procedure is compulsory for medicinal products derived from biotechnology. This procedure is available at the request of companies for other innovative new products. Applications for new drugs are submitted directly to the EMEA at its London offices. The scientific evaluation is undertaken and a decision rendered in 210 days within the agency. The opinion of the scientific committee is transmitted to the European Commission to be transformed into a single market authorization applying to the whole European Union.

The decentralized procedure (or mutual recognition procedure) is used to approve the majority of conventional medicinal products. It is based on the principle of mutual recognition of national authorizations, meaning that a drug accepted by one member country is accepted by all the members of the European Union. This approach provides for the extension of a marketing authorization granted by one member state to one or more other member states identified by the applicant. Where the original national authorization cannot be recognized, the points in dispute are submitted to the EMEA for arbitration.

The European Commission adopts the final decision in both cases with the assistance of a standing committee or, in the event of serious disagreement among the member states, by the Council of the European Union. Purely national authorizations remain available for medicinal products to be marketed in one member state.

The Kosheisho: The Japan Ministry of Health and Welfare

The Kosheisho was established after World War II, and a look at its Web site *(www.mhw.go.jp/english/)* suggests that this is as much a world-class bureaucracy as its Western counterparts. Most interesting is that this agency not only controls drug approval and monitors the public health effects of medications but also administers the reimbursement of physicians. A further review of the site reveals that this agency functions along the same lines as Medicare does in the United States, that is, by administering a national health insurance program, regulating the water supply for hospitals, and addressing other social welfare and public safety issues.

Japanese law requires that drug companies do clinical effectiveness and safety studies on a population of Japanese patients. This makes it difficult for foreign companies to introduce new drugs, but this is a policy that looks to be eased now, as have the barriers to entry of foreign companies, as long as their entry into the market includes a joint venture to comarket, codevelop, or cross-license products with a Japanese company.

The Key Differences in the Markets

The main difference is the time to approval. The FDA and the Kosheisho do not guarantee any time frame to approval, while the EMEA approves its decisions, according to the information on its Web site, in 210 days, or seven months. From an investor's point of view, this time lag in the United States and Japan may have a significant impact on the company's earnings. This sometimes affects the price of the stock and at other times does not, as different companies are more efficient in their business strategies and use different methods to hedge their exposure to international risks (this is discussed later).

The Japanese marketplace is traditionally more safety conscious than geared toward efficacy, which also leads to slower approval and to lower drug dosages. Thus companies that compete in Japan must essentially customize their products to the Japanese culture, and more careful market research is often required here.

Drug companies pay user fees to the FDA that are governed by strict and sometimes seemingly capricious rules that are beyond the scope of this discussion. The EMEA and the Kosheisho have a more standardized and less cumbersome fee schedule, with the Kosheisho's being the least expensive. The EMEA charges an annual maintenance fee.

European marketing licenses last five years, and the product is reviewed and relicensed every five years with new fees being levied. The entire marketing costs for the European Union have been capped at $250,000 as of 1997.

Most interesting, using these 1997 data from the previously mentioned Vilas-Boas and Tharp article, it costs a company $937,000 to keep a single-dosage form of a product in the United States for five years, compared to $262,500 in Europe. This is only what the drug company pays the government agencies and does not take marketing and other expenses into account. Drug companies must also deal with the fact that governments set the prices for drugs all over the world, except in the United Kingdom and the United States.

Summary

In this chapter, I have introduced the macro aspects of biotechnology; the history, politics, and role of the FDA and international regulatory agencies; the role of central banks; and sources of information for investors. My goal has been to demystify the shroud of science and to frame it in a context that makes it easy to appreciate and understand why this is the investment theme of the future.

History is a part of what we are. If we do not understand the past, we cannot decipher the future or savor the fruits of our labor.

Thus the historical perspective was presented to bring you to a common place from which to start what I believe will be a grand adventure into discovery—not only a discovery of how to invest in biotechnology stocks, which I expect will be extremely profitable for those with a longer-term time horizon, but also a discovery of your own ability to learn and implement your hard-earned knowledge and experience. This is a discovery of a self-confidence and self-reliance that is balanced by a healthy respect for the wild animal called the stock market. Only those who are armed with the correct knowledge about what it really means when a company discovers a new gene or creates a new drug can make long-term decisions about stocks. Only those who can live through the inevitable rough spots in the biotechnology sector will reap the long-term rewards.

The discoveries mentioned here will be exquisitely rewarding only to those who truly grasp the key concepts of what biotechnology really is and what it is trying to do. There is too much at stake to limit the discussion to just buying and selling stocks. Anyone can learn to do that. Only the few armed with the right information will be able to make decisions that can make the difference between making them very rich, not so rich, or poor, in both money and spirit.

For example, if company X announces that it has just discovered a new technique and the stock rallies, a well-informed investor can quickly gauge whether Wall Street is really correct in its enthusiasm. By the same token, if a company receives a setback, such as in the Cephalon example, a well-informed investor would make the decision not to sell by knowing that the company's efforts to expand the drug's uses were not limited to just one indication. Knowledge of the company's pipeline would also be reassuring since more products in the future could lead to a prolonged profit cycle.

If you know where to find the right information and can decide that the product is not as landmark as the hype is making it out to be, a big rally could be an opportunity to sell into what could be the highest price for the stock in several months to years.

The combination of technical and market analysis (to be discussed later), along with the knowledge of history and the basic knowledge of science in this book, is intended to help investors make the decisions that could make the difference between a thousand-dollar profit and a potential million-dollar one.

We now know that biotechnology is a new science whose growth into the dominant branch of biology has spanned less than three decades. In other words, in the time that it takes to be born, grow up, and graduate from college, the science has advanced from the production of human growth hormone by induced bacteria to the verge of the potential for curing many of the world's illnesses and even the prolongation of life beyond the current expectation.

Armed with this knowledge, we can now begin to learn the key concepts in the science before moving on to the companies, how the markets work, and how to pick stocks.

CHAPTER

2

Basic Science Applied

The goal of this chapter is to build on the knowledge obtained in chapter 1. Thus special care was taken to carefully research information that is commonly used in the media when reporting on biotechnology and drug companies.

Science can be daunting, but it doesn't have to be. As a member of the science community, I always marvel at the difficulty that's infused into science and technology reporting. Even as a board-certified anesthesiologist, I often have to carefully research a company's methodology and assess its potential relevance because the news releases and the reporting are often so full of gibberish. Thus I went to great lengths to simplify the concepts presented in this chapter while still presenting a complete picture of the processes involved in biotechnology. This is not meant to be a complete "state of the art" science textbook. But the information here is quite fresh and is geared toward providing you with an excellent conversational background in the science involved.

The perfect proof that investors do not need a medical or scientific background to make money in biotechnology is the story of Anthony Guilford, who manages the Munder Farmington Health Care Fund. Guilford was the captain of the bridge team at Oxford University, where he studied Latin, Greek, Roman history, and philosophy. He credits his experience as a card player in college as excellent preparation for picking biotechnology stocks.

In an article in the September 25, 2000, edition of *Barron's*, Guilford describes his style as similar to the one described in this book. He homes in on companies that are growing rapidly when they look cheap. His fund, according to *Barron's*, had returned an average 37.5 percent per year in the three years prior to writing the article and ranked in the top 10 percent of its class.

If a bridge-playing philosopher can pick biotech stocks, then it is possible for lawyers, accountants, and just about anyone who can read and learn to do so as well. This is not a knock on Guilford, whose intellect is obviously top notch. It is just an illustration of the potential simplicity of learning the concepts and then applying them successfully.

An investor in biotechnology needs to grasp a seemingly complex yet simple set of concepts before proceeding on his or her journey. At its most basic, the whole science of biotechnology can be summarized in four steps:

1. The discovery and isolation of a new organism, gene, compound, or combination thereof

2. The extraction of the key portion of the organism, gene, or compound that makes the desired effect

3. The development of the compound in the laboratory

4. Mass production

Companies that excel in these four areas or form strong and stable partnerships will be successful. Thus the well-trained investor, armed with a solid knowledge base, can base his or her efforts in culling out companies who can execute, either on their own or with partners, the four strategies needed to succeed.

In chapter 1, we learned the basics about biotechnology, the impact on our daily lives, and the process of taking an idea and turning it into a successful drug. This chapter will lay down the foundation from which we will move into how markets work and how to eventually pick winning biotechnology stocks. But in order to be able to pick stocks and to time their purchase and, more important, their sale, investors need to become familiar with the science, language, and methodology of biotechnology.

The chapter is organized in a logical sequence that takes you from the basics of cell biology through the intricate lattice of the multidisciplinary environment that is the foundation for biotechnology. The basic themes are explored with clear modern-day examples of real companies whose ongoing research or product cycle is unique and appropriate to the topic. This was a very difficult chapter to research, compile, and write. But the finished product is worthwhile, as it delivers a well-condensed version of the key processes involved in the production of drugs in biotechnology.

The terms and themes explored and described here are commonly used in the financial media and news releases. Thus I recommend that you become very familiar with the content in this chapter. Finally, I want to point out that this chapter does not cover the technical or fundamental analysis of markets or stocks, but it will prepare you for that section of the book.

The Cell

In chapter 1, I discussed how science can be a big eye-glazer to the nonscientifically oriented. I also noted that one of the problems that science has with attracting the public's attention to the inner beauty of the discipline is the high-brow language that is used and the difficulty encountered by scientists in using plain language. But some science is inescapable, even in an investing book. After all, this is a book about investing in science. Thus it is important to understand the basics of what a cell is since most of biotechnology stems from the function of cells and the goings-on in different parts of the cells.

Most nonscientists have heard only part of the story about biotechnology since the press deals mostly with the sensational angles of the story, such as the discoveries regarding DNA. But while DNA is an important part of the cell, there are other key components that cannot be excluded if this is to be a complete manual. As I said earlier, the information included in the science chapters is meant as a guide for investors—to serve as a quick reference when the investor is faced with having to decipher information in news releases and biotechnology-related announcements.

Thus in the following paragraphs I'll give you what may seem a dry summary of the components of the cell. If it seems like you're reading a textbook at times, I apologize. But it is an important reference point, without which this book would be less effective. If I didn't mention some of these concepts and instead dove right into a discussion of the companies, it would be like sending you into a racing car not just without a helmet and fireproof clothes but also without the brakes.

I promise you that after reading this section, you won't be in any danger of being considered for a Nobel Prize in molecular biology. My goal here is to send you into the rest of this book warm and toasty, as if mom's hot chocolate were swimming around your bloodstream on a cold wintry morning. And more important, I want to give you a basis from which to understand those pesky science-heavy news releases that move biotechnology stocks 10 or 15 points up or down a few minutes after the release of the news.

The cell is the basis for biotechnology. Cells are defined as a membrane-bound portion of living matter; thus they are small sacs of fluid with specks of other small sacs sprayed throughout. They are the basic unit of structure of all animals and plants, meaning that all organisms are made of billions of these small sacs of liquid and their components.

Some organisms are made up of one single cell, while others are composed of millions and billions of cells. There are many varieties of cells within organisms, but all share the ability to make products that can be harnessed for mass production. And that is the key to biotechnology, as it is the products that are made by cells that biotechnologists harvest to make medications and other products.

For example, a discovery that a substance produced by a key organelle is the cure for lung cancer will move a stock. But after a few days, the stock may fall back. A stockholder who owns the stock and who has no knowledge of what an organelle is or what it does may make a blind decision based on the short-term volatility. But a stockholder who reads this book, and this section especially, is more likely to do more research. The research may lead to the conclusion that this discovery is so rare and so important that the stock's pullback is inappropriate and that, instead of selling, the position should be expanded. That is my intention here: to create an interest and to plant a seed, one that will make you want to be not just a stockholder but also a well-informed investor, one who can make intelligent decisions about his or her holdings.

Obviously, this is a highly idealized example. But the point is that long-term investors in any sector should become familiar with the basics of that sector, or they will almost certainly be at risk of losing large sums of money on a regular basis.

There are two basic kinds of cells: eukaryotes and prokaryotes. For simplicity's sake, everything that is not bacteria or blue-green algae, a group of species of water plants, is a eukaryote. This is important because the basic DNA for all organisms on earth is made of the same building blocks, and that is the reason that we can take products made by bacteria and use them to treat diseases in people and higher animals.

Eurkaryotic cells have nuclei and organelles. The nucleus is a membrane-enclosed structure that contains the chromosomes. Chromosomes are the structures that contain DNA. Humans have 23 pairs of chromosomes. The X and Y chromosomes determine gender, with X chromosomes determining females and Y chromosomes determining males.

This information becomes important in research into genetically derived diseases, where defects on chromosomes and genes are detected and eventually corrected by biotechnology.

Organelles are small bodies that reside outside the nucleus of the cell in an area called the cytoplasm. They are individual structures and are specialized in the production of chemicals and the storage of chemicals they produce or that are produced by other organelles. The only organelle that I'll mention here is the ribosome. This is the area where protein synthesis is carried out.

Protein synthesis is the central area of biotechnology. As we'll discuss later in this chapter, protein synthesis is the end point of all the other processes in cell function, and its perfect working order is absolutely necessary in order for organisms to function properly. Ribosomes are attached to a saclike structure, the endoplasmic reticulum, which winds its way through the cell. Proteins synthesized by the cell are stored in the endoplasmic reticulum.

Cells aren't blobs. They have a skeleton, called the cytoskeleton, which is composed of a series of protein tubules and filaments that give the cell its shape, allow for the transport of substances inside the cell, and may be involved in cell movement. The cytoskeleton is found in the cytosol, which is the liquid, jellylike portion of the cytoplasm. Many of the functions of the cytoskeleton and its components are still not known and at some point may prove useful to scientists.

To summarize, cells are sacs of fluid that are also the home to smaller sacs of fluid. The action and interaction of these microscopic structures form the basis for understanding biotechnology. The information in this section is meant to provide a foundation for further reading on the science of biotechnology. Now that didn't hurt, did it?

As figure 2.1 clearly illustrates, the focal point of biotechnology has become genetic engineering. Multiple disciplines pool their knowledge and use the methodologies that are known as genetic engineering to isolate, study, extract, modify, multiply, and then mass produce the desired product.

Genetic engineering is the deliberate manipulation of genetic material by biochemistry. The practice is quite common in plants,

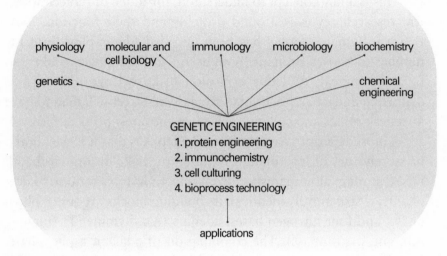

Figure 2.1. *The basic science sequence.*

where transgenics, or organisms that carry the genetic material from more than one species, are the key. This is discussed in detail later in this chapter. This process is also known as recombinant genetics and is commonly used to produce insulin and growth hormone, as discussed in chapter 1. The gene that causes the desired effect is isolated and then cloned into the host organisms, which are farmed and harvested in mass quantities using incubators and reaction tanks. The products are then extracted, and the process is repeated.

DNA

Now that we understand the big picture, we need to discuss some terms to understand the basics of DNA. DNA, deoxyribonucleic acid, is the molecule that holds the genetic code, which is expressed by the proteins that the DNA sequence causes to be manufactured. In other words, the DNA is the template, and the proteins are the messengers.

This is a key concept to understand, for much of biotechnological research revolves around proteins and their function. Now that the human genome has been decoded, the explosion in the number of known proteins (both useful and otherwise) is likely to be astronomical. And this explosion of knowledge may lead to confusion and stock price volatility, as Wall Street will tend to have knee-jerk rallies and collapses based on the latest press release.

A more descriptive way to describe DNA is that it is the library, or storehouse, of information required to make an organism. All DNA among all organisms, from the tiniest bacterium to elephants, is structurally identical. Its building blocks are sugar, phosphate, and four nitrogen bases: adenine (A), thymine (T), guanine (G), and cytosine (C). The combination of a sugar, a phosphate, and a base form the basic unit of DNA: the nucleotide.

DNA is ordered in an entwined ladderlike structure called a double helix. Within the double helix, A is always paired with T, and C is always paired with G. Two complementary strands are connected by alternating sugar and phosphate bridges and are thus twisted into the double helix. Thus, DNA can be viewed as the language of life, and its components form the words.

Continuing our language analogy, it makes sense that as long as the words and the sentences are arranged in the correct grammatical order, the final book, or organism, will be what is expected. The instructions contained in the genes are then translated into the substances that build organisms.

When this language becomes flawed, it is expressed as genetically transmitted disorders since many genetic diseases are the result of an enzyme deficiency or other protein abnormality. Thus enzymes are proteins that are coded for by DNA. Faulty genes do not allow for the production of the necessary enzyme. In turn, cells cannot function appropriately, and the genetic defect is expressed in an illness or a condition.

In other words, enzymes are messengers, and genes are the templates for the messengers. If there is a faulty gene, then either an enzyme won't get produced or a faulty enzyme that carries the wrong message or no message at all gets produced. That means that if the faulty gene or genes can be isolated and production of the missing enzyme can be instituted, much suffering can be eliminated. All these components of the cell, including DNA, work in concert, and when one or more of these or other cell components fail to work, things go wrong. Things can go wrong at every step of the process, and it takes just one small piece to unravel the entire sequence.

Success in correcting enzyme deficiencies has been encountered with cystic fibrosis, as mentioned in chapter 1. But the process is important to know in detail and can serve as a template.

Protein Synthesis

Protein synthesis, or the actual manufacturing of proteins, is the end result of what DNA's programming is about. Proteins do the hard and important work in the human body, and life without proteins is impossible. Proteins function as (1) enzymes or (2) key structural components, such as keratin and collagen, that make up skin, nails, bones, and tendons. Actin and myosin are specialized muscle proteins without which there would be no movement. Hemoglobin carries oxygen in the blood. Key membrane proteins act as filters, controlling substance traffic in and out of cells.

Thus protein synthesis is what it's all about. Here is where the genetic defects become real. It is at this stage in cell function that things go wrong that cause disease. And here is where biotechnology makes its biggest impact in drug development: through genetic engineering.

Recombinant DNA

Recombinant DNA is the most basic process by which biotechnology works. If DNA is the language, then recombination is an editing of the language. It is the end result of the alteration of an organism's genetic code. The classic example, briefly described in chapter 1, is Genentech's ability to place the human insulin gene in bacteria and induce the bacteria to produce the hormone.

The actual process is simplified by a cut-and-paste analogy. Once the gene is identified, it is then cut by the use of "scissors" proteins placed into a plasmid, which is a form of DNA found in bacteria. This insertion or placement of a DNA fragment is completed by the use of special "glue" proteins.

The plasmid, which now contains edited DNA, is then placed into the bacteria, which will then process the instructions and make insulin. More important, when the bacteria multiplies, its offspring will carry the plasmid and be able to produce insulin as well.

Genomics

Just as catalysts and enzymes speed up reactions, so did biotechnology experience its own jump into hyperspace with the development of genomics. "Genomics" is the term given to a process developed by J. Craig Venter that, simply stated, means to study not just a few genes but all of them. And that is precisely what Venter does at The Institute for Genomics Research (TIGR; *www .tigr.org*). The institute was formed with funding from Human Genome Sciences and developed the concept of the expressed sequence tag (EST).

The EST concept is based on the fact that genes are islands of functional DNA surrounded by nonfunctional DNA. Thus by extracting only the DNA that functions and sequencing the fragment, the EST was found and could be used for research. The development of ESTs, which are essentially a shortcut, was a crucial factor in the speed with which the human genome was identified.

TIGR, which is nonprofit and government funded, continues the work of unraveling the genome of any organism it can get its hands on and posts the results on its Web site. The institute also provides internships to students, provides educational resources for teachers, and holds conferences and disseminates information.

An interesting academic use of genomics with imaginative potential was the application of the EST technology to a mummy found in the Andes Mountains, dubbed "The Ice Maiden." The mummy represents the remains of a 14-year-old Incan girl who was sacrificed. Her body was entombed and was found frozen. TIGR took DNA samples and developed ESTs that were then analyzed in an attempt to discover similarities in the genome with those of living people in order to discover potential ancestry and to elucidate the possible migration pattern of her race.

The analysis revealed that the mummy's DNA was similar to that of North American natives and the Ngobe people of Panama— once again, life imitating science fiction, as in chapter 1, where it was mentioned that scientists are attempting to clone a Tasmanian tiger.

Genomics has also shown with great clarity that once nature has a successful gene in place, it doesn't alter it much as it climbs the evolutionary ladder. Thus gene X in a yeast is similar to gene X in humans. And gene X is easier to study in yeasts than in humans.

This becomes a very handy tool for investors in deciphering information in news reports. In the past, animal studies were immediately dismissed as little more than a beginning. But now, a gene-related discovery in bacteria can be as meaningful as a human discovery. This, of course, needs to be put into proper perspective. As we discussed earlier, a gene discovery is nothing more than the beginning of a long process by which compounds must be developed and then followed by clinical trials prior to a drug's being approved.

But the point is that, in the old days of Biology 101, professors often guffawed at reports of discoveries in microbes and mice. In the age of genomics, such information is stored in databases and is accessible on the Internet, sometimes free of charge. This information gives scientists nearly instant access to data with which to compare and extrapolate the relevance of a new discovery or observation. The "Net" result has been to rapidly increase the pace of both the discovery and the development of new technologies.

But not only TIGR has a vast database. Incyte Genomics
(www.incyte.com; NASDAQ:INCY) also has a vast database that
it rents to pharmaceuticals firms. Incyte is a particularly interesting
company since it has forged a partnership with IBM (NYSE:IBM).
This is not simply two technology companies coming together for
a joint venture. It is more of a glimpse into the future, as traditional silicon-based technology formally enters the arena of the biological sciences both as a provider of equipment with which to
decipher information and as a true and official partner.

On September 11, 2000, Incyte introduced its Genomic
Knowledge Platform software application, which was developed
with IBM and Seca Technologies to allow researchers to analyze
genomic data from a variety of sources simultaneously. This incredible development came about as Incyte's Genomic Knowledge
Platform incorporated IBM's DiscoveryLink data management
software. This software allows for the integration of information
from multiple data categories, such as gene sequencing and expression of the gene. The combination of data increases the speed
with which researchers can identify and characterize potential
drug targets, drug efficacy, and, most important, individual response to medication.

That last sentence is landmark, for an intricate knowledge of
the human genome will allow treatment to be custom made for
each individual in the future. This concept of personalized and
customized treatment is the basic tenet for Millennium Pharmaceuticals (NASDAQ:MLNM), one of the most promising biotechnology stocks for the next decade.

Even more important, Incyte's Genomic Knowledge Platform
allows data obtained on the genomic aspects of the subject being
studied to be linked to information about its chemical, clinical,
and postmarketing data. In essence, once Genomic Knowledge
Platform is fully implemented, it will provide scientists with one-
click access to everything they could possibly want to know about
a gene, from its function to its prospects for drug development
and how well the product may actually sell.

As figure 2.2 shows, Incyte stock failed to get much out of the announcement. This is an important point to keep in mind. When a company introduces what is likely to be a landmark product, one that is likely to revolutionize its field, and Wall Street fails to respond, there is something wrong. And there is something wrong either with the company or with Wall Street. Wall Street's main problem may be either that analysts have not covered the event well enough for brokerage firms to be promoting the stock or that the concept is either too complex or not exciting enough for mass consumption, hype, or hysteria, which is what often causes stocks to move dramatically.

But IBM did not stop at the joint venture. The company also announced that it would develop a supercomputer called "Blue Gene," which would be used to analyze and design protein structure, especially the characteristic folding of each protein molecule, which is a key part of the protein's function.

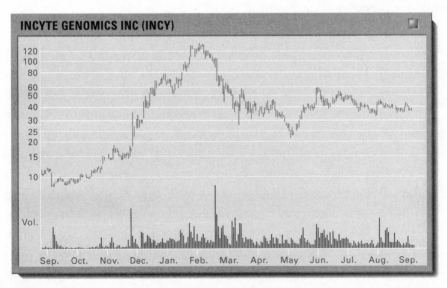

Figure 2.2. *Incyte Genomics (NASDAQ:INCY). Note the lack of movement on the good news for the stock. Courtesy of Telescan.*

Even more interesting was the announcement on October 1, 2000, by Compaq Computers (NYSE:CPQ) and reported by the Financial Times *(www.ft.com)* that it would invest $100 million in biotechnology. While IBM immediately joined the fray with a partnership with Incyte, Compaq decided to provide venture capital to start-up companies and thus create a market for itself in the long term.

My own belief is that Wall Street knows best and that the market is efficient, meaning that it prices stocks on the basis of the information it has available. But that doesn't mean that Wall Street is timely in every case. As I stated in *After-Hours Trading Made Easy,* when addressing the efficient market, the market isn't always right, but it is efficient. This means that stocks trade on the information that is available and that eventually the truth is discovered and the price adjusted.

Thus, in the case of Incyte, the information was available but was not acted on immediately by the Wall Street spin machine. In such a case, as with Incyte, it could be a great opportunity for long-term investors to enter the stock and patiently wait.

A perfect example of the efficient market occurred in September 2000, when a rapidly growing networking company called Emulex (NASDAQ:EMLX) was the target of a stock manipulation hoax. A bogus news release stated that the company's CEO was resigning in a cloud of uncertainty, and the stock lost nearly 60 percent of its value in a few minutes. The company's rebuttal led to the return of the stock to its previous levels almost by the end of the day, and the stock resumed its normal course thereafter. The perpetrator was apprehended, and life went on. But the market, albeit in knee-jerk fashion, proved that it is efficient by rapidly responding to significant news on both ends of the report.

An interesting article called "Selling DNA Data" by William Wells can be found at *www.accessexcellence.org,* a premier Web site for background information on biotechnology. In this excellent treatise, Wells notes that Incyte's director of research contends that the company is a year away from bankruptcy if it doesn't pursue any new technology on an ongoing basis. Thus, in a sense, Wall Street's apparent indifference to an impressive announcement by the company may be looked at in the same way as the boy who cried "wolf."

After all, the company is on the record as saying that it must constantly not only come up with new technology but also spin it just right in order to attract capital. Thus in the case of the IBM announcement, Wall Street just shrugged, since it was, in the eyes of the analysts, just another announcement in a long line of similar events from the company.

But the stock did not sell off, which may mean that the Genomic Knowledge Platform may develop into a significant revenue component for the company in the future and that there are enough strong hands in the stock to not sell unnecessarily. One thing is certain: From a science standpoint, the new software is indeed significant.

The previous analysis is important since it frames the discussion not only on Incyte but also on the sector as a whole. Biotechnology moves so rapidly that companies must continually scramble to attract attention and funding. Digging into Incyte's earnings, which come primarily from leasing its database to pharmaceutical companies for nearly $5 million per year, it's easy to see that competition is fierce. While the company was profitable in 1997, beginning in mid-1998 and as of June 2000, there had been six straight quarterly losses despite rising revenues. Once again, biotechnology companies burn money quickly.

The most visible of all the genomics information companies is Celera Genomics (NYSE:CRA). The company is a division of medical equipment maker PerkinElmer (NYSE:PKI). Celera, of course, is given credit for decoding the human genome. But here again, as figure 2.3 clearly points out, we note that even with the company's impressive resume, Wall Street continued to yawn. The story can once again be found in the earnings report. This time we

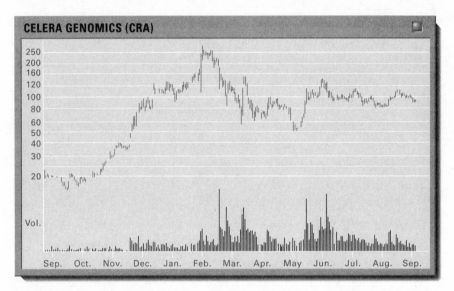

Figure 2.3. *Celera Genomics. Note the similarities in the charts for Celera Genomics and Incyte Genomics. Courtesy of Telescan.*

found that Celera had reported 12 straight quarterly losses from 1997 to 2000 despite increasing revenues.

The message here seems to be that now that the human genome has been deciphered, the information companies have little growth left in them and that attention will now be turned to those companies that can deliver the drugs, even if they do so by using the databases provided by the genomics data banks.

It is also important to note that Wall Street was betting heavily on genomics before the actual news of the decoding of the human genome. That optimism, which is well expressed in the left portion of figure 2.3, the chart of Celera Genomics, came to a grinding halt as the previously described events involving President Clinton and Prime Minister Blair unfolded.

More interesting is the realization by Celera Genomics that a database is a great asset to have but that it may have limited marketability. The company announced in the summer of 2000 that it would begin efforts to discover drugs based on its database. There is intense competition in the field, and Celera has a lot of catching up to do. Once again, the efficient market took the news in stride.

Mass Production

So far, we have discussed the salient aspects of the basic science of biotechnology, beginning with the organization and deciphering of disciplines, the structure of nucleic acids, the key process of protein synthesis, and the genomics phenomenon. The logical conclusion of the theme is to explore how drugs are manufactured.

Once the organism has been successfully induced to carry the new gene and is producing the targeted compound, the next step is to be able to produce the compound in large enough quantities to cure large numbers of people of the condition that the product was intended for and, it is hoped, to turn a profit for the company.

The process of fermentation, which is well recognized in beer, wine, and spirits manufacturing, is ironically the central method of production for biotechnology—thus our basic tenet that science doesn't have to be complicated if you keep the proper perspective. Neither should science be underestimated. After all, even after we have decoded the human genome and can access multiple databases with the click of a mouse, there are still the basics to remember. Biotechnology depends on living organisms, which undergo genetic modification and are tricked into producing what are uncharacteristic products for the species. Thus climate, temperature, and pH must be carefully controlled.

Fermentation has been known for at least 6,000 years, but its true nature was discovered by Louis Pasteur in the 1800s, when he formulated his germ theory. Pasteur is best known for his gift of "pasteurization." But his contributions to microbiology and to science overall are key concepts that must be understood and properly implemented in biotechnology if it is to be successful. Perhaps his greatest contribution was in the discovery and development of vaccines, which are a key portion of biotechnology and will be discussed later.

What Is Fermentation?

Microbiologist Christine Case's treatise on fermentation can be found at *www.accessexcellence.org*. She describes fermentation as the process that produces alcoholic beverages and acidic dairy products. Simply stated, when bacteria find something that they can break down to provide themselves with energy, they use fermentation. It is a kind of digestive process that breaks down large molecules into smaller ones, producing sugar, which in turn provides energy to the organism. The waste products of fermentation, such as alcohols, are useful to human beings and are a perfect example of how dependent all organisms on earth are to each other and how precarious the balance of life really is. Fermentation is also used in muscle tissue to produce energy and provides products like bread, yogurt, cheese, and sauerkraut, along with alcohol.

Fermentation, for the purposes of biotechnology, is conducted in an apparatus called a bioreactor. Above all things, it is important for the bioreactor to be sealed and maintained under sterile conditions in order to avoid contamination. This means that there are two kinds of bioreactors: those that function in a nonsterile environment, which are used primarily in brewing, and those that operate under sterile conditions and are used in the production of antibiotics, vitamins, and other medical products.

The organisms are placed in a water bath that is pumped full of nutrients. The temperature, acidity, and oxygen content of the mixture are meticulously maintained at the optimal level for the organism to ensure the best possible yields. Just as the nutrients are pumped in, waste products must be removed. It is in the creation of this perfect environment that the microbiologist and the chemical engineer must work closely together. The mixture of nutrients, water, gases, and organism must be perfectly mixed in order for there to be balance and the product yield to be optimal. Waste products from fermentation are put to use in sewage treatment and in the treatment of liquid wastes.

Downstream Processing

This is the final step in drug production and is almost the most important since special attention must be given to reducing waste of the product. This is a very labor-intensive process and requires high levels of manpower and state-of-the-art technology.

In summary, at this point you should have a grasp of the complexity, but also the orderly and well-structured nature, of the biotechnology sector. The science of biotechnology has taken giant leaps and bounds in the last two decades. But these major developments would not have been possible without the work of Pasteur and his colleagues in the 19th century.

The journey so far has taken us from the basics of cell function to the manufacturing of products. The next objective is to fit in other scientific processes that are crucial to the sector and to note places where information is easy to find.

Cell Culture

The organisms used for industrial purposes must be cultivated. Again, the cells—bacteria, animal, or even human—must be maintained in optimal noncontaminated environments. Many of the same principles of fermentation are adhered to, especially sterility and the avoidance of contamination from water used for the culture medium.

What Are Monoclonal Antibodies?

A discussion of the basic science of biotechnology cannot be undertaken without a detailed examination of monoclonal antibodies. Not only are these molecules a growing field of study and increasingly useful in medicine, but their production is an excellent application and review of the processes we have discussed previously in this chapter.

We are all familiar with antibodies, as they are part of our daily lives. Antibodies are proteins produced by the body's immune systems, more commonly known as the body's defenses. When we sneeze, it is because a foreign particle, like dust, has entered our nose. That foreign particle binds to special cells that produce an allergic reaction. If we have been exposed to this substance before, antibodies are mobilized, and lots of mucus is produced. The mucus is where the antibodies do their work, which is to neutralize the invader.

Antibodies are highly specific proteins. The body manufactures only one kind of antibody to fight each individual invader. Some antibodies, such as those formed against childhood diseases, confer immunity for a lifetime. Vaccines are composed of killed or weakened bacteria or viruses that induce the production of antibodies. It is this specificity that makes antibodies ideal vehicles for both the diagnosis of disease and the delivery of medication to diseased areas of the body.

Traditionally, antibodies were commercially produced in mass quantities by injecting animals with antigens. After antibodies were produced, serum, the liquid portion of the animal's blood, was collected, and the antibodies were extracted. This method, although useful, also produced impurities that were undesirable and also produced too small a yield of the substance.

The solution to the problem came as a result of cell culture techniques. Scientists discovered that a particular type of cancer cells, called myeloma cells, could live in culture indefinitely. By combining antibody-forming cells from the spleens of animals that have been injected with antigen and combining them with myeloma cells, there is now a way to mass produce antibodies. The combined cell is called a hybridoma. The result of the creation of hybridomas is a better supply of highly specific, purified antibodies.

Biotechnology is a sector in which companies use science to trick nature into changing. The nature of the change is often for the good of those who are ill. And therein lies the potential benefit of the science.

For investors, those who know the most will be able to make better decisions. Throughout this book, I'll be highlighting not just the science and the companies that I think are likely to out-perform the rest but also those that are genuinely favored by the marketplace.

But most of all, my goal is to teach you how to think for your-self when making decisions to buy or sell.

Uses for Monoclonal Antibodies

An excellent example of the therapeutic use of a monoclonal anti-body is Embrel. Embrel is a product of Immunex *(www.immunex .com;* NASDAQ:IMNX) and is marketed by Wyeth-Ayerst Phar-maceuticals, a division of drug giant American Home Products (NYSE:AHP). The relationship between the large pharmaceutical companies and the biotechnology industry is obvious. I'll expand on this relationship in great detail in a later chapter. This relation-ship should not be taken lightly, as traditional drug companies and biotechnology companies continue to work together more and more frequently. In this case, Immunex is producing a block-buster drug, and American Home Products is the marketing arm. Both are big winners because of it.

Embrel is derived by monoclonal antibody technology, which is obtained from adapting recombinant DNA technology to the Chinese hamster ovary. In other words, the gene for the antibody is inserted into the hamster ovary, which then becomes a factory for Embrel.

The drug is used in the treatment of rheumatoid arthritis and is composed of both a human immune protein and a receptor of a chemical known as tumor necrosis factor (TNF). This is a perfect example of the lock-and-key mechanism between substances such as TNF. It is not important to remember TNF per se, although some familiarity with the term will likely be useful in the future, as TNF occurs in many parts of the human body and is involved in other disease processes in which biotechnology may be involved.

The lock is the antibody, and the key is the receptor, which in reality is a chemical in itself. The body is full of receptors for all kinds of chemicals. Every time the correct key (substance) enters the lock (receptor), something happens. A common example of a substance receptor complex is movement. When we move a muscle, it is the result of a substance-receptor interaction, which triggers another set of reactions, leading to the muscle action.

The next sequence is a prototype for the way monoclonal antibodies work. There are millions of people in the United States and the world who suffer from this deforming, crippling, and painful disease. But monoclonal antibody technology is helping an increasing number of them, especially young people, whose arthritis tends to be more aggressive and devastating. Thus, this is another example of how biotechnology actually helps people.

Figure 2.4 represents a highly idealized joint in a sufferer of rheumatoid arthritis. The lower cutouts in the figure represent the receptors for TNF in the joint. The receptor is a chemical, which is the key to a reaction. When the receptor is filled with the sub-

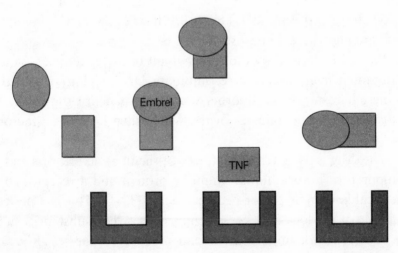

Figure 2.4. *Representation of a joint and the receptor-substance (lock-and-key) process.*

stance, which is the key, something happens. The rectangles are TNF, the substance that makes something happen, in this case pain and suffering. The ovals represent Embrel. Embrel is the treatment whose function is to trick the TNF into thinking that it is the joint. Normally, TNF binds to the joint tissue and triggers a reaction that causes the joint to become highly inflamed, causing pain and the other symptoms of rheumatoid arthritis.

But Embrel competes with the receptor and pulls away much of the TNF. This causes a decrease in the lock-and-key mechanism, and the joint becomes less inflamed. In other words, the door remains locked. The bottom line is that the patient feels better. Embrel does not necessarily reverse the process of rheumatoid arthritis, but it does delay the long-term effects and gives people a chance to have a better life. The science here is beautiful, as Embrel fools the TNF into thinking that it is the joint and binds it, preventing it from causing harm.

The example of Embrel is quite useful, as it brings together many of the concepts introduced earlier and provides a useful preview of what I'll be discussing later. The major concept is that monoclonal antibodies are crucial to the biotechnology sector. This basic knowledge can be useful when evaluating companies and news reports. It is useful to file away company names and their basic way of doing business. I recommend keeping a file, either on a computer or on file cards, of which companies make what kinds of drugs and which methods they have been successful using.

Immunex is a rare type of biotechnology company and one worth becoming very familiar with. Not only does it have successful products, but it is using leading-edge technology in conjunction with strong marketing partnerships and is concentrating its efforts in areas that are not only useful but highly visible as well. This, then, is a good benchmark company to use as a comparison when reading a news release, especially about monoclonal antibodies. A great place to research the basics of a company online is Hoover's *(www.hoovers.com)*.

Another great example of how biotechnology companies use monoclonal antibodies is Immunogen's (NASDAQ:IMGN) TAP protocol. Chemotherapy for cancer is often very toxic to normal tissues since the cancer cells and the noncancerous tissues are killed by these potent chemotherapeutic agents once they are injected into the body.

TAP is short for "tumor-activated prodrugs." Monoclonal antibodies, by definition, are highly specific, meaning that they bind to only one specific antigen. The surfaces of cancer cells are dotted with rare, unusual antigens that are almost never found on noncancerous cells. This makes them easy targets for drugs that are configured for interaction with the antigens.

A TAP is a combination of a monoclonal antibody to the surface antigen of cancer cells and a chemotherapy agent. When the monoclonal antibody attaches to the cancer cell, the cell engulfs the TAP. Once inside the cell, the medication is released, and the cancer cell is killed, preserving the normal tissue, leading to fewer side effects and perhaps greater cure rates.

Again, here is a company on the cutting edge of technology using monoclonal antibodies as the vehicle for a more specific and potentially better treatment against a life-threatening illness. I see even more potential in the development of TAP-like substances that could deliver different kinds of treatments that in the future may be used for illnesses that are now cured only by surgery. We can take a few seconds and imagine curing appendicitis by injecting a TAP-like substance into the bloodstream and having it kill the infection instead of having to undergo surgery. Interesting indeed.

Transgenic Animals

The final key concept is that of transgenic animals. These are genetically engineered versions of the normal animals with which we are familiar: pigs, cattle, and sheep. The most famous of all transgenic animals is Dolly, the cloned sheep. Her main purpose for being created was to see if cloning could actually be carried out successfully on a large scale.

But there is more to the transgenic animal story. Herman the bull was created in a laboratory where a bull embryo was genetically engineered at an early stage of development. The gene that is necessary for lactoferrin production was inserted into Herman's DNA. Lactoferrin is a protein that is essential for infant growth but is not present in cow's milk. The hope was that when Herman bred, he would transfer the lactoferrin gene to his progeny and produce cows that in turn would produce lactoferrin-containing milk. The enhanced cows would then be used for improving nutrition, especially in underdeveloped countries.

Of course, it worked, and Herman has produced several calves that have the gene. But Herman and most transgenic animals are still in the laboratory, for there are many unresolved issues, both ethical and regulatory. Most people still fear the Frankenstein-like aspects of transgenic animals. And most people are still concerned about genetically enhanced animals and even vegetables turning up at the supermarket, although much of what we eat and drink is composed of biotechnologically derived substrates.

The purpose of including transgenic animals in this discussion is first, that they exist. Transgenic mice are used all the time in the production of monoclonal antibodies. Transgenic bacteria produce insulin and growth hormone. The products of Herman and his lactoferrin-producing herd may still be a decade away from being found on supermarket shelves, but they are coming.

More important from the drug development and investment standpoint will be the company or companies that can successfully produce superior strains of transgenic organisms and which company or companies will be the one to convince regulators and the public that, when used properly, transgenic animals both are safe and can enhance life.

Figure 2.5 is for Genencor International, a biotechnology company that went public in July 2000 and that has a significant stake in transgenic animals. First, we should note that the stock traded higher after its initial public offering (IPO). This is a rare event, as many companies tend to fade after the IPO. This suggests that there is significant interest in what the company is doing from investors who may be fairly patient. As we will see later, this is a good sign, as a higher stock price is an indication that a company inspires confidence.

Genencor has interests in agriculture, pharmaceuticals, and health care markets. Among its interests in the health care market is the development of a strain of transgenic mice that can mimic the human immune system. As a result, the company, if successful, will have a model with which to study the function of the immune system as well as the responses of the immune system to drugs and the development of drugs through knowledge of the immune system.

Genencor also serves to illustrate several examples of how the biotechnology industry works. First, it is a research firm. As such, it will use funding from its non-correlated work to fund its fundamental mission. Part of the company's funding comes from gov-

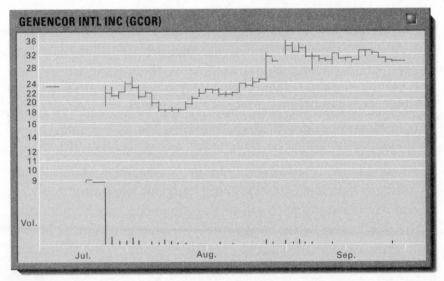

Figure 2.5. *Genencor (NASDAQ:GCOR). The company has a significant stake in transgenic animals. Courtesy of Telescan.*

ernment grants, such as the $17 million it received to develop an enzyme that could increase the alcohol yield from corn. This is an alternative fuel study, which is not untimely given the rising price of oil and the almost certain possibility that, as supplies are harder to find and exploit as time progresses, there could be significant energy shocks around the world.

More important is the leveraging of the immune platform that the company has built. It is in a partnership with Procter & Gamble (NYSE:PG) to develop hypoallergenic consumer products, including cosmetics and detergents.

Thus, Genencor is becoming a leader in its own niche of biotechnology, which encompasses a well-diversified portfolio of science with wide commercial implications for the private and public sectors, with the unifying force of eventually leading to products that can be used by consumers. This is the kind of company that we will be describing in great detail, starting in chapter 3, where we begin to look at company dynamics.

Excellent Sources of Information

If you are like me, by the time you've reached this point in the book, you have become intrigued and want to see if some of the things mentioned are true. I think this is an excellent time to get some hands-on Web surfing done. Therefore, this last section will be about some of the places where information is easy to gather on the Internet. This means that if you aren't already an online investor, this is a great time to start doing some research, at least about where free or relatively cheap information about biotechnology can be found.

Table 2.1 is divided into two sections. The upper section is dedicated to biotechnology information. The five links provided are by no means all that are available, but they are representative. Accessexcellence.org is a purely educational site that has information geared toward high school teachers. It provides excellent reviews of the key scientific processes involved in biotechnology and, more important, has excellent review articles, provides historical perspectives, and delves into ethical and moral issues. The site was used extensively in the preparation of this book and is highly recommended for anyone who wants to learn more about the science of the biotechnology sector.

The Food and Drug Administration (FDA) site is also important since this is where information about what is on the regulatory docket can be found. It is a difficult site to navigate at times because of the amount of information on it. But I recommend getting a feel for the site, as a serious investor in biotechnology needs to have some idea as to what the FDA is up to.

The Institute for Genomics Research site is an excellent source of free information that can be used as background for the latest technology in the public service. The institute offers lectures to the public that may be worth attending as well. The site is well worth the time spent on it.

Yahoo's Biotechnology Industry News site is a well-documented and frequently updated site with the latest news available. In the biotechnology sector, more than in other sectors, news is important, as it can really move stocks and present either a buying or a selling opportunity.

Finally, the University of Galveston Medical Branch site offers an alphabetized and comprehensive directory of biotechnology companies. The site provides a brief description of the company and a link to the company's Web site. As I mentioned earlier, company Web sites offer a great deal of useful information about drug pipelines and clinical trial stages and results. When this information is combined with a strong knowledge of market mechanisms and technical analysis, investors should be well armed for the biotechnology stock wars.

The second part of the table is dedicated to financial Web sites. These sites contain charts, news, and indicators. Most are free of charge, while some offer premium services. Serious investors will have to spend some money in order to have access to

Table 2.1 *Free Biotechnology Information, Internet Charting, and Financial Editorial Sites*

Biotechnology Information Site	Web Address
AccessExcellence	www.accessexcellence.org
Food and Drug Administration	www.fda.gov
The Institute for Genomics Research	www.tigr.org
Yahoo Biotechnology Industry News	biz.yahoo.com/news/biotechnology.html
The University of Galveston Medical Branch Biotechnology Companies	marlin.utmb.edu/~jwhill/bio.htm

Financial Site	Indicators Available	News Available	Premium Service	Web Address
Hoovers.com	Yes	Available	No	www.hoovers.com
MarketMavens.com	No	Available	No	www.marketmavens.com
Market Sentiment Central	Yes	Not Available	No	www.wallstdet.com
CBS Marketwatch.com	Yes	Available	No	www.cbsmarketwatch.com
AfterHourTrades.com	Yes	Available	No	www.afterhourtrades.com
On24 Audio News	No	Available	No	www.on24.com
E-charts.com	Yes	Available	Yes	www.echarts.com
Askresearch.com	Yes	CBS MarketWatch	Yes	www.askresearch.com
Wallstreetcity.com	Yes	Comtex	Yes	www.wallstreetcity.com
Prophetcharts.com	Yes	Available	Yes	www.prophetfinance.com
BigCharts.com	Yes	Not Available	No	www.bigcharts.com
Investorlinks.com	Yes	Available	No	www.investorlinks.com
CNBC.com	Yes	MSNBC and CNBC	No	www.cnbc.com
wsj.com	Yes	Wall Street Journal	Yes	www.wsj.com
SmartMoney.com	Yes	Dow Jones	No	www.smartmoney.com
CNNfn	Yes	CNN and Reuters	No	www.cnnfn.com
TheStreet.com	Yes	TheStreet.com	Yes	www.thestreet.com

the best information in a timely manner, as only those who get into and out of stocks at the right time will be able to maximize profits. These are the online sites that I find useful. More details about the sites mentioned are provided in the appendices.

It should also be noted that the volatility in the biotechnology sector makes it an ideal place for day trading. Day trading is not something that I recommend for everyone, as it is a high-risk proposition. In a later chapter, I'll discuss the pitfalls and solutions for day trading biotechnology stocks. Here, I'll mention that day trading offers the best results to those with a very fast broadband Internet connection, a powerful computing system, and professional day-trading software.

Although table 2.1 is by no means a complete list of financial information sites, it is a list in which biotechnology-related information can be found by looking for stock charts and editorials (including my syndicated columns, which appear on some of the sites listed) or, as in the case of Hoover's, where excellent company summaries are available.

I find Hoover's capsules the best for company summaries. I like the easy-to-follow, well-written, and concise summaries and the links to both news and the company sites. Most company sites for biotechnology offer excellent summaries of their business, their pipelines, and their earnings. Joining the biotech companies' mailing lists is also a good idea. This can be done on their individual Web sites.

Another excellent site for information is the Wall Street Journal online *(www.wsj.com)*. This is a premium site that is well worth the price. Excellent news and perspective articles are always available, as are options data for those interested in the market timing aspects of trading as well as index summaries, after-hours news, and so on. For after-hours information, I also suggest AfterHourTrades.com *(www.afterhourtrades.com)*.

Wallstreetcity.com *(www.wallstreetcity.com)* offers the best index charts on the Web and is closely rivaled by BigCharts.com *(www.bigcharts.com)*. The difference for me is that Wallstreetcity's charts are offered in different sizes. Thus, I can fit more facts on my screen as I'm trying to make decisions. For day trading, professional strength real-time data is the best option and can be found on the Internet for reasonable prices.

For free news and play-by-play on the market, it's hard to beat CBS Marketwatch.com *(www.cbsmarketwatch.com)*. This site's resources are unrivaled, and its news coverage is excellent. The main strength of Marketwatch, however, is its huge editorial staff, which is always reporting on what's happening.

Summary

This chapter has built on the information provided in chapter 1, which focused on both the history of biotechnology and the steps necessary for a company to develop and market products such as drugs. We began this chapter by discussing the basics of cell biology and ended with online investment information sites.

My goal is to work on several levels at the same time since this is what a biotechnology investor has to do to be successful: to be able to multitask as well as gather information from multiple places and gauge the chances of success or failure based on the click of a mouse or a call to a broker. The biotechnology investor first has to understand the key concepts of biology and the related science. Thus we covered the basics of cell biology, concentrating on protein synthesis and its central role in the science.

The examples of stocks and their movements given in this chapter were of cutting-edge genomics-based companies (Incyte Genomics and Celera Genomics). We saw how their stocks rose dramatically, only to fall as President Clinton and Prime Minister Blair committed their political faux pas. Then we noted that despite important announcements, the stocks remained fairly stable in consolidation patterns.

The two stocks illustrate what a real-life investment in biotechnology could be like—companies with great stories in strong bull markets leading the way. At some point, it is important to know when to separate the science from the investing. But if you do not become accustomed to looking at both areas simultaneously, then investment decisions will be difficult to make. Thus, whenever possible, I'll continue to bring together both areas.

As I'll discuss in a later chapter, the era of genomics is much further along as an investment theme than most people realize, at least on a research basis. This means that Wall Street is less likely to be impressed with the discovery of a new gene since there really aren't any new human genes to discover in a macro sense. Now, the bar has been raised, and stocks will rise on the expectations of new products that will come from the use of research and discovery. As genomics moves to its next level, the new theme for stocks that will move on research news will be that of proteomics or the actual study of proteins as a means to develop drugs instead of studying genes.

Thus my heavy emphasis on cell biology and protein synthesis. Their role, when looked at in this new context of proteomics, is important because protein synthesis is the process in which defects in the genetic code are usually expressed. So, that is where scientists will now do most of the work in biotechnology, trying to find proteins that can be used either to study conditions or to develop drugs. If you understand the important parts of protein synthesis, it will be easier to listen to or read a news release about a company that is touting its new product or drug.

When a company makes an announcement in biotechnology, there is a high probability that the stock will move, often violently. This move can also spread to the whole sector and may be temporary since Wall Street often acts before it thinks. After all, an ax murderer may be efficient, just like the market, but neither is always pleasant to be around. Thus the goal of this book is to teach you the important concepts that will allow you to make decisions not just on stocks, which are trending, but on those that may offer a great buying or selling opportunity based on news.

If you had difficulty with the section on protein synthesis, I suggest another pass through it. A lack of understanding about protein synthesis and its central role may make it difficult to understand proteomics, genomics, transgenic animals, monoclonal antibodies, and the role of these seemingly esoteric molecules in stocks and in their effect on your pocketbook and portfolio.

The other key scientific processes listed included fermentation, monoclonal antibodies, genomics, cloning, recombinant DNA, and transgenic animals. These are the basic processes that can be used to catalog companies, as I'll discuss in a later chapter. A working knowledge of these concepts is paramount in biotechnology investing.

By no means do I believe that this treatise will make you a Nobel laureate. But I do hope that after reading this book, the mystery of biotechnology will be unraveled, in terms of both science and investing. Thus it should be your goal to understand and associate the basics of the science with the basics of the investing.

At this stage of the book, you should be comfortable with the fact that biotechnology has been around for thousands of years but that the greatest advances have come since 1977. The science of biotechnology is composed of many disciplines, ranging from biology and chemistry to state-of-the-art brewing techniques adapted to scientific purposes by the use of highly specialized fermenting machines called bioreactors.

The most important advance since 1999 has been the decoding of the human genome, but that may soon be eclipsed by the emerging phenomenon of proteomics. The unraveling of the human genome was accomplished by a process called genomics, which shotgunned gene studies and moved the science forward by many years in a short period. In turn, genomics has set the stage for the emergence of proteomics, the next logical step. The advent of the Internet and the rapid advances in computer technology are likely to keep the sector in hyperdrive for at least the next decade, especially now that major technology companies like Compaq and IBM have sensed the potential for a lucrative market.

With this in mind, we can move to the next chapter, where we will discuss the details of a biotechnology company before moving on to how the financial markets work and affect biotechnology.

CHAPTER 3

The Investment Basics

In chapters 1 and 2, I discussed the watershed dynamic that is represented by biotechnology and the external and internal influences that will weigh on the sector. It is this confluence of seemingly independent but actually converging vectors that will eventually influence the final expression of the juggernaut that was created by nature and initially harnessed by humanity thousands of years ago. This tidal wave of science and evolving technology was spurred in the 19th century by the legendary Louis Pasteur and catalyzed in the late 20th by the application of microprocessor technology and the Internet, culminating in the spring of the year 2000 with the unraveling of the human genome.

But this is only the beginning, for the potential for growth, as expressed in financial, scientific, and in tangible everyday results, is nearly limitless, given the fact that nature's variations on the theme of life are too numerous to catalog despite relentless and continuous study by humanity. This chapter will build on this principle as we begin the journey into making sense of the big puzzle.

From an investment standpoint, we must be able to wonder at the beauty of the science but also gauge which companies and which technology will actually make the cut and lead us to picking winning stocks. Management decisions, public relations, partnerships, and the all-important Food and Drug Administration (FDA) are all key internal factors. When we factor in governments and the central banks, the equation can become rather complex and daunting for the average investor, who has to work a full day to support a family. Thus, in this chapter the focus will be on describing the building blocks of biotechnology companies, the stages of their development, and what often separates the winners from the losers. The information presented here will serve as a reference point and another building block for the sections on technical analysis and stock picking. In this volatile sector, stock picking without the proper background is little more than gambling.

We will begin this chapter with a look at what could be the defining moment in investing for the next decade, as money begins to flow out of companies in the traditional technology sector and into biotechnology, where the growth prospects currently are much greater. In my opinion, this is a secular dynamic, meaning that it is likely to translate into a long-term phenomenon. This analysis does not predict or guarantee a straight-line increase in the price of biotechnology company shares. But if I'm correct, the money that comes out of traditional technology, along with new money, will find its way into biotechnology.

This is a similar dynamic to that of the 1990s in which money came out of the IBMs of the world and made its way into companies like Dell and Microsoft and later into the Internet and cellular phone companies, only to eventually leave those areas and begin to search for a new home. That is what Wall Street does above all. The efficient market continues to search for new areas where growth is maximal and where the very powerful, but not so limber or nimble, institutional behemoths can park large sums for periods of many years in order to maximize their profits. Each decade has its major theme or themes that attract the imagination and money of the institutions. I believe that the first decade of the 21st century belongs to biotechnology.

The Big Picture: The Transition Arrives

As I described earlier, the scientific revolution has been sparked by computer technology and the ability to rapidly disseminate information through the Internet. Nowhere has the vote of confidence for the scientific revolution ring louder than in the NASDAQ Composite Index, as shown in figure 3.1. The index, which rose on the strength of the stocks of major companies like Intel, Microsoft, Oracle, Cisco Systems, Dell Computers, and Sun Microsystems, shows the power of a strong idea, its implementation during a generation, and the fulfillment of the promise. This is a key statement, for it is the starting point of where we begin our journey into biotechnology investing. Our goal is to decipher the megatrend for the next decade and perhaps beyond and to place our money in the best companies of the best sectors, with the goal of managing the position or positions for a period of several years. The best

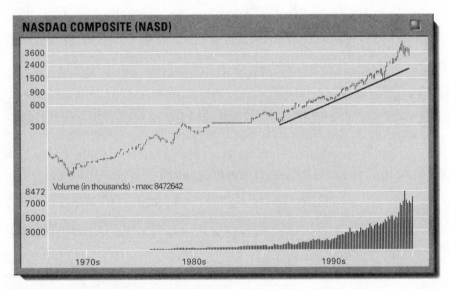

Figure 3.1. *The NASDAQ Composite (COMP). The long-term view. Courtesy of Telescan.*

place to decipher ideas is the market itself, for ideas, as I discussed in chapter 1, are where drug developers begin. Those biotechnology companies that have the best ideas and can promote them most effectively are the ones that will attract the venture capital and be able to continue. These are the same companies that the large institutions are looking for, those companies that have the infrastructure and the know-how to deliver the goods for the next decade.

In his books and in the newspaper he founded, *Investor's Business Daily*, William O'Neil, a master stock picker, focuses all his resources on finding stocks that have the technology that will drive the engine of growth. O'Neil, as I am, is a great believer that in a free society, with reasonable access to information and a well-organized plan, the average investor can realize riches beyond his or her wildest dreams. But in order to do so, the major investment themes for the era must be culled out early, and the plan must be implemented with discipline.

The theme for investing in the 1990s was obvious. The combination of microprocessor technology, software, hardware, and the ability to make them all work faster and harder while at the same time connecting them through the Internet at the speed of light through fiberoptics has been a powerful force, both for the advancement of our ability to communicate and for making money. Investors who had the foresight and the ability to make the right decision at the right time have been well rewarded. While every age has its messiahs, such as Bill Gates, Michael Dell, Larry Ellison, and the rest of the visionaries, each individual investor had the chance to make money if he or she could pick the companies and continue to think for the long term.

I believe that biotechnology is now at a point similar to where computing was in the early 1990s, when the NASDAQ Composite was near 300. Since then, the index rose as high as 5,000 before entering into a major bear market. The catalyst for the last stage of the bull run was the Internet and its promise of finally making the dream come together. The potential for nearly instant access to information and the ability to use it for work, research, and recreation was finally a reality. A feeding frenzy on technology stocks occurred and ended badly, when all the companies that led the way up were cut down to size. Investors had to suddenly grapple with the sobering reality that microchips will get smaller and work harder but that PCs became such a large part of the landscape that, like refrigerators and television sets, everyone has one. They are wonderful, but they are a little more than a wonderful part of the furniture, in an investment sense.

The decade of the 1990s for the NASDAQ Composite (see figure 3.1) has a trend line that I drew to illustrate several points. First, the month of October 2000 shows what can happen to any index when it becomes extremely overextended. Second, I want to avoid the temptation to call the so-called tech wreck an end to all bull markets in technology because, although the advance has stalled, there is plenty of room for the index to rebound. The main point of the chart shown in the figure helps frame the discussion for what I believe is a rough transition into a new era of investing. The main point, thus, is that much of the gain in the technology stocks could evaporate. This is important, for I don't want to give the impression that chips are dead. This chart is saying that the technology stocks may have hit an inflection, or transition, point: a point where established technologies are so readily available that growth potential has slowed. Therefore, investors are reevaluating their long-term commitment to the traditional technology sector and transferring it to other areas.

For example, investors have to factor in the fact that aside from PCs as the main object of their technological desires, now we have the emerging technologies of handheld devices, such as Palm Pilots and Handspring Visors. Cell phones have gone digital, and the new generation will sport larger screens, so that graphic-heavy PC-style visibility could be achieved on a handheld device. Wireless technology is making it easy to access information on the run, as two-way paging is increasing in popularity, thus increasing the potential for constant access to information, increasing productivity, and once more increasing the speed with which business advances.

The promise of riches now belongs to biotechnology, as the hard work of companies like Intel, Microsoft, and the imitators and innovators that their achievements have sparked has created a new gold rush, as the technological revolution has increased the speed with which researchers can make new discoveries and transmit the data more efficiently, both privately and publicly. The technology revolution has found a home alongside the realm of real-time quotes and Java charts, and it is this gold rush that I intend to decipher and place in the proper perspective. Just as the NASDAQ Composite ran out of gas in October 2000, even if time proves that it will be only in the short to intermediate term, so will biotechnology, as an investment, eventually meet its Waterloo.

What makes biotechnology much more attractive at this time in human history is that as a theme it is more global and has a greater connection on a gut level to humanity. Sure, PCs are everywhere, but many people still don't understand how they work or how to use them, unless they are engineers, while most people have had a friend or loved one who has had cancer. And many of them have survived, often as a result of a biotechnologically derived or influenced medication. It is this ability to connect with people on their own terms that makes the potential for an investment boom, even bigger than that created by the wondrous PC.

Thus as the promise of biotechnology is much grander on a cosmic scale, so is it likely that the surge in the value of the stock of companies in the sector will be just as grand, until, of course, reality sets in. The bottom line is that biotechnology can lead humanity to the mastery of the environment. If harnessed and managed properly, the dynamics of the sector can lead to a nearly inexhaustible supply of food, fuel, and medications as well as the potential for the prolongation of life beyond any benchmark currently entertained. The potential is there, and thanks to the advances in traditional technology, the reality of a better world for all is increasing despite the persistence and the presence of ideological differences in key political hot spots.

But the rise to full potential is not going to be a straight line up. There will be very difficult periods in which investors will have to carefully evaluate their portfolios and their commitment to investing in the dream that the industry offers. Already the sector has proven to be vulnerable to government scrutiny, both on a daily and a workmanlike basis, as when the FDA fails to approve a product, or government officials such as President Clinton make off-the-cuff remarks about the sector. It is not my intent to sour investors about this wonderful sector. But I think it would be irresponsible if I didn't reinforce the fact that history will repeat itself and that biotechnology will have its negative periods. At this stage, however, the sector is near its most explosive stage ever, and its potential to create millionaires is much greater than that offered by the PC, software, and microprocessor dynamic, where, as I'll discuss shortly, the potential for slower growth has been manifested by heavy selling.

In my opinion, much of the money that came out of PC-related technology found its way into biotechnology. This is illustrated in striking detail in figures 3.2 and 3.3. The AMEX Biotechnology Index (BTK), shown in figure 3.2, is a relative sea of calm compared to the Philadelphia Semiconductor Index (SOX), shown in figure 3.3.

The relentless selling in the chip stocks took the semiconductor sector, as measured by the SOX index, below the 700 area by October 11, which was ironically a significant bottom in the U.S. stock market in 1990, when oil prices were rising, unrest in the Middle East was in the headlines, and there was a very prominent Bush in the vicinity of Pennsylvania Avenue.

The absurdity of the selling is demonstrated when we look at table 3.1, which lists the component stocks of the index. I say absurd because markets tend to overreact. A 50 percent decline in an index such as SOX often precedes a significant buying opportunity. A huge

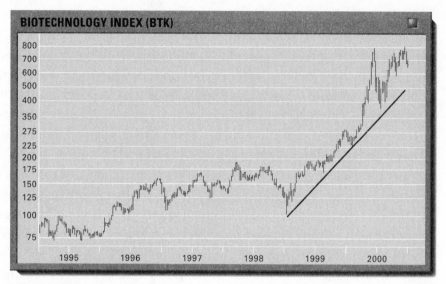

Figure 3.2. *The AMEX Biotechnology Index (BTK). The beginning of a gold rush. Courtesy of Telescan.*

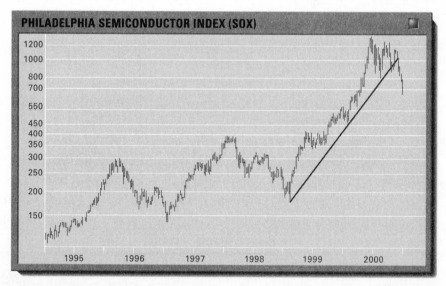

Figure 3.3. *The Philadelphia Semiconductor Index (SOX). The index break below a rising trend line down suggests that money is flowing out of semiconductor stocks. Courtesy of Telescan.*

Table 3.1 *The Philadelphia Semiconductor Index*

Xilinx

Rambus

Applied Materials

Lattice Semiconductors

Linear Technology

Micron Technology

Intel Corporation

Texas Instruments

Teradyne

Novellus Systems

Altera

KLA-Tencor

National Semiconductor

LSI Logic

Motorola

Advanced Microdevices

Reproduced from The Wall Street Detective's Market Sentiment Central *(www.wallstdet.com)*. Courtesy of the Philadelphia Stock Exchange *(www.phlx.com)*.

cut in the price of the stocks in companies of this caliber is factoring in a catastrophic decline in their ability to produce relevant products, and it basically discounted a total crash in the industry. While it is too early to tell whether the efficient market was right, as investors we have to be able to look at reality. PCs are not going away, which means that Intel and those companies that survive the October 2000 drubbing will have business for a while yet to come.

The SOX index is the most widely followed sector index on Wall Street and is the undisputed bellwether in technology. I personally use it so much as a bellwether and in my daily stock market commentary and analysis that I dedicated an entire page to it on Market Sentiment Central, and it happens to be one of the most heavily trafficked pages on the site.

As the table clearly shows, the SOX index is composed of a "who's who" of semiconductor manufacturing powerhouses. But in October 2000, the potential for lower earnings as a result of sluggish European economic growth and multiple production and management missteps from sector bellwether Intel, shown in figure 3.4, began a cascade of negative developments that culminated in heavy selling of traditional technology stocks. While only the future can tell whether the sector will return to its former glory, an intermediate-term analysis can lead to only one conclusion: Things have changed.

The fate of the chip stocks in October was best summarized by the action in the leader of the group, Intel. The stock, as figure 3.4 shows, broke below a 10-year trend line. By comparison, the leader of the genomics movement, Human Genome Sciences,

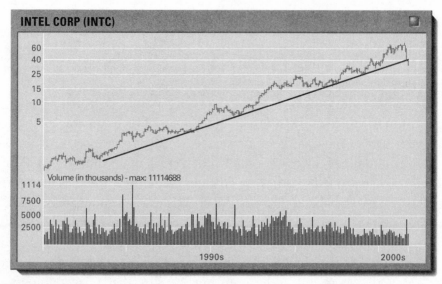

Figure 3.4. *Intel broke a 10-year trend line. Courtesy of Telescan.*

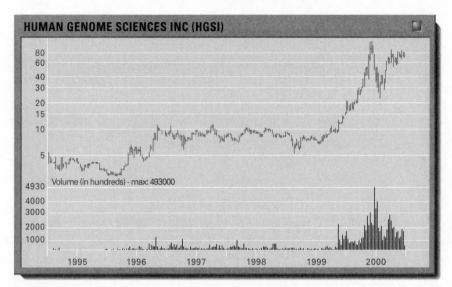

Figure 3.5. *Five-year chart of Human Genome Sciences. Note the consolidation pattern and the relative strength exhibited by the stock compared to Intel.*

shown in figure 3.5, on the same day shows that the stock is near an all-time high and instead of collapsing is consolidating its recent gains. The message is clear on both the sector and the individual stock level and validates our point. Money came out of traditional technology in October 2000 and went into the new leadership group for the early part of the 21st century: biotechnology.

The way of the markets is usually in a stepwise and often violent fashion. Thus, while a sector may get some of its luster back, once the dynamic that drove it higher has been diminished, it is usually never the same. A perfect example is that of Xerox (NYSE:XRX), shown in figure 3.6.

In the late 1960s, Xerox was among the technology leaders and a charter member of the so-called Nifty 50 stocks—growth vehicles that, according to market wisdom, could never fall since their technology at the time was so revolutionary that it could never be replaced. Well, in came Canon, which made better (or at

Figure 3.6. *Xerox (NYSE:XRX), a nearly 30-year history. Note the near extinction of the company in the late 1990s. Courtesy of Telescan.*

least as good) copiers, and in came Sharp and then Hewlett Packard with dot matrix printers, and the PC revolution took off. While Xerox rallied to new highs in the late 1990s, it fell once again and may go the way of the Edsel if management does not take appropriate steps. Sure, Xerox's problems were operations-related to a great degree. But the message is clear: No stock goes up forever.

Thus, the breakdown of Intel is significant for several reasons. First, it is another rough reminder that any stock is vulnerable if it fails to live up to Wall Street expectations. Second, it shows that in today's market, where information travels at the speed of light and where the Securities and Exchange Commission has cracked down on selective disclosure rules, by which companies would re-lease sensitive news to analysts before they did so to the public, stocks can be severely damaged in a matter of hours to days, as the unfiltered news leads to violent price markdowns.

It should also be noted that as of October 11, 2000, Intel broke below a ten-year technical support level. From an intermediate-term standpoint, this potentially is a deathblow to the stock of a leader and thus is worthy of note. It does not mean that the technology sector is dying, but it is significant and will be something to monitor in the next few years. Perhaps the grimmest message regarding where most of the money is coming out of in the technology sector is found in figures 3.7 and 3.8, of Dell Computers and Microsoft.

The stocks of these two giants have seen better times. While Dell found itself in a business with decreasing growth potential and equally decreasing profit margins, Microsoft and its monopolistic business practices (as far as the judgment, yet to be appealed, against it is concerned), got the rest of the software industry quite angry. The results were catastrophic. Founder Bill Gates abdicated the throne and went back to the development table, and its highly touted Windows 2000 operating system ran

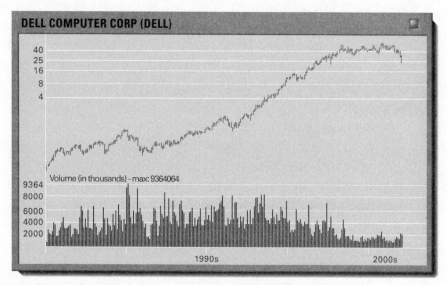

Figure 3.7. *Dell Computers breaks down. Courtesy of Telescan.*

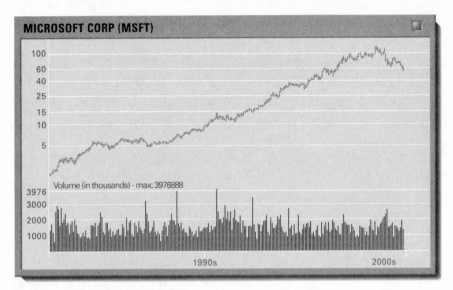

Figure 3.8. *Microsoft breaks down. Courtesy of Telescan.*

into resistance from the emerging Linux operating system. But be-yond the politics, the charts don't lie. Money also came out of these stocks and went into biotechnology, and the stocks had such large amounts going into them that even if no new money was to go into biotechnology, the rally sparked by flows out of these wounded dragons was so large that a biotech rally could well be just as legendary.

Comparing figures 3.3 and 3.4, we can see that the SOX index was heavily influenced by the action of Intel and that the trend line for the SOX index was broken, meaning that the rising trend was violated for the whole sector, and not just Intel. This offers an interesting similarity between the traditional technology sector and biotechnology, as a problem for one stock in the sector can lead to "me too" declines, as Wall Street starts to factor in the fact that similar problems could be duplicated in similar companies. An FDA denial or an earnings shortfall in a major biotechnology company can spread throughout the entire sector just as well.

Now that we have noted important individual stocks and have touched on the change in the flow of money, it is important to compare the BTK and SOX index charts in detail, for this is a classic study in intersector and intermarket analysis, an approach first described by master technical analysts John Murphy and Martin Pring.

First, we note that both indexes began impressive rallies in 1998. We note that during the period, interest rates were rising but had little effect on either sector, at least until late 2000, when it became evident that the interest rate increases might be having a slowing effect on the economy. Both indexes rose impressively until January 2000, when both made tops. But the subtle differences began to creep in soon thereafter, as the SOX index began to assume a weaker posture, while the BTK index bounced off its trend line more robustly and, more important, in weak moments managed to remain stronger than the chip index. Finally, the breakdown in SOX is in contrast to the BTK index chart, where the index has given in to the general market weakness but remains in a rising trend, again clearly documenting that money is flowing out of the chips and into the biotechnology sector.

Thus the charts of the NASDAQ Composite and those of the BTK index and of the SOX index clearly support the theme that money is coming out of traditional technology, especially PC and traditional software stocks, and finding its way, albeit slowly at this stage, into biotechnology. The BTK index is noticeably rising above a trend line that began in 1998, as the potential for the decoding of the human genome became the dominant theme in the sector.

The BTK index rose eightfold in nearly two years, prior to the generalized market weakness in late 2000, just on the expectation that something big was about to happen. Thus, it is understandable that some backing and filling will occur after such a huge move. Also important is the effect of higher interest rates and tough talk from the Federal Reserve, rising oil prices, and general seasonal tendencies for stocks to fall in the September–October period.

Support and resistance are key points in technical analysis on which I'll expand later. But at this stage of our discussion, *resistance* is a chart point above which a stock or an index has trouble rising. *Support* is a chart level below which a stock or an index has difficulty falling. Resistance means that there are sellers waiting, while support means that there are buyers waiting.

I also note that the trend line on the Biotechnology Index suggests that even if the index falls, there is plenty of support at the 500 area. As a technical analyst, and as I'll discuss in a later chapter, I am a firm believer in the power of trend lines, as they are crucial in the decision-making process of when to buy or sell a stock.

Thus far, I've discussed the dynamics of a secular move, or a long-term move in a sector of the stock market. A secular move lasts for many years and sometimes for over a decade. The best example of a recent secular move began in the late 1960s, when the Nifty 50 stocks, such as Xerox, set the stage for what was to become the legendary rally in the semiconductor and PC-related stocks that truly gathered steam in the 1980s and lasted at least until 2000. The jury is still out on whether the chips and PCs could mount another comeback.

Biotechnology is in the early stages of what could be a multi-decade move up. Already, the unraveling of the human genome and the emergence of genomics from the lab to the world stage are the dominant themes that are capturing the imagination and the money flow from institutional investors and, to a lesser degree, from the public.

The future of biotechnology will lie in the next two stages. The development of genomics-based drugs and the emergence of proteomics, or the actual use of proteins to make drugs. Before we dive into these dynamic topics, a clear blueprint for company analysis must be established.

Now that we understand the dynamics of a secular move, we can move on to the dynamics of biotechnology. The best way to

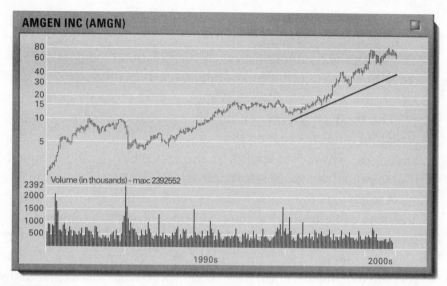

Figure 3.9. *Amgen's long-term price chart.*

understand a biotechnology company is to look at the sector bellwether, Amgen, whose lifetime stock price as of October 2000 is shown in figure 3.9.

A quick glance at Yahoo's Biotechnology Industry page *(biz .yahoo.com/research/indgrp/med_biomed_gene.html)* reveals that of the hundreds of biotechnology companies listed, only 33 of them are profitable. As we get into company profiles, we will list the key ones in detail. But at this point, I'll concentrate on the first biotechnology company to have products and to become profitable.

Amgen Is the Benchmark

Amgen is the yardstick by which the biotechnology sector is measured. From its humble beginnings to its rise as a member of the Standard & Poor's (S&P) 500 index, a significant milestone for any company but especially for a biotechnology company, the company has proven to be a class act in its ability to deliver the goods to both the medical community and its investors.

Amgen is the world's largest independent biotechnology company, having been founded in 1980. As the company's mission on its Web site *(www.amgen.com)* clearly illustrates, its goal is to discover and develop "both naturally occurring proteins, and small molecules" in order to develop drugs.

The connection between the pharmaceuticals industry and the emerging biotechnology industry in the late 1980s was quite clear at Amgen, whose first chairman and CEO, George B. Rathmann, Ph.D., came from Abbott Laboratories.

Amgen was the brainchild of scientists and venture capitalists and was initially funded by a $19 million private equity placement in 1981. It went public in 1983 and placed secondary offerings in 1986 and 1987. Its second CEO was Gordon Binder, who remained in place until May 2000, when he was replaced by Kevin W. Sharer. The company grew from a staff of seven in 1981 to a staff of 6,400 in 1999 and has established a global presence, with offices, factories, and distribution centers in California, Kentucky, Europe, Asia, Canada, and Puerto Rico.

Its fiscal 1999 revenues totaled $3 billion, growing rapidly from the prior year's $2.7 billion. The company's research budget for 1999 was $823 million. Net income was $1.1 billion.

The rise of a company from a small office with seven staff members to an empire is worth exploring and can be divided into six stages, which are listed in Table 3.2. In the examples of the technology stocks I described previously, we saw many of these stages as well, and I'll go back to them as necessary.

Stage 1: The Dream

The dream stage is the earliest stage for a company. It starts when the founder or founders meet in a coffee shop somewhere and wish that their lives were better. The entrepreneurial spirit takes hold, and more dreamers are drafted. If there are enough dreamers and others that sign on, the company moves ahead to something more tangible than a dream. But most companies never make it past the dream

---

Table 3.2 *The Six Stages of a Biotech Company*

Stage 1: The Dream

Stage 2: The Discovery of the Dream

Stage 3: The Stumble

Stage 4: The Recovery

Stage 5: The Reality

Stage 6: Life Goes On—Mergers and Acquisitions

---

stage, and most entrepreneurs never realize their business dreams. But a handful of dreamers make it to the next level, and they are usually driven by the pure, unadulterated desire to succeed.

It is at this stage when the right amount of luck and skill are required, for capital is the absolute necessity at this stage. Offices must be rented. Furnishings, telephones, PCs, and other electronics must be bought. And customers must be courted, along with outside money.

This is where Amgen was in 1981 with its seven staffers. As the history of Amgen shows, there is hope for the right dream and for those who know how to make it come true.

Stage 2: The Discovery of the Dream

Stage 2 refers to the publicity stage, when the company moves beyond the initial dream and establishes some sort of tangible research and perhaps even a small production line. It is at this point where the venture capitalists who helped found the company begin to promote the company to Wall Street, first in private meetings. This is followed by the offer for the company to be underwritten and to go public. Biotechnology companies often go public before other companies because their cash needs are so high. And the market often gives them the benefit of the doubt since the promise for a big payoff is often huge.

But companies at this stage, especially in biotechnology, need to have made some sort of discovery or have convincing research results that may have even been published in scientific journals. Convincing preclinical trial research and/or early clinical trial research is important and usually is sufficient evidence that the company has a real chance to make it to the next stage. Most important is at least one endorsement from a major pharmaceutical company that has formed an alliance with the small company. Government grants also help solidify the credibility of the company and provide much-needed cash.

The discovery of the dream culminates with the wide acceptance of the company's research platform or early product by Wall Street and the initial public offering (IPO), in which the company's and the founder's pockets are replenished and they are finally paid for their troubles.

But the IPO is really only the beginning. Amgen went public in 1983, and its first product, Epogen, was patented in 1987. Epogen was finally approved in 1989 by the FDA. By 1999, Epogen sales were $1.8 billion. The point here, which I'll continue to repeat for the rest of the book, is that biotechnology investors, above all, need to be patient.

Amgen's dream stage and the discovery of the dream took many years to develop. Human Genome Sciences, a company that in 2000 is in the middle stages of the dream stage, has yet to produce a drug. But, as of September 2000, it had entered into phase 3 clinical trials.

The dream must also be eloquently communicated, and no one is better at keeping the market abreast of significant developments than Human Genome Sciences CEO Michael Haseltine, M.D. Dr. Haseltine is frequently seen on CNBC and other significant media outlets. His face has become synonymous with genomics and is likely to become synonymous with proteomics, the next dream in biotechnology.

The next step for a dream-stage company, if its product is successful in the clinical trials, is FDA approval. It is after approval that the real test will come because the expectations for the company to deliver were already built into the price of the stock. Thus, when the first drug comes out, Wall Street will expect a huge surge in profits, which will be carefully watched over the first few quarters for signs of growth.

Stage 3: The Stumble

Like any highly anticipated event, after the excitement comes stage 3: the stumble. The stumble presents itself in two ways: FDA approval and/or the failure of critical clinical trials or the disappointment of an expected blockbuster drug's not delivering earnings to Wall Street's expectations.

All companies stumble after the dream stage, and Human Genome Sciences will likely stumble as well, not because the company will necessarily fail or because its management will be inadequate. Although those things are within the realm of possibility, the stumble will come more because, after several years of the stock rising on the expectations of becoming profitable, Wall Street will sell on the fact, just like it bought on the rumor. The stumble may present itself as a long-term buying opportunity and is worth watching for.

The perfect example of the stumble is shown in the 15-year chart of IBM, shown in figure 3.10, whose fortunes changed drastically when Dell, Apple (NASDAQ:AAPL), Gateway (NYSE:GTW), Compaq (NYSE:CPQ), and the rest of the clones burst onto the scene en masse. IBM was still largely dependent on revenue from its mainframe business and enjoyed a significant portion of the still-infant PC market. But when competition hit and management missed several chances to rally around the new challenge, the stock was pulverized.

As will happen with quality companies, new management, new direction, or both are found, and both the company and the stock make a comeback. Today's IBM makes a significant portion

Figure 3.10. *IBM stumbles and recovers.*

of its money from business consulting, and the future may be in biotechnology. I point this out because when compared to the chart of Dell Computers, whose action I described earlier and which has no exposure to biotechnology, IBM looks great, fluctuating in what currently looks to be a consolidation pattern.

An even more representative example of the life and times of a biotechnology company is the chart of Cephalon, shown in figure 3.11, a company that was mentioned in some detail earlier. First is the overall choppy nature of the chart, as the company's fortunes have risen and fallen. The left side of the chart, from 1992 to late 1995, depicts what I would call a lackluster and protracted dream stage.

The company had sound research with its drug Provigil but not a widespread market. Thus, Wall Street rewarded the company with capital via an initial public offering in order to allow the company to continue operations. Provigil is a drug that keeps patients who suffer from narcolepsy from falling asleep. While the product is excellent, the market is small.

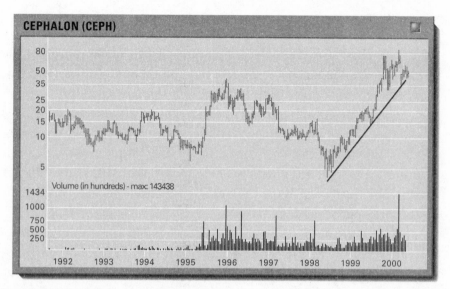

Figure 3.11. *Cephalon's stumble-and-recovery cycle. Courtesy of Telescan.*

Now, the trick is to stay in business long enough to leverage the drug into other uses. And that's what Cephalon started to do in 1996, when the new dream, or the use of Provigil for broader uses (such as sleep apnea, another sleep-related disorder), was sought from the FDA.

But again in 1996, 1997, and 1998, the dream turned into a nightmare. Finally, clinical trial data became encouraging, and by late 1998 the dream was back on, and the stock rose both on increasing sales of Provigil for narcolepsy and on the renewed promise of diversified use. Unfortunately, as the chart shows, in mid-2000 the FDA denied the use of Provigil for sleep apnea, and the stock stumbled again.

By now, the uninitiated reader may be getting better at reading charts and might have noted that Cephalon, despite its 2000 stumble, does remain in an up trend, as highlighted by the rising trend line. That means that the stock is still alive and that Wall Street is confident that the company will survive long enough to either make it on its own or be bought by a rival.

Stage 4: The Recovery

As the charts of IBM and Cephalon clearly illustrate, after the stumble, if management rallies and the company does the right things, such as refocusing its research, improving its public relations, and diversifying their pipeline, the stock will recover. This is the true test of management's ability to lead, and this is where institutions make the decision whether they want to stay for another long-term stint with management. With IBM, the answer was obviously yes. With Cephalon, the answer is less certain but certainly encouraging.

In biotechnology, the key to success will be the ability to anticipate what the nearly profitable companies with huge pipeline potential will do when the money starts to roll in. Will they continue their research efforts to their full power? Will they expand by acquisition? Worst of all, will they just sit on their laurels?

The best way to maintain a strong recovery, and the benchmark for staying with a company, is the ability of the company to continue to grow responsibly by both acquisition as well as internal growth from a strong drug pipeline. We want to see them expand the sales force and make the right alliances, and we want them to meet or beat expectations every time. With one miscue, they will find themselves back in stage 3, much as Cephalon did in the previous example.

Stage 5: The Reality

Stage 5 is the point at which a company matures and goes about its business. The prototype stage 5 biotechnology company is Amgen, which is now considered as much a pharmaceuticals company as a biotechnology company. The reality is that as long as Amgen can deliver the goods, Wall Street is likely to be kind to it. That does not guarantee that the stock will go up forever. Just as happened to Intel and to IBM and Xerox, Wall Street can definitely lose its patience. But the dynamic of the sector, and the ability with which Amgen has navigated some rough seas, suggests that its leadership position is safe for now.

Reality comes in two ways. First, it could be that the company's products and management are inadequate, and that is almost a final reality unless the company makes drastic changes. Second, and a topic which I'll expand upon in a later chapter, is the reality of the market, as it befell Gemini Genomics (see figure 3.12).

Gemini's management has a dream: to discover proteins that cause diseases and to use them to find treatments or cures for them. The dream has been discovered, as Wall Street financed an initial public offering. The public offering came as the company's research on twins has revealed at least 10 proteins related to chronic diseases. Furthermore, the company has developed a test that it has licensed to Affymetrix to detect the presence of a protein found in patients with osteoporosis, which could serve as a diagnostic marker and may be used to identify patients with the potential to develop the disease.

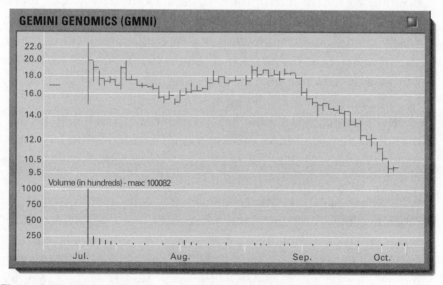

Figure 3.12. *Gemini Genomics (NASDAQ:GMNI) and reality.*

Thus the company meets the previously outlined criteria for a solid study. The company had a dream. The dream was accepted. The research is sound. The goals are worthy. And the stock gets sold vehemently, even as much of the sector remains reasonably stable.

What happened? Reality came in and delivered a bear market in stocks. Margin calls, which I'll discuss later, came in. Investors had to sell or have their brokers sell at least the speculative stocks in their portfolio.

Summary

This chapter was designed to give investors a broad look at the investment landscape for the first two decades of the 21st century. I discussed the macrodynamic of money flowing out of the traditional technology stocks and finding its way into biotechnology. Despite the fact that computers are not going away, PCs as we know them are not likely to provide the growth for profits and revenues that they delivered in the two decades prior.

Thus biotechnology stocks in the year 2000 are in a similar position to where microprocessor and PC-related stocks found themselves in the early 1980s—as entities with sustainable and nearly predictable double-digit-plus growth for the next ten to twenty years. It is this fact that is central to my expectation for the sector, and it is one that is becoming increasingly accepted by money managers on a daily basis.

By this time, you should have a solid understanding of the history, the science, and the basic workings of a biotechnology company. You should also have a basic knowledge of some of the Internet sites where information is available and be comfortable with the stages of development and behavior exhibited by biotechnology companies and what to expect from management when things go wrong. But we are not ready to look at companies in detail, nor are we ready to learn how to make buying and selling decisions. Before we delve into those aspects of the game, we must understand how the markets work.

As I wrote this chapter, another Middle East oil-related crisis developed, and many familiar aspects of how markets behave and how they affect individual sectors unfolded. In the next chapter, this unfortunate but serious development will be used and supported by other events as an illustration of how the financial markets work.

CHAPTER
4

The Markets

In the prior three chapters I have presented three major concepts. In chapter 1, I discussed the history of the biotechnology sector. It became obvious that the sector provides something old and something new. The main point was that as long as the individual investor can stay focused on the fact that biotechnology is as old as the earth itself and as old fashioned, in a sense, as the art of brewing, the sector is less threatening. Thus by framing the discussion properly and attaining a more relaxed mind-set about the complexity of the sector, you should feel more comfortable with the science, which can be difficult to understand if it's not properly condensed. Chapter 1 also described the role of the Food and Drug Administration, which is the single most important step in drug development once the discovery and research phases are done.

Chapter 2 provided a basic knowledge of the key terms and processes involved in the science of biotechnology. The thrust of the chapter was to provide enough information to the nonscientist to prepare one to interpret news releases that may affect the price of an owned stock. Here we began with basic terms describing the cell's anatomy. We discussed the key concepts, beginning with DNA and ending with the central concept of the science: protein synthesis. We discussed genomics and set the stage for a later discussion on the next key concept in biotechnology—proteomics—where I believe serious action will take place over the next ten years.

Chapter 3 shifted gears and began a discussion on companies. We discussed the secular dynamic that unfolded in the fall of 2000 in which money poured out of the traditional technology sector and made its way into biotechnology. The chapter also prefaced the discussion of technical analysis in chapter 7, where I'll discuss the art of chart reading and indicator analysis. Chapter 3 concluded with a detailed review of the history of Amgen, the bellwether company for the entire sector. This set the stage for a discussion of the six stages in the development of a company. In a later chapter, we'll discuss how this analysis should be incorporated into making buying and selling decisions.

The goal of the three prior chapters was to provide a working background for investors with a nonscientific background on what biotechnology is all about, how it got there, what it takes for a company to become successful in biotechnology, and what the next decade holds for patient investors with a long-term time horizon.

Thus, armed with a strong background on the key internal concepts of the biotechnology sector, this chapter will introduce and detail the key external, nonscientific concepts that affect the price patterns of stocks, not just in our sector but in all sectors as well.

The goal of this chapter is to begin to add knowledge of the markets to our knowledge of the science. I'll do so by introducing and developing the concept of Intellectual Inclusion, which is a key to the success of sector investing. The concept works by training investors to piece together knowledge from different areas and then apply it to investing. By the use of these techniques, you will be able to act more quickly and make more sound decisions.

Intellectual Inclusion

I coined the principle of Intellectual Inclusion when I was a chief anesthesiologist in Dallas, Texas. It was a tumultuous period, one when the pressures of managed care were weighing heavily on patients, hospitals, physicians, and other health care providers. I volunteered to give a talk on teamwork to the department heads of the hospital where I worked at the time. I discovered that the key to teamwork is for the team to learn to analyze situations correctly, in a uniform fashion, and to carry out the solution by the use of well-defined protocols.

That does not mean that people become automatons. Instead, the principle, when applied correctly, allows each individual to act on a situation by drawing on his or her own experience and then plugging that experience into the choices provided by the principle for each situation. The full explanation of this concept is beyond the scope of this book and is intricate enough to deserve its own treatise. But the basics of it can serve as a template for making stock market decisions and can serve as a platform from which the rest of the chapter and the book is built.

In summary, a person's actions on a day-to-day basis are the sum of the expression of the interaction of his or her genetic makeup, environmental influences, and experience. Therefore, when any of us respond to a situation, we are unconsciously integrating the three major influences. The result is the response, which can be extremely positive or disastrously negative. Intellectual Inclusion simply brings the content of the subconscious to the forefront and forces the individual to make a conscious decision by literally clicking through the possibilities in his or her mind's eye.

This is by no means a cultish form of mind control. There are no donations to cloak-and-dagger organizations to make, and there are no one-on-one sessions with gurus who have made it through a rigorous course. Intellectual Integration is designed only to improve the thought process and to create a conscious set of thought processes that can be used in similar situations. The result is greater confidence in a person's ability to interact with the environment and more consistent and successful trading and investing.

This philosophy will come in extremely useful on that fateful day when a biotechnology company in your portfolio makes that fateful announcement that the Food and Drug Administration (FDA) denied its application, and the bottom falls out. Certainly, some of us will have sell stops in place that will limit our risk. But others will be more long-term oriented and will be holding a stock that has lost a great deal of value and will have to make a decision as to what to do next. While I'll deal with this in great detail in later chapters, I'll mention here that those who practice Intellectual Inclusion are likely to be better prepared for the event since they will have studied similar cases in the past and will have already devised several strategies that fit their experience and personality.

At the center of the concept is becoming acquainted, either personally or vicariously, with as many experiences as possible, both in trading stocks and in real life. The financial markets, just like real life, are expressions of human behavior that, in turn, are derived by the interaction among genetics, environment, and experience. By watching friends, co-workers, and relatives as well as living our own lives, we become exposed to huge amounts of live real-time data in the form of interpersonal interaction, with both positive and negative outcomes. Unfortunately, our brains have been trained to ignore much of what we see and hear. Television and much of technology can dull the cognitive process if allowed to do so.

Intellectual Inclusion works on the premise that we should always have at least part of our conscious mind paying attention and collecting data. Our senses are like radar screens with very efficient "broadband" connections to the brain, which is an organic filing system. Once the data are collected, they should be consciously sorted and stored. That which is useful should always be ready to be retrieved and used at a moment's notice, and that requires practice.

One of my favorite exercises on long drives is to pretend that I'm being interviewed on a major talk show. I imagine the guest host as an intimidating monster whose job it is to make me say and do the wrong thing. Thus I steel myself and practice my responses. I'm not someone who goes to the lengths that presidential candidates go to in order to give politically correct responses. Instead, I use the exercise not just to practice my diction and manner but to also sort through the data and consciously remove that which is no longer relevant.

A simple exercise is to go through my portfolio mentally as the nasty host asks me what stocks I own and why. If I can still talk myself into owning the stock, I keep it. If I can't convince the host, the stock is usually a sell. For example, I have owned shares in Starbucks (NASDAQ:SBUX) in my personal account and in several client accounts for over a year as of this writing. The stock has been in a protracted trading range. But as I walk into my neighborhood shop once or twice a week, the place is always full. The company continues to report steady growth of 10 percent in same-store sales. Whenever I walk in, I see smiling customers relaxing over their drinks. I see a wide range of ages, from high school students to retired people. I see construction workers and "Goths" with pierced ears and noses waiting in line next to fur-coat-clad socialites and executives who drive luxury cars. And I see many of the same faces every time I walk in. When I go to the shop two miles down the road, I see the same thing. And when I go to the shop at the mall, guess what? I see more of the same.

The conclusion is that something is happening there, something that is worth waiting for. As long as the stock remains within my prescribed parameters, I will own it. If things change, it will be time to sell.

This is a simple exercise in Intellectual Inclusion. It is using what I know and what I see, adapted to and added to my knowledge of the financial markets. I like coffee, and I know that millions of other people share my vice. I see them all flocking to get their daily dose, and I see no evidence of a slowing in growth for the trend. In fact, I see that the world is beginning to discover Starbucks, suggesting that, barring unforeseen problems, the company is on solid footing and that eventually Wall Street will recognize the dynamic once again and the stock will eventually rise. If I'm wrong, by keeping tabs on the store traffic and by watching the stock's price action, I will sell—dispassionately, efficiently, and quickly.

Another great way to gather data is to observe what happens at the office. The personal interactions you see could also, in principle, be applied to the stock market. For example, if a colleague is a gambler and loses everything on a penny stock, that should be stored and cataloged, as it will become useful when that $5 stock dances across your favorite Web site. If the colleague will talk about it, you might learn something about faulty thought processes and discover tendencies in yourself that could be corrected. Not all $5 stocks are dogs, but the ones that don't become $6 and $10 stocks at a reasonable pace are likely to be dogs.

By the same token, Intellectual Inclusion means that skills learned in one area should be applied to other areas. For example, when reading charts, why not apply some of your knowledge of physics? After all, a stock chart is just the same as a rocket, which eventually succumbs to the pull of gravity. My experience as an anesthesiologist has come in handy in trading, investing, and money management. For example, when stocks are likely to be heading into trouble, I get the same feeling that I get when I'm running into trouble with a patient on the operating room table.

In the operating room, my job is to manage the patient's airway and maintain unconsciousness and unawareness of pain during an operation. I do so by constantly monitoring a circuit that begins with the patient's positioning on the operating room table and helps prevent nerve injuries if they are positioned in a way that is unnatural. I then make sure that all my monitors are placed correctly so that the readings on the oscilloscope and other consoles are accurate. I monitor the connection to the breathing circuit, as leaks can be hazardous to the patient and the operating room personnel. I watch the monitors, which keep a running total on heartbeat, the level of oxygenation of the blood, blood pressure, and the level of anesthetic being administered. At each step of the way, I have to make both minor and major adjustments.

That vigilance is what makes me a good anesthesiologist. The same skills, down to reading vital signs, is what makes me a successful investor and trader. By using the same analytic skills and transferring them to a different arena and coupling them with new training, anyone can make a transition to a new occupation or vocation.

Of course, I don't enjoy watching markets crash. My goal, which I have been quite successful at obtaining, is to be as much out of stocks as possible when the markets take a tumble. But, in a case where things happen suddenly, it is good to have solid options and protocols ready to unleash.

In the operating room, I use the Advanced Cardiac Life Support (ACLS) protocols when trouble arises. In investing, I use technical analysis. The principles are the same. When something bad happens, I'm ready for it because I have purposely prepared and have practiced. More important for me is the fact that I have had the privilege of having saved lives as well as the sorrow of not having been as fortunate in other cases where the patient was much too ill to survive a lifesaving emergency operation. This spectrum has given me perspective to deal with the volatility of the markets. Even if I lose some money, I haven't watched a patient die. The next day, I'm back in front of the trading screen.

Finally, Intellectual Inclusion means that we should become more in tune with our feelings. If you are looking at a stock and the thought of owning it gives you a racing heart and a tight stomach, it's time to take a step back and remember the last time you felt this way. If the experience that came up in your mind's eye is unpleasant, this is not a stock to own.

Thus, as you go through this book, I encourage you to spend time letting the concept take its natural course. What is discussed in one chapter will be connected to something in another chapter. Be inclusive. Encapsulate the experience. Store it. And retrieve it later. Then train your mind to do the same when looking at a stock chart. Practice talking to a difficult talk show host. If you can't convince him or yourself, it's time to do some serious research and consider selling. If a stock's trading pattern seems familiar, that's because chart patterns tend to repeat themselves. Regardless of the stock, outcomes tend to be similar in similar situations. Write notes in a diary about an interesting and successful or unsuccessful trade. Go back and review it. If you made a mistake in the past and are about to make it again, this could save you both heartache and money.

If you read a news release that is similar to one you read last week, remember what happened to the company after the similar incident. Go online and look at the charts. Compare them. If the outcome last week was negative, it likely will be this week, even if the companies are different. Biotechnology stocks often move in tandem, much like traditional technology stocks. They also have relationships both with one another and with similar partners in the pharmaceutical or other industries. Negative events have ripple effects.

In short, Intellectual Inclusion, and the ability to order and retrieve our past experience, makes us better investors. It often helps us to be more thoughtful people. With this basic premise in mind, we can move on to the most important external influences on the financial markets: the Federal Reserve and interest rates.

The Federal Reserve and Interest Rates

The greatest fallacy of financial market analysis is to place the stock market above the bond market in importance. This is not to say that billions of dollars are not exchanged in stocks on a daily basis. But the fact is that over a trillion dollars per day exchange hands in the U.S. Treasury bond market alone. Thus, the entire outstanding debt of the United States gets turned over in the Treasury market in the space of a week.

The bond market is a poorly understood instrument by most investors because it is not glamorous. It does not have the appeal that owning technology or biotechnology stocks does, and it certainly does not make for snappy cocktail party banter. But it is the foundation of the financial system, as the business world revolves around the ease with which money can be borrowed. More important, the bond market is the field agent of the central banks, for central banks raise or lower interest rates by buying or selling

Treasury securities in the open market and thus adjusting liquidity in the system.

How the Federal Reserve and other central banks actually make the monetary system work is beyond the scope of this book. But the fact remains that those investors who ignore the potential effect of the bond market, the Federal Reserve, and other central banks on their portfolios are asking for trouble.

History may show that the year 2000 was the year in which the biotechnology sector made it to the top of Wall Street's most-wanted list as a sector. But history also shows that the most constant influence on stock prices is the Federal Reserve.

The Circle of Life

As the father of a five-year-old, I have had an intimate experience with the Disney catchphrase "the circle of life," which was the theme of the hit movie *The Lion King*. But the stock market itself has its own version of the circle, with three main players: interest rates, market sentiment, and the flow of money.

In *After-Hours Trading Made Easy,* I fully described the relationship and thus will only reprise it here to a smaller degree.

The Federal Reserve monitors economic conditions in response to its double-edged mandate from Congress: low inflation and full employment. The central bank attempts to meet these goals by raising or dropping interest rates. The main effect on the economy is that higher interest rates make it more difficult for businesses and individuals to borrow money, with the intended effect being an economic slowdown and a decrease in inflationary expectations.

The economic expansion of the late 1990s, which may have ended in 2000 at least at its above-average rate of rise, was boosted by the promise of increased productivity of the Internet. The premise of the so-called new paradigm was that technology would allow for more work to be done by fewer people, more economically, or cheaper when looked at from a productivity standpoint. Simply said, people could produce more goods and services in the same amount of time for less money. This was expected to increase profits infinitely and lead us all to an economic Nirvana.

Of course, history shows that anytime everyone starts to yell that this time is different, something bad is about to happen. The bad thing this time was that the "irrational exuberance" that Federal Reserve Chairman Alan Greenspan referred to in a now infamous speech eventually came to pass. As the Internet stocks rallied to incredible heights, ones that obviously were out of proportion with reality, the paper wealth created by the false valuations of businesses that had no earnings and low chances of ever making any money fueled economic growth, which made the Fed uncomfortable. It will never be truly known whether the so-called Internet bubble would have led to an economic catastrophe because the Federal Reserve began raising interest rates, and eventually Internet companies could no longer borrow money or issue any more stock to finance operations. As a result, the entire technology sector collapsed, as I have discussed.

It is important to note that the Federal Reserve had to raise interest rates for a long period of time in order to achieve its objectives of slowing at least the rate of growth in the Internet sector, as it began raising the discount rate in August 1999 and raised it four more times, for a total of five rate hikes. As of November 2000, the Fed was not very likely to raise interest rates much further as the economy began to show signs of slowing.

The moral of the story is that just when most people began to think that this time was different, in fact it wasn't as different as they thought it was. The Federal Reserve can still slow the economy and wring excessive speculation out of the stock market, even if it takes longer than anyone expects.

The net effect of the higher interest rates is an increase in bearish market sentiment. Market sentiment is essentially a measure of the mood of market participants and will be discussed in more detail later. But when the market's mood becomes too bullish, as when the Internet stocks were at their peak, the market becomes vulnerable to external events, such as interest rate increases and earnings disappointments. As stocks fall, participants become more gloomy and sell stock. Eventually, negative sentiment reaches a climax, the selling stops, and all the money that has flowed out of stocks finds its way back in, making stocks rise again.

This is the circle of life, and it is the most important concept in market analysis.

The Federal Reserve

The Federal Reserve is at the center of the circle of life, and it has done an excellent job under Alan Greenspan despite multiple stock market crashes. Despite boom-and-bust periods, the United States has not fallen into a depression like Japan and Southeast Asia did when Japan's central bank raised interest rates in 1989. In 1989, Japan was at the top of the world, with their business models being adopted by many countries. Its markets were the envy of the rest of the world—until its central bank raised interest rates. Suddenly, the golden economy that could do no wrong was exposed for what it was: not a transparent market but an intricate sham and a remnant of a feudal lord system in which cronyism and cover-ups were the rule. Of course, there has now been some reform in Japan, but much more remains to be done. That is the main lesson to learn from all markets. They all rise on expectations that feed on themselves and become unrealistic beyond anything that resembles normalcy. Eventually, they all fall when the emperor's clothes are exposed for what they are: nothing.

The Federal Reserve was established in 1913 to prevent booms and busts in the economy. Prior to the Fed, private banks were the only source of funds for a largely agricultural society that depended on the weather and the dynamics of supply and demand for farm products to survive until the industrial revolution added new potential for growth, which for a while just amplified the boom-and-bust cycle. For a period of time in the 19th and early 20th centuries, booms and busts were dependent on the goodwill from famous bankers like J. P. Morgan. Thus, it seems ironic that it took until the late 1980s for a Fed chairman to emerge with the insight to navigate the incredibly murky waters of the current global economy with nearly minimal effect on the U.S. economy. When you add the intangibles brought on by the shenanigans of Congress and the White House as well as the political turmoil caused by conflicting ideology and bumbling tyrants all over the world, the Federal Reserve may well deserve honorary canonization.

But central banks are not immune from making mistakes. The greatest danger of central banks is that they become politicized, as was the central bank of Japan in the 1980s and as former U.S. Feds were alleged to be prior to Paul Volcker's and Alan Greenspan's tenures. A politicized central bank loses credibility and leads to market chaos.

Major central bank mistakes occurred in 1929, when the Great Depression was brought on by too tight a money policy; in 1989 in Japan, for the same reason; and in 1992 in Europe, when a weak economy was flogged by Germany's Bundesbank and triggered a global currency crisis.

Thus the Federal Reserve is the world's leading central bank, and Alan Greenspan is considered to be the greatest central banker of all time, as he has perfected the art of quenching speculation, wringing out excessive inflation, and keeping the U.S. economy moving forward. His political acumen is more revered than his economic judgment, which often is questioned by pundits, rivals, and politicians. But the fact remains that it is this kind of stewardship that, if maintained, even by a Greenspan successor, can nurture the development of periodic bull markets in stocks and keep the U.S. economy moving forward.

The Bond Market

The bond market is a huge beast when you account for treasuries, quasi-treasuries (e.g., mortgage-backed securities sold by agencies like Fannie Mae), corporate bonds, and bonds issued in the municipal market by states, cities, and other municipalities. For our purposes, we'll concentrate on the U.S. 30-year Treasury bond, which for all intents and purposes is viewed as a global benchmark. Bonds are measured by yield, or how much interest they pay. As the price rises on the bond, the yield drops. As I discussed previously, lower interest rates are usually good for stocks. This is a result of market participants looking for the highest rate possible for their money. As bond yields fall, bonds are less attractive, and money flows into stocks.

The Federal Reserve and the bond market work together, as the bond market essentially validates or protests the Fed's actions. If the bond market does not approve of what the Fed is doing, it will protest by going against the Fed. For example, if bonds are selling off and market rates are rising and the Fed raises rates but the bond market thinks that the Fed should have done more, bonds will continue to sell off. Eventually, the Fed will acknowledge the bond market, and the relationship will be back in equilibrium.

A basic understanding of the bond market is important in investing in all sectors of the stock market, as all stocks are eventually interest rate sensitive, meaning that if rates rise high enough, the stock market will eventually fall.

How the Bond Market Affects Stocks

Figure 4.1 clearly shows that the overall trend for market interest rates over the five-year period of 1995 to 2000 was down, as the U.S. 30-year Treasury bond yield (left) fell to 5.7 percent from a high of 7.2 percent in 1997. This rapid fall in yields was the result of a flight to safety in the global marketplace, as the Asian crisis extended into 1998 and the Russian crisis followed. When the Asian crisis erupted, there was a high potential for a global economic crisis.

Thus, Alan Greenspan, having learned the lessons of history, did the right thing by easing U.S. interest rates and making it known that the Federal Reserve was ready to be the lender of last resort.

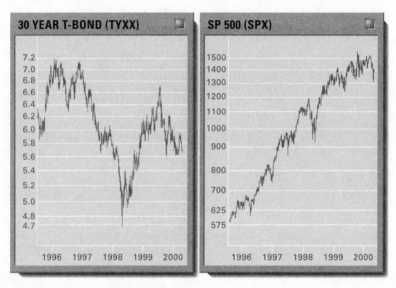

Figure 4.1. *The S&P 500 and the U.S. Treasury bond yield side-by-side comparison. A five-year history. Courtesy of Telescan.*

The Standard & Poor's (S&P) 500 (right) responded to lower interest rates by rallying. In 1998, as the Fed eased again, the S&P 500 initially fell in response to the second leg of the Asian crisis, which now involved Russia. This time, the Fed eased interest rates. But the bond market had seen enough and thought that the Fed had gone too far, and yields began to rise on the 30-year Treasury bond. This was a signal to the Fed that the bond market thought that the Fed had gone too far and was now potentially fueling inflation.

The chart in figure 4.2 shows that although biotechnology stocks rose as a whole during the five-year period, 1998 was a tough year, at least for a while. The dip in the sector was a response to the Asian crisis. But once the Fed eased, the biotechnology stocks, which were headed for a historical set of developments with genomics and the unraveling of the human genome, took off and never looked back, even as interest rates rallied.

This is an important chart to keep in mind, for it represents a key concept in market analysis. As interest rates began to rise, the

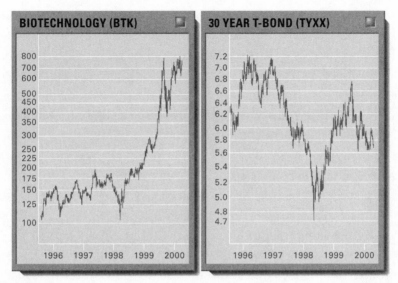

Figure 4.2. *Five-year comparison between the AMEX Biotechnology Index (BTK, left) and the U.S. 30-year Treasury bond yield. Courtesy of Telescan.*

biotechnology sector began to rally in late 1998 and into 1999. History clearly shows that higher interest rates are negative for stocks, especially companies that rely on borrowed money or the sale of equity in order to finance operations. Thus the keen observer would analyze this divergence from the norm as a sign that the market must know something that is so powerful that even rising interest rates cannot affect it.

Of course, as more time passed, the genomics dynamic began to unfold, and it was eventually known what the excitement was all about. My point here should not be lost. Even if the market is falling, each sector, and each stock in each sector, must be looked at individually and compared to the market itself. Mark Seleznov, a master day trader and managing partner of Trend Trader.com *(www.trendtrader.com)*, sums this concept up better than anyone I know: "Trade the chart." This means that during a period of rising interest rates, investors should be extremely cautious. But they should also be very vigilant, for a very significant story could be developing, and those who can catch a trend at its early point and ride it as long as it lasts will be greatly rewarded.

In this case, the biotechnology sector ignored many of the Fed rate hikes. Again, that suggested that there was something special going on since the sector is interest rate sensitive to some degree because of its dependence on borrowed money, and under normal circumstances it would have fallen like other stocks. This, then, could be interpreted as a once-in-a-generation opportunity, as the early stages of a new set of discoveries were strong enough to blunt the negative effects of rising interest rates.

By the same token, this analysis should not necessarily be confused by investors to mean that the biotechnology sector is immune from higher interest rates. Even a strong sector that marches to its own drum and runs on its own incredible dynamic will eventually be vulnerable to higher interest rates. The Fed should not be ignored. Just think back to the chapter on the technology sector, which also met its Waterloo. Instead, I suggest that the biotechnology sector is somewhat insulated from the market because of its amazing potential and that investors should keep a close eye on the Fed and act only if the sector responds negatively to higher rates. I also suggest a high degree of suspicion every time the Fed raises rates in the future, as any rate increase could be the one that knocks down a strong sector that has been resistant in the past.

The major lesson to keep in mind is that biotechnology stocks live on borrowed money either until they are profitable on their own merits or until someone buys them. Thus by definition they are interest rate sensitive. The experience of the late 1990s and early 2000 should not be used as a benchmark but should be looked at as a potential rare occurrence in the future. At some point, just as it happened in the Internet sector and in the chip stocks, biotechnology stocks will fall if interest rates rise high enough. More important, if biotechnology continues to rise in the face of higher interest rate periods in the future, investors should be even more keenly aware of any subtle changes in the sector, for a small crack could turn into the earthquake that sinks the entire sector, much like the America Online merger with Time Warner precipitated further trouble for the Internet stocks, which were already weakened.

Interest Rates and Drug Stocks

The AMEX Pharmaceuticals Index (DRG) is home to many of the world's giant drug companies. These large companies are, in a sense, the parents or at least the guardians of the biotechnology sector. The truth is that most biotechnology companies want to grow up to be large pharmaceutical entities. Thus we can call the drug group the "senior circuit" (no offense meant). These large companies are excellent sources of capital, as well as of guidance, to the start-up biotechnology firms and are very involved in the sector through either joint ventures, alliances, licensing agreements, or even directly as owners, wholly or partially, of many biotechnology firms.

The drug sector is a traditional haven from the claws of bear markets. These large, well-capitalized companies usually have a global presence, and because they produce medications that many people cannot do without—without risking death or serious injury—they usually maintain steady or steadily growing earnings.

Figure 4.3 shows that higher interest rates can also take their toll on these giants, as the 1999 rise in bond yields led to a decline in the DRG. More important as a negative during the period was the intensity with which managed care insurance companies fought price increases from the drug makers. In my opinion, this was more of a drag on the sector than interest rates. More interesting is the way that the drug industry dealt with managed care, as they lobbied heavily against the insurance industry and invested in drug delivery systems and other areas of technology in order to diversify their earnings stream. Merck (NYSE:MRK), a component of the Dow Jones Industrial Average, bought a pharmacy wholesale and distribution unit that has become one of the most profitable parts of the company.

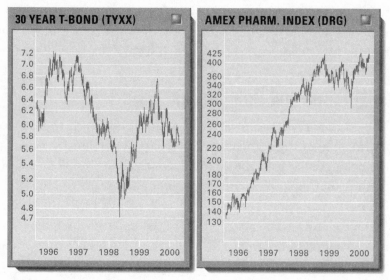

Figure 4.3. *Five-year side-by-side comparison of the AMEX Pharmaceuticals Index (DRG, right) and the U.S. 30-year Treasury bond yield.*

The major point here is that drug stocks tend to fall less than the rest of the market with higher interest rates but that it is also important to look at the whole picture before deciding why a sector is falling. In the late 1990s, despite higher interest rates, the effects of aggressive price controls from managed care were more of a drag on the drug stocks. When the managed care bubble burst, as Aetna–U.S. Healthcare (NYSE:AET) all but collapsed from the weight of lawsuits and boardroom disarray, the drug stocks began to rise.

Why Are Drug Companies Important to the Biotechnology Sector?

The performance of the drug sector is extremely important to biotechnology. First, biotechnology companies, by and large, are really aspiring drug companies, aside from those that make equipment and are sources of information. Second, a great deal of financing for the operations of a biotechnology company comes from investment by the large drug companies as well as licensing income and strategic partnerships. Finally, it is important from an investor's standpoint to note that merger and acquisition frenzies usually appear when the price of the stock of the acquiring company is rising, since this makes stock swap deals easier to make.

Thus the health of the biotechnology sector is clearly tied to the pharmaceuticals sector. If higher interest rates tend to be less harmful to the drug sector, it becomes easier to be patient and hold on to a stock for the long term.

How to Predict Interest Rates

We now have a clear understanding that interest rates, as influenced by the Federal Reserve and its interplay with the bond market, are the centerpiece of the circle of life, or the relationship between market sentiment and money flows into and out of the markets. One of the most common fallacies in investing is that most people still believe that the direction of interest rates is not predictable.

I had the pleasure of running into Bill Donoghue at a Trader's Online World Expo *(www.otexpo.com)*, which both of us attended in October 2000. After we exchanged books and talked for a while, I thanked Bill for his influence, which was purely coincidental but has been very useful to me over the years. On the Financial News Network, Bill had discussed the average maturity of the money funds indicator during an interview. I discussed the indicator in detail in *After-Hours Trading Made Easy*, but it is so useful that I'll again discuss it at length here as well as update the chart that documents its accuracy.

The average maturity of money market funds is a measure of the supply and demand in the money markets. It is expressed as a weekly number, which is published by iMoney Net, Inc., formerly IBC Inc. (508-616-6600). The number is reproduced in *Barron's* Market Lab section under the heading "Money Fund Report."

Most people have never heard of this indicator, and it is largely ignored by the market, at its own risk.

The money markets are where companies trade what is known as commercial paper, or short-term corporate debt, which is the private market's equivalent of U.S. Treasury bills. The fund managers in this market are the best interest rate timers in the world, and their actions speak louder than words. More important, when this group's actions begin to trend, it is almost a 100 percent accurate predictor of where interest rates are headed.

Thus this indicator is a window into the soul of the beast. It tells you whether money is easy or hard to borrow. That means that it usually predicts whether interest rates are going to rise or fall based on the simple principle that if the economy is strengthening, then borrowing costs are going to rise. This makes the maturities fall.

When the maturities fall, it means that money managers shorten the amount of time during which they are willing to lend corporations money. For example, if Lucent Technologies (NYSE: LU) wanted to repair a plant, it would do so with borrowed money, but it won't want to issue a 5- or 10-year bond, so it taps the money markets.

But in a strong economy, Amgen also wants to improve its capacity. Thus it wants to tap the money market. The fund manager at Fidelity's flagship money market fund wants to help but also wants to get the best return for his fund. He knows that both companies want to borrow. So he is willing to lend the highest bidder the money for the shortest period of time possible, since the economy is strong, and he expects to lend the money to someone else next month for a higher return. The fund doesn't lend the money directly; it actually buys the commercial paper on the market, although private financing is also possible. But the net effect is that supply and demand are at the root of this indicator.

The state of the supply-and-demand equation is reflected in the average maturity of money funds. As the number of days in the maturity decreases, the chances for higher interest rates increase, as companies need to borrow, and money market funds want to get the highest return possible. Thus the money manager lends the money for the shortest amount of time possible, in expectations that in a short period of time, he will be able to get an even higher return for his money.

Let's return to the Lucent-Amgen example. The fund may arrange to buy Amgen commercial paper, which pays 5 percent for 30 days. Once that money comes through, Amgen may want to sell some more paper. The fund will ask for 5.1 percent and be willing to hold the paper for only 28 days, sensing that the market is still leaning toward demand. If Amgen agrees, this means that the market is indeed leaning toward demand.

When Lucent's 5 percent paper comes due in 30 days, the fund manager may return to the market and say, sure, I'll buy some more 30-day paper. But knowing that Amgen was willing to pay 5.1 percent, the manager may push the envelope and ask Lucent for 5.2 percent and hold the paper for only 26 days. Already the dynamics become obvious. In a short period of time, the fund manager has managed to extract 0.2 percent more from his money and has held the paper for a shorter period of time.

If the market slows down the next month, the same fund manager may buy Amgen or Lucent's short-term paper and receive only 4.9 percent. The manager, realizing that this is a good return, will lengthen his maturities to 32 days.

When this kind of action is occurring thousands of times per day, it eventually emerges as a broad picture that is expressed in the average maturities of money market funds indicator, which I use. Figure 4.4 updates the action in the average maturities until October 2000. The upper line is the average maturities plotted on a weekly basis, using the figure obtained in *Barron's*. Directly beneath it is the 13-week moving average.

The moving average smoothes out the volatility and gives "buy" and "sell" signals. A buy signal occurs when the indicator line rises above the 13-week moving average. This means that fund managers are willing to lend money for as long they can, knowing that this is the best possible return at the time and that

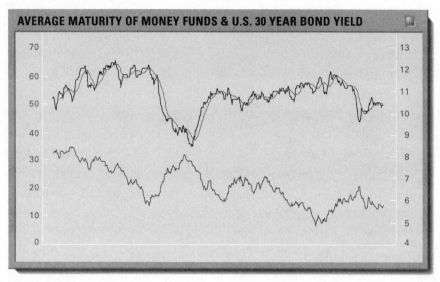

Figure 4.4. *The average maturity of money market funds (upper jagged line, left scale), the 13-week moving average of the average maturities (upper smooth line, left scale), and the 30-year U.S. Treasury bond yield (lower line, right scale). Note the inverse relationship between the average maturities and the bond yields. Note also the accuracy with which trend changes in the maturities mark significant trend changes in bond yields.*

the future holds even lower returns. This is the best time to be buying stocks, as interest rates are falling.

A sell signal is the opposite. The indicator falls below the 13-week moving average, suggesting that fund managers want to hold on to the paper for shorter periods of time, knowing that in the near future they will be able to get a better return for their money.

The lower line signifies the U.S. 30-year Treasury bond yield. Note the uncanny ability of the rises and falls in the average maturity to coincide with tops and bottoms in interest rates. I wonder why all economists, fund managers, and individual investors don't use this simple indicator instead of flying by the seat of their pants. This is a pure expression of the supply and demand for money. Although I don't know this for a fact, I would bet large sums of money that the Federal Reserve keeps close tabs on this indicator.

In summary, if you should ever run into anyone who says that the direction of interest rates can't be predicted, you should politely point out that in fact it is possible to predict both the direction and the timing of changes in interest rates.

Internal Influences on the Price of Stocks

On a rainy Sunday afternoon in October 2000, I had an enlightening conversation with trend trader Mark Seleznov. Mark is not only a master day trader; he was also a market maker on the Philadelphia Stock Exchange and has traded just about anything under the sun successfully. Mark is the managing partner of TrendTrader.com *(www.trendtrader.com)*. His firm offers online trading both for professionals and for individual investors. His seminars are well known for, as he puts it, "telling it like it is."

Mark's message is that "Wall Street has the advantage." Wall Street will always have the advantage, and if you want to win in trading or investing, you must live with that rule and learn how the markets truly work. This is sound advice, especially coming from someone who's been on both sides of the aisle and has been successful.

Traditional books and treatises on "how the market really works" reproduce almost word for word the mantra from the exchanges. There is a big difference between how the New York Stock Exchange (NYSE) and the NASDAQ markets work, and it is important for investors in biotechnology to know these important differences, especially when doing short-term trading.

It is important to understand that the NYSE specialists are slightly less competitive with the individual investor than are the NASDAQ market makers. This is by design, as the NASDAQ's electronic system is designed to clearly give the market makers every advantage possible. This is not an accident, as without certain advantages the market makers would likely go out of business on a regular basis given the volatility of many of the stocks that trade on the NASDAQ.

One of Seleznov's favorite concepts is that of market makers moving stocks on news in the thin after-hours market, a concept that I discussed in *After-Hours Trading Made Easy*. The way the game is played, and the way that it accounts for a great deal of volatility, is that a news event occurs in the after hours. Market makers do their job and factor in the news, bidding the stock higher and higher in the thin session. Even though few people actually buy this stock at these prices on many occasions, the price stays high until the morning after, when the retail investor comes in with market orders. At that time, the market makers factor in the demand, and invariably the stock price falls. When the price of the stock eventually stabilizes, it is often because the market makers are buying the stock back at a lower price for their own account, waiting for the next potential frenzy.

A perfect example of how to use this phenomenon to your advantage comes from a personal fortunate story. On October 23, 2000, I bought Genzyme (NASDAQ:GENZ). I had been analyzing the stock, and I liked its business model, as I'll discuss in a later chapter. The stock had been moving steadily higher and had successfully remained above its 20-day moving average, the curving line traveling in the middle of the chart. Also important to note is that the stock remained above the rising trend line. This is a technique that I'll discuss in chapter 7 on technical analysis. But for this example, let's say that this stock was acting right.

I bought the stock at $75.31, five minutes after I had bought it for a client at $75.12. As an investment adviser, I always buy and sell my shares after the clients. That way they are usually assured of getting a better price in and a better price out than I am. It's not only ethical but legal and required, as is full disclosure to the client.

That small uptick on my shares was a good sign of things to come, as on November 1, at 5:39 P.M. Eastern time, the company announced that U.S. regulators were to bypass an advisory committee review of a drug that the company had submitted. This was a great development, meaning that the drug was almost guaranteed approval. As the news hit, the stock began to rally in the

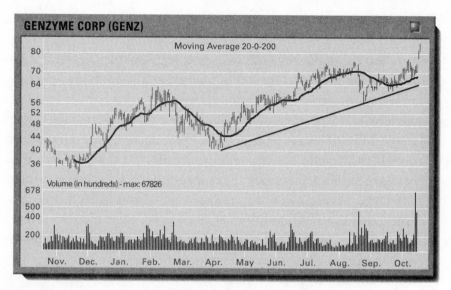

Figure 4.5. *Genzyme (NASDAQ:GENZ) and its response to news.*

after hours. By the next morning when the public woke up, the stock was trading at $80, and by November 3, the stock had added another six points. I sold my client's shares and mine in the afternoon as the stock was stalling, and both he and I made a nifty little sum in a few days.

The first fact is that the movement in the stock was telling you that something was up. The second fact is that a small stock like Genzyme could be very volatile. After two days of huge gains, it was bound to come back down. Thus a little profit taking was in order.

Another example occurred in another stock which I owned at the time: Palm (NASDAQ:PALM), the leading handheld computer company. On November 3, 2000, as the market was near the close, the stock rose over seven points, as fund managers who mimic the NASDAQ 100 index of stocks had to buy shares. The stock was being added to the index at the close. This is a common phenomenon. What is also a common phenomenon is what happened to Palm on the following Monday, as the demand for the stock dried up and the market makers continued to mark the stock down in order to make a market. By midday, the stock had given up over $5 of the prior Friday's gain.

What the market makers do is not illegal, but it does tend to exaggerate the underlying trend in many cases. It certainly is not unfair from the simple standpoint that the information has been publicly disclosed in many textbooks, and no one is making threats on the lives of those who disclose these facts to the public. The trade I made could be executed by anyone who learns to look for the characteristics in a stock that suggest that a big move is coming.

In my opinion, it's not the market's fault that people lose money. It's the public's fault for not taking the time to learn the rules of the game. The Securities and Exchange Commission *(www.sec.gov)* goes to great lengths to provide the public with information and to make sure that the broker-dealers also provide information. No one says that the information has to be easy to read or easy to find. But it is definitely available, and it's the investor's responsibility to find it, read it, and use it.

There's a misconception that funny business is going on in the markets, which is why I'm going to great trouble here to illustrate these concepts. Yes, there are crooked brokers, and they are also often arrested, prosecuted, and punished, just like crooked car dealers, doctors, and politicians. As a trader and an investor, the risk of losing money on bad trading decisions is the big danger. The market makers and the specialists have the advantage. But the investor has the responsibility to find out how to beat the advantage of the insiders.

Biotechnology stocks are small companies with small amounts of stock available for trading. They are the source of a great deal of news being released, as the example I just described illustrates. The market makers and the specialists are well aware of this and use the tools available to them to make a market, a very volatile market that is full of risk for those who don't take a longer-term view and who fail to learn the rules of the game.

Don't be fooled by the NYSE, which is just as dangerous. The exchange, on its Web site *(www.nyse.com)*, describes the job of the NYSE specialists as one of making an orderly market. Yet I see stocks getting cut in half on a regular basis for missing their earnings estimates by one or two cents. This is hardly orderly, in my opinion. In fact, it is rather disorderly and dangerous for the individual investor if he or she is not aware of how the market truly works. But it is not illegal, and as I mentioned earlier, in the broad sense it isn't really unfair. After all, the specialists and the market makers are entitled to make a living. Those who don't like the rules should probably not trade. It's much easier to learn to live within the system and exploit it for your own profit.

Instead of complaining after I've made a bad trade, I try to learn from it. A perfect example is a trade I made a few months prior to the Genzyme trade, involving a similar company named Chiron (NASDAQ:CHIR). The company made a positive announcement and rallied for two days. Instead of taking my profits and moving along to the next trade, I watched the stock fall below where I bought it and let it lie there for several days before I sold it. The stock is still where I sold it. I studied that trade and learned that a big move in a small biotechnology stock is likely to be short in duration because of the small float and the nature of the markets. So when I saw the huge two-day move in Genzyme, the decision to take an 11-point gain in a little over a week was easy.

I believe that it's up to the investor to understand how the markets work and to know how to defend him- or herself against the predatory nature of the markets. I prefer to focus on accepting the fact that the specialists and the market makers have the advantage, and my goal is to try to outwit them. That is the intellectual challenge. That is why a winning trade is so sweet, as it means that I just beat nearly impossible odds against a Goliath who is sitting in a cage full of data that tell him exactly what the supply-and-demand status of my stock is. When I got my 11 points out of Genzyme, I also knew that one day the Goliath will get even. That is the nature of trading.

By the same token, I do not adhere to the conspiracy theories that abound about the market being rigged. As Mark Seleznov says, "Wall Street has the advantage." The advantage is that the

NYSE specialists and the NASDAQ market makers have access to all the information on buy and sell orders for all the stocks in which they make a market. They clearly see who wants to buy and sell and at what price, and they are given up to 15 seconds in certain circumstances to match your order. Even more important to know is that when stock falls precipitously, they are always there to buy it on the cheap, and they are always willing to sell it at a higher price, even if it is stock from their own account.

It is also legal for specialists and market makers to hedge their positions with options, which they often will do to protect themselves. Thus, the investor should be clear on the fact that the market makers and the specialists can influence the market in the regular session as they do in the after hours. They can make the price of stocks rise or fall in response to news, earnings, and general supply and demand. The market makers are always there when a stock drops far enough to buy it back for their own account at a cheaper price, only to sell it later when they entice the market with a higher price. It's what making a market is all about.

This is not at all illegal. It's just that they have the advantage. Any one of us would do the same thing given the opportunity. It's not a conspiracy—it's human nature. It's competition at its purest and most lethal, and the buyer should be fully informed.

According to Seleznov, market makers and specialists begin to test what a stock will do at the initial public offering. Immediately, they begin to push the envelope in order to develop a beta, which measures the volatility of a stock. Betas range from 0 to 2, with 0 meaning the stock doesn't move and 2 meaning that the stock is extremely volatile. The market has a beta of 1, and most people equate the S&P 500 to the market. Betas are relative, meaning that if the S&P 500 is having a very volatile year, then high-volatility stocks will tend to magnify that volatility. The beta is not something that is known until a stock goes public and is solely developed by the response that the market has to the market maker or specialist's bid and ask prices on the stock. Again I note that the amount of stock available for trading and the interest in that stock are the basis for the development of a beta. What is absolutely true is that the specialists and the market makers will try to exploit the high-beta stocks to their full advantage based on the information available and the market's response to the information.

Another great clue as to how a stock will move is the liquidity ratio, which is a measure of how much dollar volume is required to move a stock's price up or down by one percentage point. A high ratio indicates a stock that requires relatively heavy trading to move its price. A low liquidity ratio indicates a stock that moves on relatively light volume. The ratio is calculated by adding the daily percentage changes of a stock's closing price for each trading day of the month. Then the total dollar volume for the month is divided by this total-percentage-change figure. This ratio is not necessary to calculate and is included only to document how a specialist or market can move a stock.

According to Smart Money.com *(www.smartmoney.com)*, Human Genome Sciences had a liquidity ratio of 52,858 on November 3, 2000. The company's float was 109,708,000 shares. The range for that trading day was 95.06 to 100.88, a spread of over five points. That means that it takes 52,858 shares to move this stock one percentage point and that the market maker will have a lot of fun moving the bid-and-ask and matching orders, especially on volatile days.

On the same day, SBC Communications (NYSE:SBC), a stock that I owned at the time, had a liquidity ratio of 223,194.50. That means that it took over four times as many shares of SBC to move its shares by one percentage point. This is due to the number of outstanding shares, which was 3,389,562,000. The daily range of SBC was from 55.31 to 57.06.

The bottom line is that it's the specialists and market maker's job to move the stock wherever the market will accept. If the market will accept that stock A will move in a broad range on any given day, then the specialist and the market maker will do their best to give the market what it wants. It's all about what the market will take. This is particularly important in very volatile stocks like Human Genome

Sciences, whose daily price will fluctuate in the range of 5 to 10 points or more, especially on days in which news is released.

The Analysts

Finally, one of the major influences on stock prices are the comments made by Wall Street analysts. By and large, these are very bright, honest people who are trying to do a good job. Unfortunately, they work for the same brokerage firms that underwrite many of the stocks they follow. Furthermore, the companies that employ the analysts are the same brokerage firms that are specialists and market makers in the stocks that are being rated. The companies are required to make full disclosure, which is better than nothing, but does not really add to the atmosphere of conflicting interests.

On occasion, an analyst will make a call that is obviously not the result of a conflict of interest. But more often than not, analyst comments are not very helpful, except to increase volatility in a stock or a sector. In my opinion, though, the presence of analysts just makes the whole thing more exciting. It's just another uncertainty that requires that we as investors raise our game one more notch.

As the section on market makers and specialists shows, market makers and specialists are competing with the individual investor in order to survive in the cruel game of Wall Street. The conflict of interest is obvious, and it can theoretically affect the timeliness of a call by an analyst. I say theoretically because I have no personal knowledge of such activity, and the analysts, the brokerage firms, and all of Wall Street will deny any such conflicts vehemently. They often say that the analyst side and the brokerage side are acting independently. But ill-timed calls happen so often that it is more of a rule than an exception.

To me, it looks the same as if a guy had two wives. He could love both of them dearly. The two families are both well fed and clothed, and he spends time with both of them. He is a model father to both households. But in Western society, he is still a bigamist. Wall Street analysts are excellent sources of information, but there is nothing to compare with your own research. The example in this paragraph is extreme, but I'm trying to make a point. Wall Street analysts are often late in downgrading and upgrading stocks after the stock has had a big move. Why they do it is not important. The facts are out there and are quite responsible for the changes in disclosure rules recently enacted by the Securities and Exchange Commission, which now bars companies from making selective disclosure to their favorite analysts.

The analyst factor is another reason why investors should become well versed in technical analysis, in which signals of a shift in trend can often be seen before stocks break out to new highs or crash down to earth. Therefore, my solution is to be my own analyst, and that's what I recommend to you. This book has the tools to help you become your own analyst. I recommend using these tools.

Summary

In this chapter, I've prepared you to finally tackle the myriad of companies that need to be analyzed in order to make sense of biotechnology. My stepwise approach began with the history of biotechnology and worked its way through the basics of cell biology, progressing through the science in the first three chapters.

Now we understand how the external and internal forces of the market work to give us the constant price movements summarized in stock charts. I introduced the concept of Intellectual Inclusion, my own creation, in which you take knowledge from one area and apply it to another. This is a concept that should be practiced by analyzing your trading habits, as I'll discuss in more detail later. But at this point, you should be getting used to the idea that there is a method and that this method requires some retraining of both the senses and native behavior patterns.

I also discussed the fact that equally important to the actions of the Federal Reserve and its role in setting interest rates is the ability to understand how the market makers and specialists factor in all the information available to them in a single instant and how they use it to move stocks and make the market dance to their tune. There is nothing illegal as to how these astute market participants work. But there is also nothing illegal in my telling you how to be a better player in this tough game.

Throughout this chapter are intermixed trading anecdotes involving both biotechnology and nonbiotechnology stocks. These are meant to illustrate both trading strategies and how the principle of Intellectual Inclusion is exercised, bringing the experience from one trading arena to the next. A stock is a stock is a stock. When faced with decision making, the investor, just like the physician in a critical care situation, must have already thought about what he or she will do when finding him- or herself in a specific set of circumstances. For example, in the description of my Genzyme trade, I was not greedy, and I took my profits as the stock moved aggressively ahead. I was well rewarded on the following Monday when the stock fell several points.

Genzyme, as a result of that successful trade, became a stock that I analyze on a regular basis, looking for similar opportunity to reappear. By the same token, when I discussed Palm in the same passage, I knew that, because of my knowledge of how the market makers work, Palm would fall on the following trading session. That is a perfect illustration of Intellectual Inclusion, as I was able to apply a similar line of analysis to two stocks, in two very different sectors, both of which went up sharply on the same day for different reasons. Genzyme rose on positive news, while Palm rose artificially on institutional buying. But on the next trading day, both behaved equally because of the way the markets work. Thus the contents of this chapter are meant to be additive to the contents of the prior chapter and are meant to be incorporated into the whole system of analysis required to make money in biotechnology.

Next, we'll look at the giant pharmaceutical companies—their strengths, their weaknesses, and the role they play in the rapidly growing biotechnology sector.

5

The Pharmaceuticals Industry

T hus far, we have looked at the history and basic science of biotechnology and the external factors affecting the financial markets and the biotechnology sector. We have also looked at the basic stages in the development of a biotechnology company. We will use our knowledge of this intricate web as the basis with which to make decisions for buying and selling biotechnology stocks.

We have made our transition from the broader subjects that will serve as our foundation of knowledge about this wonderful sector to the more precise content that will allow us to make intelligent decisions about companies. Even though you might focus on the short- and intermediate-term trading aspects of this book, which I'll describe in a later chapter, there is no substitute for grasping the traits of a company and its management that make a winner.

Once you are comfortable with the characteristics of the core companies and business practices of the traditional drug and biotechnology sector, it will become much easier to evaluate individual companies and make decisions about stock ownership. The basic method of analysis can also be adapted to other sectors in the stock market by applying the principles of Intellectual

Inclusion, where information and experience can be adapted to similar situations.

There are two ways to invest in biotechnology: directly and indirectly. Direct investing is buying shares in pure biotechnology companies, which I'll discuss in the next chapter. Indirect investing is accomplished by buying those large pharmaceutical companies that have a significant biotechnology strategy. By owning the large pharmaceuticals, which are well positioned in biotechnology, investors are buying diversification and a moderate degree of security, as biotechnology is only a part of what makes the large pharmaceutical company attractive. The drawback is that the potential gain in the large drug stock giants may be less than that which would be provided by a direct investment.

For example, if Company X is a top 10 drug company and derives 2 percent of its profits from biotechnology, the stock may or may not rise or fall vigorously in response to news from that division, unless it is a very significant piece of news. The flip side is obvious for a pure biotechnology company, whose fortunes often depend on the results of one or two products or even the results of clinical trials.

Time and time again, in my own trading, I have made the right decision to buy and sell a stock, not just on the basis of the technicals but also on the basis of knowledge about management and management's ability to execute their business plan. This is accomplished by reviewing certain criteria on a company's history and their ability to meet or beat expectations for sales and, to a lesser but still important degree, profits. It is not as important to understand the nuances of a particular company as it is to develop a feel for management's ability to deliver.

Thus if we are to understand the true nature of the biotechnology sector as it pertains to the drug industry, a great place to start is with the current giants in the drug industry itself. These companies provide a template for what most biotechnology companies want to become and are also big providers of financing for the biotechnology industry. Most important, these companies have built a record and have a history of management decisions as well as the transparency that allows us to build at least a generic profile of a winner.

Therefore, in this chapter, I'll be profiling the largest drug companies in the world. I'll be looking at their business strategies, their drug pipelines, and their ability to deliver on their promise to investors. Aside from profiling these giants, I'll also be looking at how they fit into the biotechnology sector in order to provide a road map into the future, as the traditional drug industry begins to both assimilate and transform the biotechnology sector.

It is not my intent here to highlight which companies you should own. This chapter is about learning what to look for and how to decipher the information. It is also meant to illustrate the increasingly blurring landscape between biotechnology and the traditional drug sector, as most large drug companies either own their own biotechnology division, are significant investors in biotechnology companies, or are involved in partnerships and/or joint ventures with biotechnology companies.

The key questions to answer about a pharmaceutical company are the following:

1. *Does the company have an existing product base that is profitable?*

This is important for obvious reasons. A drug company without products that are making money is not to be included in the list. Furthermore, it is important to examine how well diversified the product mix is. A major strategy in the drug industry is to smooth out the ups and downs that can occur when a company's patents expire and sales of a blockbuster dry up by investing in consumer products and by releasing non-prescription-strength versions of the drugs. This is best exemplified with the popular pain relievers like Motrin IB and Advil, which are non-prescription-strength versions of former blockbuster drugs. Drug companies also diversify their holdings by owning cosmetics and hair care product lines and by producing pharmaceuticals for the animal market. This is not something that biotechnology companies do on a regular basis, but it is a potential development as the larger companies mature and look to diversify their holdings.

By answering this question, we also get a glimpse into the ability of management to leverage and guide the company's product portfolio. The timing of a company's leaps into the diversification process is also an excellent clue as to what management is thinking, which I'll discuss in detail when I profile Pfizer later in this chapter. This leads into the question of a drug pipeline.

2. Does the company have a viable drug pipeline?

The pipeline is the future, as patents on drugs expire in seven years. That means that a company has to make as much money as possible from a blockbuster before its exclusivity expires and the generic drug can be manufactured. What we want to see here is balance between an obvious easy winner, such as a new generation of the same old drug that has worked before, and a totally new direction. Most companies will follow a blockbuster with a new-and-improved version of the drug. This practice allows the company to leverage its product line to a friendly audience. A perfect example was in the 1970s and 1980s, when the beta-blocker class of anti–high blood pressure medications were all the rage.

Beta blockers are compounds that lower blood pressure by slowing the patient's heart rate. The original beta blockers had many side effects, which included dizziness, sexual dysfunction, and irregular heartbeats. But constant modification of the drugs created better compounds that kept a loyal following, both in patients and in doctors, since the drugs are very effective at controlling blood pressure. The drug industry also modified the use of the beta blockers to include treatment for chest pain related to coronary artery disease (angina pectoris) and migraine headaches and even developed beta-blocker eyedrops to treat glaucoma, where increased pressure in the eyeballs can lead to blindness.

When a biotechnology company has a successful product, I always look to see how it is expanding the product's use. A perfect example of this is Cephalon, as I described earlier, with its drug Provigil. Cephalon continues to look for ways to expand the use of the drug in order to leverage its investment and prolong the profitable life of the product.

This is like recording a record album, where the artist has to balance giving the fans what they want with satisfying his or her own need to explore. At the same time, the artist continues to play live shows, which include the classics as well as new music. This analogy works well and should be kept in mind.

One way to prime the pipeline is to grow it internally. Here the large pharmaceuticals have a huge advantage if they own their own laboratories and research centers, as I'll describe in each case where this applies. Another way to prime the pipeline is to go out and buy a pipeline, which is also fairly common. This is the way that the huge players grow; they just buy what they need and make it part of the company.

Analysts love to write about the pipeline and to punish companies that aren't minding this portion of the business. I should note here that very few major pharmaceutical companies remain that do not have serious in-house pipeline potential, either through arrangements with biotechnology companies or through mergers and acquisitions, as the drug industry had to consolidate in order to adapt to managed care and the squeeze on profits.

I recommend frequent sweeps of the company's Web site and subscribing to their mailing list in order to keep up with developments.

3. *Does the market recognize the company's efforts by owning the stock and maintaining it in an uptrend?*

We want to own stocks that the market recognizes as leaders. With the large drug stocks, most of them rise and fall as a sector in most instances. Thus those stocks that don't keep up with the sector are the ones to avoid. I'll discuss more details in chapter 7. Even better is to own the stocks that are ahead of the sector and that are building a full head of steam.

4. *Does management have a clear vision, and is it executing the business plan?*

The best way to evaluate this is to visit the company's Web site and determine whether the stock price is consistently moving with the company's guidance. This is not to say that I'm a believer in hanging on to every utterance from an analyst. My views on analysts have not changed. Most do a good job and are trying to be honest. But many of their calls are questionable based on their timing. I prefer to get a capsule of what all analysts are saying as a group. It is simple enough to turn on CNBC and get that information casually, as the anchors and reporters are always citing the analyst community. Again, I'm not saying that I recommend following the comments of Wall Street's analysts. But if the analysts happen to be saying good things about a stock, the market makers will factor that into their machinations, and the stock will eventually rise.

The day that the business plan is tested is usually on earnings announcement day. If the earnings are good, the market's reaction will tell you what's next. If a stock falls after a great earnings report, this is usually a sign that an analyst said something like the next quarter looks bad, the company's pipeline looks weak, management is indecisive, and so on.

My point is that the relationship between the drug companies and the analyst community, which is often based on the spin that the company puts on its operations, will move the stock. The perfect example of what can happen when a company disappoints the analyst community is visible in the chart of Lucent Technologies (NYSE:LU), which, until the day it missed its earnings report, was the leader of the networking sector.

The chart of Lucent Technologies (figure 5.1) tells the grim tale of why it is important for companies to deliver the goods. The chart clearly shows that news does matter and that the comments of analysts are important. Lucent committed the most cardinal of sins for a publicly held company in the year 2000. It warned analysts in January, and the stock dropped. The CEO at the time, Richard McGinn, went on the business talk show circuit and said

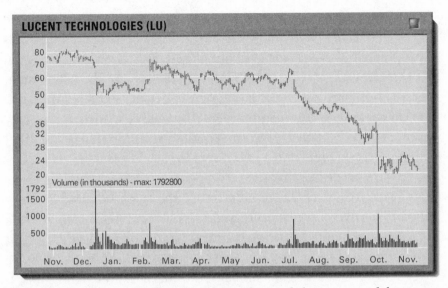

Figure 5.1. *Lucent Technologies (NYSE:LU) and the price paid for not executing its business plan and disappointing the analysts.*

that the problems were temporary. Analysts bought the story after an initially negative response, and the stock held on, even mounting a countertrend rally into the spring.

But in July, the company warned again, and the bottom fell out and continued falling, as the analysts ganged up on the stock. Eventually, all the damage was revealed in October as it became obvious that the company was not in any shape to compete with the smaller, more focused, and more aggressive emerging giants of the networking industry.

The point here is that the company warned but essentially lied to the analysts. Of course, anyone who does technical analysis would have bailed out of the stock after the first warning and failure to rally, a point that I'll expand on later. But the point is that it is important to keep your hand on the pulse of the chatter about a company and then compare it to the chart. Talk about good news that is not backed by a good-looking chart is a clear sign of trouble. The reverse is also true, as analyst chatter about bad things, while a stock is rising, suggests that Wall Street has it all wrong.

Closer to home, a similar story developed in Amgen in late October, as the company warned of trouble in its upcoming quarter (figure 5.2). The stock fell out of bed, as is often the case when a company warns of trouble and the analysts join the bandwagon instead of warning clients based on their own research. To be fair, excellent calls are sometimes made by analysts, such as the very prescient calls made by the semiconductor sector analysts in 2000 that correctly predicted a slowdown in the chip market, as we discussed in an earlier chapter.

As the chart of Amgen illustrates, the stock bounced and rallied. This was no accident, as by November the company had begun to promote its five-year strategy based on new products that at the time were in the Food and Drug Administration's (FDA's) regulatory process. The company did many things right. First, it warned about trouble. But then it put together a very credible plan and gave itself ample time to execute the strategy.

In the plan, the company addressed all the major concerns that Wall Street had. First, it stated that it would refocus itself on

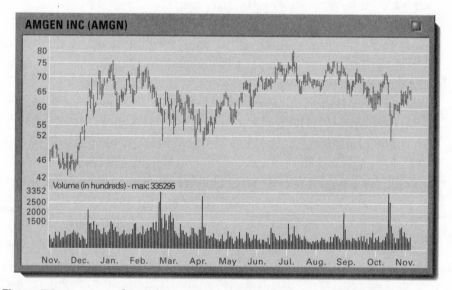

Figure 5.2. *Amgen's disappointing news and Wall Street's response.*

development of drugs based on proteins, antibodies, and small proteins. In essence, the company showed that it was finally keeping up with the times and moving away from its old strategies to the new area of proteomics and monoclonal antibodies.

Next, the company reaffirmed its commitment to research by promising to spend more than anyone else in the industry based on a percentage of sales. The company also pledged to "aggressively build and advance the pipeline" and to invest aggressively to support new product launches. Wall Street loves this kind of talk, which says that the company is confident. It is believable when it comes from the company that defined the sector, but it doesn't always work with lesser-known companies.

The company also promised to attract and retain the best people and to balance near-term earnings with investment for long-term growth. This last statement is crucial, as the company clearly states that it will make enough money to keep analysts and stockholders happy but that it will not be caught with its pants down.

This is the kind of fire and brimstone that I like to see from a company. Such companies know their audience, address their concerns, and leave enough wiggle room to execute their strategy. This is why Amgen is the leader in the field. Compared to the woeful state of Lucent Technologies, whose management was blindsided by a rapidly changing fiber-optics industry (which, ironically, it defined), Amgen dodged a bullet.

Does Amgen's slick public relations mean that the stock will go up forever? Absolutely not. If the company does not deliver, it will get hammered, just the same. But the chart illustrates that the pep talk worked initially and that management understands the rules of the game and is willing to commit itself to a new world with new rules.

5. Does the company have a viable biotechnology strategy?

Finally, if a big drug company has great management, a good relationship with the analysts, a fantastic pipeline, and a well-diversified earnings stream, the final step is to evaluate whether it is keeping up with the times. Most drug companies now understand that biotechnology is their cash cow for the next decade and beyond, so they have some sort of commitment to the sector. The question to answer is how sensible and how serious they are to the commitment.

In the first company profiled, Abbott Laboratories, we will be answering all these questions in a systematic fashion. In the examples that follow, I'll be taking a more general approach to discussing the company's businesses. The strengths and weaknesses of the company will be highlighted and expanded on when appropriate. This is not meant to be a chapter about stock recommendations but more of an in-depth background check on the drug industry and what investors in biotechnology should be looking for when analyzing companies in the sector.

The information in these company capsules will then be used to create a profile of a winning major pharmaceutical company against which you can match your stock picks.

Abbott Pharmaceuticals (NYSE:ABT)

We start our profiles with a bang, with Abbott Laboratories *(www.abbott.com)*, which perhaps is best known through its infant formula (Similac) and its nutritional supplements (Ensure). Abbott is actually a major biotechnologically oriented pharmaceuticals company. It is a leading maker of antimicrobial drugs (drugs that treat infections), including leading antibiotics, such as Biaxin, which is widely used to treat upper-respiratory infections, such as those in the sinuses and ears. But in the biotechnology area, Abbott has a leading position in the fight against AIDS. The company's anti-HIV (AIDS) virus drug, Norvir, inhibits an enzyme that the AIDS virus uses to reproduce. As we discussed in an earlier chapter, enzymes are special proteins that make things happen inside cells. Norvir blocks the action of a very important enzyme in the virus' life cycle, and the virus can't reproduce. This leads to a decreased viral count, prolongs the life of the patient, and improves one's quality of life.

But Abbott has really gone the distance with biotechnology in its partnership with MedImmune (NASDAQ:MEDI). Abbott's management has shown a significant amount of foresight and thoughtfulness in its choice of biotechnology partners, as Synagis, the drug that it jointly markets with MedImmune, treats a viral infection in children called respiratory syncytial virus (RSV). RSV causes a condition that acts like asthma. That means that when a child is infected with RSV, the virus makes it difficult for the affected child to breathe, and wheezing and fever are present. RSV is among the most common causes of shortness of breath in children and is contagious and thus can spread rapidly.

Here is where Abbott's management gets kudos. The company carefully piggybacked its foray into biotechnology onto its already successful infant formula. Children usually will go to the same pediatrician for many years under normal circumstances. Abbott will usually give free formula samples to the pediatrician. This makes mom and dad happy since they save a little money. This builds trust between the family and the physician, who is glad to give something to his or her patients, especially the needy ones. At the same time, it builds brand loyalty, and when there is brand loyalty, new drugs are easier to introduce. A doctor who is happy with a company is a doctor who is likely to try a new product.

The strategy is also apparent in the company's foray into AIDS, which is a debilitating disease in which sales of the nutritional supplements could be increased by targeting the AIDS market. The target audience here is the specialist in infectious diseases, who is already familiar with Abbott's other antibiotics. Since AIDS has become a subspecialty area, the marketing of the drug is also easier, as there is already a relationship with the doctor of infectious disease.

Abbott uses a wonderful marketing plan, building on its strengths and carefully choosing its sales approach to an audience that is a much easier sell than if they were starting on a whole new product category. This kind of leveraging of its areas of strength makes Abbott a potential winner in incorporating biotechnology into its already existing product mix. This is an excellent business model to keep in mind when analyzing a drug or biotechnology company.

Clearly, Abbott has an existing product base that is profitable. The market recognizes the company's ability to execute, as it is included in the AMEX Pharmaceuticals Index (DRG), meaning that the company is recognized as one of a handful in the industry that can be used as a benchmark. The stock also has a long-term stock price performance in which it is obvious to the observer that the company rises and falls along with the markets but has an upward bias in rising markets.

Management's vision is clear from its long-term performance as well as its displayed ability to recognize its strengths and build on those strengths through its moves into AIDS and RSV treatments. Management understands that a natural move into an area of strength, that of infectious disease management, is more sensible than breaking into new ground, such as cosmetics.

Here is a perfect example of Intellectual Inclusion, as my own experience with drug companies and their sales forces gives me insight into which are better at selling their products. I suggest that you develop your own analysis pipeline. Ask your doctor and pharmacist which drug company's salespeople they like best. Then do some research on the company and ask the five questions posed in the prior section. If all the answers fall on the same side, the company is worth doing research on. This is a subjective assessment, but it does give you a great idea as to which companies are likely to be more successful than others in selling products. There is no doubt about it: If there are two competing drugs that are just as good, the sales rep who is better liked by the doctor is the one who gets the sale.

Abbott's future direction is appropriate, as evidenced by the report on the company's Web site that clearly states that the company is engaged in developing new technologies and is involved in genomics research as well as in the study of proteins and their structure.

In table 5.1, I have posted Abbott's revenues and earnings for the quarters beginning in 1997 through 2000. This information is available online, often through discount brokers. Abbreviated versions may be available at no charge on some Web sites. A five-quarter snapshot is available at SmartMoney.com *(www.smartmoney.com)* under the Financials link. This snapshot is a fair representation of the recent trend and can be used by individual investors.

The earnings and revenue trend for Abbott is steady, although not particularly robust in the most recent quarters. This is not unusual for mature drug companies since their earnings growth tends to be less than that of a younger start-up company. It is also important to note that Abbott, like many drug companies, had a decrease in revenues because of decreased reimbursement from third-party payers as a result of managed care. But what is obvious

Table 5.1 *Revenues and Earnings for Abbott Pharmaceuticals*

REVENUES (THOUSANDS OF U.S. DOLLARS)

Quarter	1997	1998	1999	2000
March	2,999,814	3,044,913	3,313,320	3,353,178
June	2,900,408	3,066,753	3,259,211	3,370,153
September	2,865,184	3,035,767	3,120,662	3,317,895
December	3,118,056	3,330,412	3,484,432	
Total	11,883,462	12,477,845	13,177,625	

EARNINGS PER SHARE

Quarter	1997	1998	1999	2000
March	0.340	0.380	0.430	0.440
June	0.335	0.380	0.410	0.440
September	0.300	0.340	0.300	0.420
December	0.365	0.410	0.410	
Total	1.340	1.510	1.550	

Courtesy of Telescan.

is that the company makes money and that it does so consistently. Its ability to deliver stable revenues and earnings is an excellent quality.

I suggest using Abbott as a benchmark. It meets all the fundamental criteria necessary to make the list of companies that should always be considered when investing in this sector. But answering the questions and looking at the fundamentals is only the beginning. In chapter 7, I'll discuss timing when to buy drug and biotechnology stocks regardless of the fundamentals, which are usually stable, at least for the drug stocks.

I'll now profile the major players in the drug industry, focusing on their strengths and weaknesses and providing fundamental and analytical detail only when necessary but always keeping the five key questions in mind.

Alza Pharmaceuticals (NYSE:AZA)

Alza is a key player in the drug industry, as it has carved a niche in the urological market and in drug delivery systems. The company's leading drug, Ditropan, controls the urinary bladder in those who have lost the ability to remain dry. The company also has developed the increasingly popular transdermal model of drug delivery. This allows patients to receive medication by the use of a skin patch, which is usually changed once a day or less often. Alza is important to the biotechnology and the pharmaceuticals industry, as it licenses its technology to major players like Pfizer.

American Home Products (NYSE:AHP)

What strikes me most about American Home Products (www .ahp.com) is that it is everywhere. Very few people in the world who use over-the-counter medical products can escape the long arm of this company. Among its most popular brands are the lip balm Chap-Stick, headache remedies Anacin and Advil, cough syrups Dimetapp and Robitussin, and hemorrhoid treatment Preparation H.

But beneath the consumer products exterior is a serious drug company that has heavy ties to biotechnology, as I discussed earlier with its anti-arthritis drug Embrel, which is based on monoclonal antibody technology.

American Home Products markets a drug in the United States called Synvisc, which is another example of its serious commitment to biotechnology. Synvisc is manufactured by biotechnology company Biomatrix, a company that merged with Genzyme. The drug is a derivative of the combs of chickens and is injected into the knee joints of sufferers of osteoarthritis. Osteoarthritis differs from rheumatoid arthritis because it is a result of the wear and tear on the joints caused by aging. Rheumatoid arthritis is an autoimmune problem in which the body breaks down its own tissue as if it were fighting a foreign body. Synvisc replaces the natural cushioning of the joints in which it is injected for a period of time, which could last for weeks to months.

American Home Products also offers biotechnologically derived treatments for blood disorders and cancer patients.

This is a prime example of a huge company with an equally huge and open commitment to biotechnology. The company has had its problems in the past, when its antiobesity drug Phen-Fen was found to cause damage to heart valves in patients. The company has settled its lawsuits.

Astra-Zeneca (NYSE:AZN)

Astra-Zeneca *(www.astrazeneca.com)* is another major player and is European, as are many of the big players in the drug sector. The company resulted from the merger of Britain's Zeneca and Switzerland's Astra. The key to the merger was the shared interest in anesthesia. Many of the drugs that I have used on a regular basis in my work as an anesthesiologist were made by either Astra or Zeneca. Astra, prior to the merger, was the leading maker of local anesthetics, the most highly recognized being Lidocaine, which is commonly used to numb a patient's skin or other sensitive body zone prior to a procedure. Zeneca became a large player with its blockbuster anesthetic Diprivan, which is the gold standard around the world to induce general anesthesia, more commonly known as "going to sleep."

Here again, management showed a very nice touch, bringing together two leading players in related areas and creating a much stronger company. Management again did the right thing when it spun off its agribusiness division after merging it with that of Novartis, another major drug company, which I'll profile later.

A visit to Astra-Zeneca's Web site reveals that the company has six biotechnology-related ventures in the works, with universities and private and public companies. Among its partners are Affymetryx (NASDAQ:AFFX), a leader in genomics research. Astra has ongoing research in genomics, proteomics, and mouse genetics.

Most interesting is the ongoing research into pain management. If Astra or anyone else can discover a pure pain relief drug that is not addictive and has no major side effects, such as nausea and vomiting, it will surely be among the biggest blockbusters of them all.

Aventis (NYSE:AVE)

Aventis *(www.aventis.com)* is the result of the merger between France's Rhone-Poulenc and Germany's Hoechst Pharmaceuticals. The company bills itself as a "pure life sciences company," and it is in its life sciences approach that one can find both strengths and weakness. Life sciences refers to the company's involvement with both people and animals as well as crops. There is often great controversy with the drugs used to treat animal stock, including an international dispute between the United States and the European Union as a result of hormone-fed beef. I also note that Wall Street does not feel much enthusiasm for the application of biotechnology to crops and animals because of the potential for controversy and the drag on earnings. The truth is that much of what we eat and drink is more heavily influenced by biotechnology than maybe Wall Street and even the general public realizes.

Aventis is a big spender in research and development and touts its "overlapping value chain" research model as an advantage. While other companies follow a stepwise, linear research process, where the lab work is completed before the clinical stages begin, Aventis begins multiple steps of the process simultaneously, with the goal of developing products faster than its competition.

Aventis lists on its Web site that it has 80 ongoing collaborations with the biotechnology industry that, according to the company, enhance its "internal capabilities in molecular biology, functional genomics, combinatorial chemistry and bioinformatics." It is obvious that this is a significant player in the drug industry, but its involvement with biotechnology is part of a very large commitment to its entire operations.

Baxter International (NYSE:BAX)

Baxter International *(www.baxter.com)* broadly is a biotechnology company, as it is the leader in blood therapy. The company's biotechnology division is focused on the extraction and development, through recombinant methods, of plasma proteins.

Plasma is the protein component of the liquid portion of blood. It is in plasma that we normally find antibodies as well as clotting proteins. Baxter produces and extracts clotting factors with which patients who suffer from hemophilia, a genetic disease of the blood-clotting mechanism, are treated.

Baxter is also a leader in blood replacement therapy and medical equipment, with a large portion of its revenues coming from kidney dialysis centers. Once again, we note the ability of a company and its management to conquer a niche and then expand on the theme. This is another classic example to keep in mind when we begin to look at the biotechnology companies.

A key measure of management's success is to see how they can continue to add successful new businesses to their core by leveraging their current areas of success. We have already noted several examples in the companies described. We must remember that most biotechnology companies are interested in becoming drug companies or major medical equipment companies. How they adapt methods that are already successful in the drug industry to their own business is a key way to measure their potential success in the future.

Once again, this company has shown a great deal of foresight into expanding its business by targeting anesthesiologists, who are the physicians responsible for administering fluids and blood products in the operating room setting. In mid-2000, Baxter became the exclusive distributor of the PSA 4000 monitor, a device that constantly measures a patient's conscious status under general anesthesia. The device is made by Physiometrix (NASDAQ: PHYX), a small medical equipment company, and has the potential for a huge marketplace, as no operating room will be able to do without it, at least in the litigious climate of the United States.

Baxter, just like Abbott, knows its market. It knows that it is a staple in the operating room and clinical laboratory setting. Thus, its sales force already has an easier time in introducing a potentially blockbuster product to an audience that will be more likely to embrace it.

Again, in analyzing this company, I used Intellectual Inclusion. My knowledge of anesthesia and my experience in the operating room allowed me to carefully analyze Baxter and its potential blockbuster with the PSA 4000.

Bristol Myers-Squibb (NYSE:BMY)

Bristol Myers-Squibb *(www.bms.com)* is deep into biotechnology, as it is a leader in cancer therapy. The company's public relations campaign is highly recognizable, as two-time Tour de France champion Lance Armstrong survived testicular cancer as a result of the chemotherapy the company developed. But this company uses a well-known and proven formula for cash flow, as its Clairol and

Aussie brand of cosmetics and the Sea Breeze skin care line provide a steady stream of earnings from consumers. The company is also well diversified, as its Zimmer orthopedic medical products division is a leader in hardware for bone and joint surgery.

Bristol Myers-Squibb has an excellent record in its involvement in biotechnology and devotes a great deal of its Web site to promoting its involvement in genomics. The company is a member of a consortium formed by Affymetrix, Whitehead, and Millennium Pharmaceuticals in which the potential for the applications of genomics to cancer therapy and drug development is being studied.

Bristol Myers-Squibb makes no bones about it: It would like to use the technology that is on Millennium's drawing board to analyze a person's genome. Once that information is deciphered, the company would like to use the data first to pinpoint weak areas in the DNA to predict those who are likely to develop cancer and to treat them preventively or at least watch for developments aggressively. Second, if a person were to develop cancer, Millennium's intent would be able to customize treatment with drugs whose dosage and mechanism of action can be customized.

This is an incredibly revolutionary concept that I'll discuss more fully when I profile Millennium in the next chapter. But suffice it to say that customized chemotherapy, based on analysis of an individual's own DNA, is likely to work better and faster and to have fewer side effects than current methods. Bristol Myers-Squibb has an impressive potential drug pipeline near completion, with potential treatments for stroke, Alzheimer's disease, and blood clots.

The lesson here is that this is a well-diversified company, with an impressive public relations campaign, an excellent product mix, and an aggressive involvement in and commitment to biotechnology.

Glaxo Wellcome PLC (NYSE:GLX)

Glaxo *(www.glaxowellcome.com)* is a perfect example of the consolidation dynamic in the large pharmaceuticals industry, which I expect will eventually expand into the biotechnology arena as competition heats up and companies are forced to merge or perish. Glaxo Wellcome is the result of the merger between Glaxo and Burroughs-Wellcome, which had merged in 1995. Glaxo is best known for the anti-heartburn drug Zantac, which is now available in nonprescription form, showing that the company knows how to get the most out of its successful brands. Glaxo is also a leader in developing treatments for viral diseases, such as fever blisters, which are caused by the herpes simplex virus. The company also produces drugs for treating AIDS.

The company's business model is solid, as is its ability to deliver. This is a large blue chip company that expands through acquisition, as with its merger with Wellcome and its proposed merger with SmithKline Beecham (NYSE:SBH).

Glaxo's commitment to biotechnology is significant, as the company developed the Genetics Directorate, led by Dr. Allen Roses, whose team at Duke University discovered the first gene associated with a person's potential to develop Alzheimer's disease. Glaxo's Web site has extensive documentation of its gigantic involvement in genetics research, including the company's extensive involvement in the SNP (single nucleotide polymorphism) Consortium *(www.snp.com)*, a nonprofit organization whose mission is to locate portions of the human genome and make it available to the public.

The SNP Consortium is composed of the Wellcome Trust and the following 14 pharmaceutical and technological companies:

- Wellcome Trust
- APBiotech
- Astra-Zeneca PLC
- Aventis
- Bayer AG
- Bristol Myers-Squibb Company
- F. Hoffman-La Roche

- Glaxo Wellcome PLC

- IBM

- Motorola

- Novartis

- Pfizer Inc.

- Searle

- SmithKline Beecham PLC

The SNP Consortium has two members that come from outside the drug industry but whose presence validates and gives credence to the emergence of biotechnology as the science of the future. Both IBM's and Motorola's (NYSE:MOT) presence suggests that these two technology giants are well aware of the potential to combine organic and mechanical technology in the treatment of disease as well as adding their technical expertise to the obtainment and dissemination of information.

Glaxo's mission is clearly stated on its Web site and involves four steps:

1. Identifying susceptibility genes, or those genes that make someone prone to developing a disease but don't necessarily guarantee that the person will develop the disease

2. Translating the information into targets for further development

3. Applying the genetic method to the development of new medicines

4. "Representing genetics accurately" within Glaxo Wellcome and to the business community, governments, health care providers, and the public

This clearly stated mission is a benchmark not just for Glaxo but also for what the goals of the pharmaceuticals industry are regarding the use of biotechnology. It is a particularly good move for the company to include step 4, as it gives the company an air of social responsibility that the company backs by being a contributor to the educational community through grants both for research and for continuing medical education.

Glaxo's research method is unique in the industry, as it searches for susceptibility genes by studying the genes of families that are prone to develop inherited diseases. The company then forms networks of facilities that study and share the information gathered from carefully coded and confidential blood samples of family members. As of December 2000, there were networks established for asthma, early-onset heart disease, metabolic syndrome, and osteoarthritis.

Of particular interest is the network for metabolic syndrome, which is a condition in which patients suffer from diabetes, obesity, high blood pressure, and high cholesterol at the same time. The combination of other medical problems that arise from this eventually lethal combination of conditions includes heart disease, kidney failure, strokes, heart attacks, and several other problems. Any potential treatments for this condition would likely lead to a significant reduction in the incidence of the other conditions and could significantly improve the health of thousands of patients as well as reduce medical costs significantly. Glaxo also participates in research about Parkinson's disease and migraine headaches.

Glaxo's corporate strategy is familiar but nevertheless well thought out. Its merger with SmithKline Beecham gives Glaxo a well-established stable of nonprescription brands, including vitamin supplement Geritol, antismoking nicotine patches, Aqua Fresh toothpaste, and leading antacid brand Tums. More important is the fact that SmithKline Beecham has agreements in place with Human Genome Sciences, which can fortify Glaxo's already ambitious biotechnology platform. SmithKline Beecham's prescription drugs are also popular and include a leading antibiotic to treat ear infections in children, Augmentin, as well as leading antidepressant Paxil.

Johnson & Johnson (NYSE:JNJ)

Johnson & Johnson *(www.jnj.com)* is more of a mutual fund in disguise than a drug company. From Band-Aids to recombinant DNA–based blockbuster drugs and medical equipment for whatever ails anyone, this company has a hand in it. This is a behemoth of a company with a huge involvement in biotechnology through its Centocor unit, which it bought in 1999, as well as its lesser-known but very large and successful Janssen subsidiary, which Johnson & Johnson has owned since the 1950s. Centocor is a leading producer of monoclonal antibodies and has annual revenues of over $100 million. This was a significant move on the part of Johnson & Johnson that clearly validated the biotechnology sector and its potential contribution to the future of medicine.

Interesting is the historical tidbit that it was Johnson & Johnson and its Janssen unit that teamed up with Amgen and pushed the development of Amgen's blockbuster Epogen and Eprex, the latter Johnson & Johnson's version of the protein erythropoetin. Erythropoetin is made in the kidneys and helps the bone marrow turn out red blood cells. Patients with kidney failure can't make erythropoetin and thus suffer from anemia, or low red blood cell numbers. These drugs help keep the red blood cell numbers at a higher level than they would be otherwise, improving the patient's quality of life. Janssen also developed a yeast-produced drug that helps heal the nonhealing ulcers caused by diabetes.

Johnson & Johnson never builds anything from the ground up. When it sees something it likes, it just buys it. Thus, this is a company with shrewd management on whose wisdom the rest of us can at least piggyback our ideas from time to time. As I'll discuss later, there is one biotechnology company that is modeling itself after Johnson & Johnson. Genzyme is among the few biotechnology companies that operate several divisions and are aggressive buyers of technology and assets from other biotechnology companies.

The lesson here is that, once again, the relationship between the old-line companies and the biotechnology industry has been in place from day one. It's also fitting that Johnson & Johnson's money was right on top of the developing new sector when it formed its alliance with Amgen, which is the largest and most successful of all the freestanding biotechnology companies.

Also important to note is the fact that there is a great deal of biotechnology research going on in the divisions and subsidiaries of these very large entities, such as Johnson & Johnson. Just because these divisions are not followed by analysts doesn't mean that they can't produce a blockbuster that can be a significant driver of the stock of the mother company.

Again, I turn to Centocor, which is a leader in monoclonal antibody research. One of Centocor's greatest failures was its antisepsis drug in the 1980s that sank both the company and the sector when clinical trials failed. But Centocor has come back and has developed Reopro, a leading drug in the treatment of coronary artery blood clots, which cause heart attacks. Without the financial and corporate support of Johnson & Johnson, Centocor might have never fulfilled its promise.

Intellectual Inclusion would suggest that the concept of looking under the hood in the big companies is one to remember. In other words, a great clue to success in biotechnology is what and when key acquisitions are made by the biotechnology companies, as the winning biotechnology companies will be the ones that can copy the strategies of the winning pharmaceutical companies.

In my opinion, it is just a matter of time before a company like Amgen, Genentech, or another leader makes a jump into a consumer products company. In order for this leap to work, there has to be synergy. It can't just be a soap company or a cosmetics company; it must be a consumer company with the proper biotechnology twist in order for it to work. This makes sense as these companies continue to make the leap from start-ups to leading biotechnology companies and eventually to the "Galaxy Class" of pharmaceutical companies.

Eli Lilly & Company (NYSE:LLY)

Eli Lilly *(www.lilly.com)* is another prototype drug company. Its climb to the top echelon came from its blockbuster antidepressant drug Prozac. But its involvement with biotechnology stretches to the beginning, when it partnered with Genentech to produce Humulin, the human insulin produced by bacteria. This was a landmark agreement and an equally important application of recombinant DNA technology, where a human gene was inserted into a bacteria and the bacteria was thus chemically coaxed into producing the desired product, in this case human insulin.

Lilly has a well-earned reputation for delivering the goods and has plenty of firepower in its arsenal, as it is leading the race in the fight against a blood-borne infection called sepsis, which is the most frequent killer in the intensive care setting. The early trials on Lilly's sepsis drug were very encouraging. If the company can bring the drug to market and it is successful, it should be a blockbuster. Prior attempts by others in the field have been resounding failures.

Lilly's pipeline is always evolving along the two major lines of improving the old and bringing about something new. Lilly's Web site is not particularly helpful, as the company is very guarded of its pipeline information, and the site has many hurdles, with many registrations and forms standing in the way.

Merck & Company Inc. (NYSE:MRK)

Merck *(www.merck.com)* is the number one drug company in the world and a member of the Dow Jones Industrial Average. Merck's list of current blockbusters include drugs to treat prostate enlargement, hair loss, high blood pressure, asthma, high cholesterol, and arthritis. As would be expected, Merck sponsors a major biotechnological endeavor, the Merck Gene Index, whose function is to decipher and clone gene sequences. Merck has sponsored a huge contribution to the known gene sequences, as it has provided over 300,000 gene sequences to the public gene database Genbank.

Merck's community involvement is unique, as it is the provider of large volumes of information, including the well-known medical book the *Merck Manual* and its funding of an arrangement with Lexicon Genetics (NASDAQ:LEXG). Merck paid Lexicon $8 million to sponsor the development of mouse models with genetic conditions. The mice are given to scientists who request them for research at no charge.

Merck's ace in the hole is its Medco division, which is a drug wholesaler that provides 50 percent of the company's sales. Here is a very original idea, one that could be used as a benchmark by emerging biotechnology companies in order to both diversify their income stream and separate themselves from the other companies. It is this kind of innovative thinking that has allowed Merck to grow more rapidly than other companies in its class.

The company's strategy is quite simple. It provides resources for a broad variety of biotechnology-related entities yet does not incur any of the major risks of actually running a risky enterprise. When a development is significant, the company is there with large sums of money ready to move in.

Novo Nordisk (NYSE:NVO)

Novo Nordisk *(www.novonordisk.com)* is a major European player and a leader in the treatment and research of diabetes. It is unique in its approach, as it relies very heavily and openly on biotechnology for its research and product line. Novo sells hormone replacement products aimed at the postmenopausal woman as well as growth hormone used in the treatment of growth-retarded children. The company uses genetically engineered blood proteins to treat sufferers of bleeding disorders, an approach similar to that of Baxter International, which I described earlier. Novo also produced enzymes for the industrial market but has spun off that business to concentrate on the medical business.

Taking a page from the Abbott and Baxter playbook, Novo also manufactures devices that help deliver its medication, including injection devices that are meant to deliver drugs with less discomfort than syringes and infusion pumps and can be worn by the patient as the drug is delivered under the skin in a timed fashion. This is particularly useful for insulin-dependent diabetics.

Novo recognizes the potential for concentrating on its niche and servicing all the needs of that patient population. It built on its diabetes franchise, leveraging to other hormone-related areas, realizing that doctors who treat diabetes will also treat other major hormone disorders. Again, this shows that management has a clear understanding of its market and how to remain successful in it.

Novo's commitment to biotechnology is obvious, as it has spun off its Zymogenetics subsidiary in late 2000. Zymogenetics is an emerging big player in proteomics, having patented over 500 gene sequences and having developed many of Novo's biotechnologically derived product. As an independent subsidiary, Zymogenetics will be able to raise more capital and begin to develop a broader range of alliances, thus furthering its business plan while Novo maintains the rights to some of Zymogenetics' product line and pipeline.

Zymogenetics has a big start in proteomics and will be heard from in the next decade, barring poor decision making by its management, as it plans to use the $150 million raised in the spin-off to establish facilities and begin clinical trials on its pipeline.

This is a pure example of how the biotechnology and traditional pharmaceuticals sector is increasingly tied together. The drug companies nurture the start-ups and in turn receive a pipeline and benefits along the way.

Novartis (NYSE:NVS)

Switzerland's Novartis *(www.novartis.com)* resulted from the merger of Ciba and Sandoz, two huge pharmaceutical firms. The merger brought together a combination that has proven uneasy to the marketplace. While the drug side has been well enough received, the agrochemical portion of the company had to be spun off as a result of the European rejection of bioengineered foods.

This is a troublesome sign, as the merger could be construed as having been ill conceived. The need to repackage a weak portion of the business as a result of a negative response suggests that the company's management may have acted somewhat irrationally in creating this merger. For that reason, Novartis' actions in this merger should be used as a benchmark for evaluating management decisions.

Two points are important here. First, the agricultural side of biotechnology is not very popular with investors. Wall Street's lack of interest could set off an intellectual argument about the ethics and morals of the dynamic. But that is beyond our scope here. If we take the analysis of this company's business practices at face value, the agribusiness side should never have been bought from a business standpoint.

When we compare this approach to growth and this company's involvement with biotechnology to that of more focused and detailed plans, such as those displayed by Novo Nordisk, Merck, Johnson & Johnson, and American Home Products, it is clearly less effective. Therefore, the message to take here is that a more focused approach to growth, built on synergy and common ground, will be well rewarded by Wall Street and global investors instead of what may be a well-meaning but difficult-to-execute strategy.

Novartis has many established brands, but they all face competition. For example, Ritalin, which is used in attention deficit disorder, could be facing a challenge from a Cephalon drug, as I noted earlier. Other drugs are facing challenges as well.

To its credit, Novartis has a very large generics pharmaceuticals operation. Generics are drugs that are produced when the brand name goes off patent, which is usually seven years. This is an ingenious way to diversify revenues and does give a few points back to Novartis' management.

Novartis is in the process of establishing the Novartis Institute for Functional Genomics (NIFG), for which it is spending $250 million and will have fully implemented in 10 years. Here again, we note that this company is getting a late start. Novartis goes to great length on its Web site to discuss its leap into genomics and proteomics, but after some digging through the cumbersome site, I finally found that the company also has a partnership with Chiron, which is a profitable biotechnology company that also has had problems with its ability to deliver.

I am not deliberately beating up on Novartis here. It is a fine company, one that produces many medications that make people's lives better. But when I compared the smooth and nearly seamless practices of integrating a biotechnology strategy used by other companies, Novartis is clearly stumbling and is being forced to spend $250 million to catch up. In contrast, Merck's modest $8 million expenditure is well within that company's way of doing business. It is a huge conglomerate, one that can afford to assume the role of a philanthropist to the science community. Merck knows that it could have a moral and perhaps even legal claim to any product that is developed as a result of its philanthropy.

When this seamless strategy displayed by Merck is compared to Novartis' continual going against the grain, we can see why Merck is the number one drug company in the world. This is not to say that Novartis is not going to be successful in its quest for drugs developed from genomics and proteomics. My point is that as investors, it is our job to see which company is likely to succeed the earliest and have staying power. By the same token, Merck's strategy may not succeed indefinitely. Thus the stock could fall, at which time it would be important to keep an eye on Novartis, whose strategy may be starting to pay off.

Pfizer (NYSE:PFE)

Pfizer *(www.pfizer.com)* read the playbook when it fought hard to merge with Warner Lambert and bring the steady cash flow of consumer products and over-the-counter medications on line with the blockbuster lineup of Pfizer drugs, which include the highly publicized impotence drug Viagra.

Pfizer's biotechnology adventure began during World War II, when the company invented a more efficient way to produce penicillin. Pfizer developed a specialized fermentation process with which to mass-produce the antibiotic. Here again, we use Intellectual Inclusion to jot down the key word "fermentation," which is the key process in drug production. Pfizer's penicillin success was a crucial turning point in the history of the science.

The company went on and began doing research on soil samples, leading to the development of Terramycin, one of the original broad spectrum antibiotics. In fact, once Terramycin was approved in 1950, the company's business model, which until then had been to mass-produce chemicals for other companies to sell through their own labels, changed to one of producing and marketing its own products under its own name.

Pfizer knows how to leverage its pipeline, as its latest antibiotic Trovan received approval from the FDA to treat 14 separate conditions in 1998. This is the broadest approval for an antibiotic granted by the FDA and is a key benchmark to keep in mind, as the race to produce more aggressive and broadly effective antibiotics is a key dynamic in the drug industry and is a recurrent theme, one that I'll discuss in detail in the next chapter.

Pfizer was also a pioneer in international expansion, as its aggressive global moves in the 1950s also created a benchmark for other companies. This is an important characteristic to keep in mind when evaluating up-and-coming companies in the drug and biotechnology sectors, as a well-diversified global strategy could be the difference in delivering profits. Pfizer derives 45 percent of its profits outside the United States.

Pfizer also recognized that it had to diversify its portfolio beyond antibiotics and has developed blockbuster drugs to treat high blood pressure, diabetes, and arthritis. It was one of the first companies to incorporate robotics in its research process, thus reducing the amount of time involved in discovering new compounds.

Pfizer owns Auguron Pharmaceuticals, a biotechnology company whose goal is to engineer synthetic drugs based on the study of protein structure. This is a roundabout way to attack the biotechnology puzzle but is a key departure from the mainstream of drug discovery, as Auguron's focus is to design drugs that interact with a receptor site on tissues to inactivate a disease process.

This is similar to a lock and key. Auguron's drugs are the key, while the receptor on the tissue is the lock. Organs, tissues, and, most important, cancer cells and viruses work in a way that takes a lock-and-key complex to turn on and turn off a reaction. If the reaction is turned on, a disease works its evil. But if a drug that fits into the key also works, it can turn off or decrease the effect of the disease process, giving the body a chance to heal. This lock-and-key analogy is the main concept I presented earlier when I discussed the arthritis drug Embrel, which is a monoclonal antibody that works by blocking the receptors in joints, leading to a cascade of events that causes the tissue breakdown and pain of arthritis.

Although Auguron may seem like a departure for Pfizer, this is a company that has a long history of taking chances and making them pay off eventually. Again I note that one of the keys to developing a successful profile of a winning biotechnology company is to note the strategies of winning drug companies and their ability to execute them. Pfizer's history is full of instances in which the company went against the grain and made it work. This is a perfect opportunity to compare Pfizer's against-the-grain strategy to the difficulties faced by Novartis that I described earlier.

Pfizer's use of automation in their drug discovery makes Auguron's use of a technique called x-ray crystallography a beautiful extension of the mother company's philosophy about expanding science. Auguron looks at compounds with x-ray crystallography and builds a map of the three-dimensional structure of the protein. In this way, it can figure out where the best potential receptor blockers will come from. This is yet another example of a sensible way to leverage knowledge and philosophy. Pfizer's management could see that the potential synergy of leveraging its technological tendencies would not be a total threat to its staff scientists or its bureaucracy. This kind of sensible strategy can make what looks to be an "against the grain" move work out well.

Even more incredible is the fact that Auguron uses genetic engineering techniques not to produce drugs but to produce drug targets. Thus its tests tend to have a high grade of reliability, as they are manufacturing the receptor and then working backward to produce the drug that best fits that receptor.

Auguron's methods have already yielded two anti-AIDS drugs, Viracept and Rescriptor, both of which function by blocking key protein receptors that disrupt the life cycle of the AIDS virus. More important is the huge potential product pipeline, which can be found at Auguron's Web site at *www.auguron.com*.

The message here is quite simple. Pfizer is a model of consistency in the way it runs its business and is a great blend of the traditional and the new. It goes against the grain when management sees an opportunity that makes sense. It is also willing to fight a fight that it feels it can win. It is a globally diversified company, one that offers a great blend of established drugs as well as its share of blockbusters. Its conventional pipeline remains robust, while its biotechnology subsidiary Auguron continues to provide impressive results.

Schering Plough (NYSE:SGP)

Schering Plough *(www.sch-plough.com)* is another drug company that derives significant income from its over-the-counter strategy. The company's popular over-the-counter brands include Dr. Scholl's foot care, Afrin nasal spray, and suntan lotions Coppertone and Bain du Soleil. This is a familiar strategy that tends to smooth out the potential peaks and valleys in earnings and is employed by many of the large pharmaceutical companies.

Schering merged with Plough in 1971 and bought Scholl in 1979. In the same year, the company bought the rights to intron, a version of the protein interferon and a leading treatment for hepatitis C. Hepatitis C is a viral condition and is the most common form of chronic liver disease, affecting 2 percent of the world's population. More important, hepatitis C is the most common reason for liver transplant.

Thus Schering Plough formed an agreement with ICN Pharmaceuticals (NYSE:ICN) for first and last rights of refusal to license two antiviral drugs as well as other products in the ICN pipeline. This agreement included the rights to three hepatitis C drugs in the ICN pipeline.

This brings up two points that deal with Intellectual Inclusion, as we have seen an evolving pattern of how successful companies build future successes. Schering Plough is actually a role model of sorts for Pfizer, being a company that emerged in the late 19th century and having had many years in which to perfect its craft. Pfizer's move into health care–related consumer products, as well as its leveraging of its company personality of successfully going against the grain, is a perfect example of a company recognizing what it does right and continuing to build on it. Schering put the same principle to work, leveraging its successes, when it signed its hepatitis C agreement with ICN, a company that will be profiled in detail in the next chapter.

You can exercise Intellectual Inclusion by learning how to leverage success by piecing together these successful strategies. Aside from leveraging success into established business practices, it becomes obvious that a company that is successful in its own niche will be looking for ways to expand that niche. Thus it makes sense to keep in mind that Pfizer is a leader in antibiotics and that SCP is a leader in the fight against hepatitis C.

These are two very common areas of research, and there are plenty of news releases from small companies that are involved in this research. A way to beat the analysts to the punch is to keep in mind that antibiotics is a hot area of research. We already know that Schering Plough, Eli Lilly, and Pfizer are companies with high levels of tradition and interest in the area. It is easy to go to the Web sites of these companies and note who their alliances are and keep these companies in mind for announcements.

It is also easy to set up a portfolio of stocks to watch on any free Web site, such as the ones listed earlier. By keeping an eye on these stocks and monitoring the stock charts as well as the basics of what the company's partnerships and research are, it becomes easy to spot unusual movements in the price of the stock as they begin to appear. I'm not advocating obsession with stock price movements, but I am stating that biotechnology is a dynamic and emerging sector that requires more interaction from the individual investor.

As I have shown in the examples in this chapter, alliances, partnerships, and mergers are the rule, not the exception. The good companies make deals with other companies that share common interests and ways of doing business. Thus, the investor who practices Intellectual Inclusion and becomes familiar with situations and patterns is likely to spot opportunities earlier.

In my own research, I have noted that I'll write an article on a stock and that one to two weeks later a big Wall Street analyst will make the same call and not once mention the positive technicals. My point is not to tout my own ability to spot trends early but to teach you that preparation is the key to success in biotechnology investing.

Summary

I found this chapter my favorite to write, as it gave me the opportunity to refresh my knowledge of the bellwether companies in the drug industry. I learned many new facts and refreshed many familiar notions. Above all, in doing the research, I learned many things on a subconscious level that have already helped me become both a better analyst and a better investor and money manager.

The principle of Intellectual Inclusion works on many levels. Consciously, because it requires that meticulous attention be paid to the matter at hand, it is likely to sharpen your analytical skills.

Subconsciously, the more the technique of trying to piece together similar aspects of situations and patterns is practiced, the easier it becomes. Eventually, it becomes second nature.

But the most important contributions of this chapter are the detailed profiles of the most influential pharmaceutical companies in the world, which are intended to provide a key reference point. In addition, an identifiable pattern of the successful strategies employed by the drug companies emerged.

This pattern can be summarized as follows:

1. All successful drug companies follow a similar road to success by combining the strategies of owning a franchise of over-the-counter products and attempting to develop blockbuster prescription drugs on a timely basis.

2. The same companies tend to form alliances with biotechnology companies whose products and philosophies fit well with their own. The successful drug companies tend to develop alliances and to license products rather than to incur the risk and expense of building their own biotechnology companies.

3. Some large drug companies, like Pfizer, have bought or built their own biotechnology division but have not waited until it became obvious that biotechnology will be the dominant force in drug development.

    (In all fairness to Novartis, which I profiled in a negative light, the company does have a small alliance with Cubist Pharmaceuticals (NASDAQ:CBST), which is a very interesting biotechnology company that I'll profile in detail in the next chapter.)

4. Several companies, like Merck and Pfizer, showed great ingenuity in the way they approach biotechnology. Merck finances research through a grant program, while Pfizer has its own biotechnology company. The reason these

strategies work for these giants is that they are well within the company personality.

The bottom line is that the drug and biotechnology sectors are highly interdependent and that the lines between them are likely to continue to blur. In the next chapter, I'll put the biotechnology sector under the microscope.

6

The Biotechnology Industry

In the previous chapter, I described the interaction between the traditional drug industry and the emerging biotechnology sector. The overwhelming message is that the lines between the two continue to blur. Thus if a major drug company is to build a foundation for the future and remain as a leader in the business, it has to associate itself with one or more biotechnology companies, either through an outright purchase or through joint ventures, partnerships, or other arrangements. By the same token, because of the capital-intensive nature of their research-heavy business, biotechnology companies are also in need of associating themselves with one or more large drug companies.

This is an important relationship between the two closely related sectors because the traditional synthetic method of making drugs in the pharmaceuticals industry, which is based on the manipulation of man-made chemicals, is beginning to be matched in prevalence and in production capacity by the use of recombinant DNA and monoclonal antibodies, the two major production methods in the biotechnology industry. The result is significant, especially to patients who, as a result of biotechnology-related techniques, often receive a more pure version of the drug, with fewer potential side effects (as with the human insulin preparations for diabetics that have largely replaced the earlier insulins, which were made by purifying and chemically altering the insulin from pigs).

Equally important is the fact that drug companies have blazed a trail of successful business practices that can be used as a benchmark for analyzing management's ability to develop and execute in the biotechnology sector. As I discussed in chapter 5 and will expand on here, biotechnology companies that are able to adapt the successful and proven methods of the large drug companies are likely to do better than those that ignore such models. The bottom line is that while there are plenty of new business strategies that lend themselves to the biotechnology sector, there are key areas that are crucial at each step in the development of a biotechnology company; the proper execution of these steps can be the key to the company's success or failure.

These well-established strategies in the drug sector are based on simple principles that flow from a well-diversified revenue base of prescription drugs, medical equipment, over-the-counter products (which in many cases include cosmetics), and personal hygiene items. Drug companies also license and market other companies' products and form alliances with biotechnology companies. The major drug companies, because of their large size and capital, usually expand through acquisitions.

This chapter will profile the top pure biotechnology companies in the sector. It is not possible to cover all such companies, but appendix A provides expanded coverage of the sector through company capsules and can be used for further research. The companies in this chapter were chosen because of their uniqueness in products, business methods, and overall performance.

My goal here is to show you how these companies have arrived at their current status as a leader because of either their products or their potential. I'll focus not only on what they have done right but also on where they could improve and even on where they have made huge mistakes. This chapter is meant not as a buy-and-sell guide but more as a deep-background document that can be used as a launching pad for more research on these and other companies.

Perhaps the best way to use this chapter is to read a company summary and then conduct some current research. I have attempted to remain broad in my descriptions, as I want the information presented to be useful for several years, if possible. If my chapter design works, you'll be able to add layers of current data to my analysis in order to build a current snapshot of the company.

More important is to use these company summaries and the analysis provided as templates with which to compare similar companies in your own research.

Major Areas of Research

Before we move on to the companies, it's important to provide an overview of the major areas of the sector's products and research. Leaders in their fields will be mentioned, and details will be expanded on later when the company is profiled.

The areas with the most interest and press coverage are usually cancer and heart disease. However, there are many products already on the market that get little press but that both help patients have a better life and produce revenue and earnings for companies and their stockholders. Among such products are those for kidney disease, for whose side effects biotechnology products are on the market to treat, such as blood chemistry imbalances and anemia (low red blood cell count).

Cystic fibrosis, a disease of the lungs, is also being treated successfully with biotechnology-related treatments. Other areas of intense interest include the nervous system with Alzheimer's disease, multiple sclerosis, attention deficit disorders, and sleep disorders as well as non–nervous system ailments, such as arthritis, diabetes, organ transplant, liver disease, and especially hepatitis.

Thus it is important to begin to look at biotechnology not as something out in the ether, where research begets research, which begets no earnings. This is no longer a concept sector. These are real companies with real products on the market from the first tier of companies. But the wave of products from the emerging second tier of companies is on the verge of exploding onto the scene, as product evaluations are well along in the approval process in both the United States and Europe and to a lesser degree in Japan. The next step is to identify the companies and describe their history, their potential, and their role in the future.

Genzyme: The Benchmark for the New Biotechnology Sector

Before we delve into a discussion of individual companies, it is important to develop a benchmark by which to make comparisons. In the previous chapter, I described Abbott Labs as a company that could be used as a comparison. Abbott is a drug company whose business practices, including its involvement with biotechnology, provided an excellent benchmark for the sector. Other great benchmarks are Johnson & Johnson and Pfizer.

In my opinion, Genzyme is the blueprint for the new wave of biotechnology companies. Although Genentech proved that biotechnology was a viable sector and Amgen proved that profitability was not just possible but sustainable, in my opinion it is Genzyme General that is the model of the future. My opinion is based on the company's ability to produce blockbuster biotechnology drugs as well as on its ability to adapt the proven strategies of success from the drug sector and make them work in its own sector.

On December 6, 2000, I appeared on the *Market Mavens* radio show *(www.marketmavens.com)* with host Michael Pinson and noted that Genzyme was a diamond in the rough. I noted that the stock was really a pharmaceutical company in disguise, that it was selling at a low valuation, and that technically it was the best-looking stock in the sector. As figures 6.1 and 6.2 prove, I was right on the money, at least in the short term, as the stock moved over 10 percent in the next two days, scoring a chart breakout.

Figure 6.1. *Genzyme General breaks out. Courtesy of Telescan.*

GENZYME CORP (GENZ)					
Date	Open	High	Low	Close	Volume
12/06/00	93.500	94.312	89.375	89.500	2,328,600
12/07/00	88.687	91.750	88.687	90.437	1,105,300
12/08/00	91.875	103.750	91.687	103.00	3,822,600

Figure 6.2. *Daily quotes for Genzyme General (NASDAQ:GENZ) from December 6 to 8, 2000. Courtesy of Telescan.*

The news event that triggered the move was the ratification of a merger approval between Biomatrix and Genzyme. Biomatrix is a specialist in the production of a class of pharmaceuticals known as bioelastics. Bioelastics are used medically and surgically to replace or improve worn-out body parts. At this time, Biomatrix's leading products are Synvisc, a jelly-like substance that is injected into worn-out joints, and Hyaloform, which is used to correct facial wrinkles and depressed scars. Biomatrix also received Food and Drug Administration (FDA) approval prior to the merger for the production of a viscoelastic device to be used during sinus surgery.

This merger was a clear indication that Genzyme was thinking big, which is why the stock continued to show a rising price, even as the NASDAQ Composite was down 50 percent from its high, during the month of December 2000. The stock's strength was more impressive given the increased market volatility as a result of the political uncertainty brought about by the disputed U.S. presidential election at the time.

How big was Genzyme thinking? Try this for size. Once the merger with Biomatrix was complete, the two companies would form a publicly traded subsidiary, Genzyme Biosurgery (NASDAQ: GZSP), which would include another Genzyme subsidiary, Genzyme Tissue Repair (NASDAQ:GZTR).

Stay with me here. This is significant because Genzyme Tissue Repair's technology, in combination with that of Biomatrix and the mother company's financial backing, created the first company with a real chance to grow organs for transplant in the laboratory. As the population grows older and major illnesses are increasingly manageable or cured, the only thing left to conquer is life itself and the aging process. That's what I call thinking big. Wall Street loves a good story, and it doesn't get any better than immortality or at least the potential for living longer.

But a company like Genzyme doesn't get to a significant point in its history like this without careful planning and execution. The company started like most others in the field, namely, doing research and trying to find a niche, which it did, as it was able to produce an enzyme called Cerezyme. Biotechnology revolves around proteins, and enzymes are proteins.

Cerezyme is the brand name for the enzyme replacement administered to patients who suffer from Gaucher's disease *(www.gauchers.com)*. The sufferers of Gaucher's disease, which in Jews is as common as sickle cell anemia is in blacks, experience symptoms that can range from enlarged organs, such as the spleen and liver, to severe brain disorders, especially in very young children.

The missing enzyme, called glucocerebrocidase, breaks down certain parts of worn-out cells. When the enzyme is missing, the cells that are not broken down accumulate, causing the symptoms of the disease. The disease can affect one out of 400 to 600 Ashkenazi Jews. Cerezyme alleviates the symptoms and prolongs the life of the sufferer while improving the quality of life.

Prior to Cerezyme, there was Ceredase, which is the enzyme extracted from human placental tissue. Ceredase was the basis for Cerezyme (a product of recombinant DNA). The gene is inserted into the Chinese hamster ovary that produces the enzyme. I'm not trying to inundate you with scientific trivia here; I'm just trying to increase your familiarity with the terms and the models as we exercise our Intellectual Inclusion.

Here is a perfect example of how to produce blockbuster drugs in a stepwise fashion. First, the developers isolated the enzyme from a human placenta and then were able to apply genomics research to the compound and produce it via recombinant DNA. Again, this illustrates that it is important to understand the basics of the science.

Based on its success with Cerezyme, and using the principles for success that I outlined in chapter 5, Genzyme began to leverage its brand and to move into the upper echelon of biotechnology.

The company also tapped a familiar model from the drug industry for its Renagel product. Renagel is a product of Geltex (a smaller biotechnology company), which binds serum phosphate in patients with kidney failure who undergo dialysis. The bottom line is that dialysis filters the blood and causes problems with the blood's mineral components, called electrolytes. Phosphate is an important electrolyte, and Renagel allows for the maintenance of proper phosphate balance. Renagel was an improvement over previous methods to control phosphate in the dialysis population, as it proved to be more effective.

Genzyme saw a great opportunity to add to its blockbuster stable, just like Pfizer, Johnson & Johnson, and the rest of the big companies. There are very few examples in biotechnology where a company is the acquirer and marketer of a product. This is usually because the companies in the sector are too busy doing research to mount their own marketing efforts. But Genzyme has broken the mold.

Finally, I note that by its actions, Genzyme has successfully made the leap from being a biotechnology company to being a pharmaceuticals company. In doing so, it set a new standard by which the industry should be judged. First, it is profitable. Second, it is expanding its own drug pipeline internally but also by forming alliances with smaller companies. These are alliances in which Genzyme is the senior member of the team, and it provides marketing muscle and business guidance.

Thus, Genzyme is a perfect example of a stock in stage 2—the discovery of the dream—a time when Wall Street was beginning to realize that this company was up to something really significant and was rewarding the company by bidding the price higher. We want to own stocks that are in stage 2, as they are the ones with momentum.

The chart of Amgen shown in figure 6.3 is an example of a company in stage 5, the reality stage. The sideways action in the stock clearly summarizes the market's impression. Sure, you are a great company. Yes, you are the moral leader of the sector since you've proven that you can make money and grow steadily. But what have you done for me lately?

It is this kind of thinking that an investor needs to start developing when looking at a chart. By applying stage analysis, or at least organizing companies into this hierarchical order, investors can make better decisions. As I progress through this chapter, I

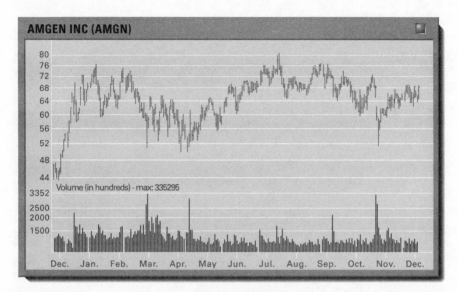

Figure 6.3. *Amgen (NASDAQ:AMGN) during the period December 6 to 8, 2000. Note that the stock advanced during the period, indicating a sector-wide move. Also note that it did not rise to the degree that Genzyme rose.*

will continue to analyze companies by using the stages described in chapter 3.

Equipment Makers and Information Brokers

Now that I have established a benchmark, let's look at some of the subsectors of biotechnology. We'll begin with the companies that provide the research tools for the rest of the industry.

Celera Genomics (NYSE:CRA)

Currently, Celera Genomics *(www.celera.com)* is a stage 3 company. Note the top and the failed rally, followed by a prolonged sell-off (see figure 6.4). This is a perfect example of a stage 3 stumble. Stage 3 is the stage in a biotechnology company where the story is out and the market is no longer interested; thus the price

Figure 6.4. *Celera Genomics, a stage 3 company in the year 2000. Courtesy of Telescan.*

goes down for what can be a protracted period of time. I am not suggesting that Celera will remain a stage 3 company indefinitely, but I am using its chart to illustrate the concept. Celera was able to unravel the mystery of the human genome, which was a great accomplishment. But it got caught with no follow-through strategy that it could implement immediately. This is a perfect example of how a company stumbles, often after its greatest triumph.

The genomics miracle gave rise to a whole new set of household names, like Human Genome Sciences and Protein Design Labs. But in order for those companies to be able to progress, they need equipment and information, and that's where the core companies entered. The most famous of all is Celera Genomics, which is credited for having deciphered the human genome.

Celera Genomics is a spin-off from Perkin-Elmer (NYSE:PKI). Celera's main purpose is to increase the speed with which drugs are developed by combining its extensive database and its proprietary technology in software, hardware, and molecular biology. Celera gives institutions access to its database for a price. The user gains access to the human genome and to all Celera's predictive information based on its already-performed statistical and mathematical models. The system also allows the user to combine the data from the public domain into its analysis, making the information virtually complete. Perhaps the most amazing aspect of Celera's database is that it is available by password access on the Internet.

Celera's strength is also its weakness. It is a database and information company in an industry where information is only part of the equation. For that reason, Celera has begun to diversify into drug discovery on its own. That is a strong long-term goal but one that will take some time to build and that may require some acquisitions and intensive capital expenses.

Affymetrix (NASDAQ:AFFX)

Affymetrix *(www.affymetrix.com)* was a stock between stages 4 and 5 in the year 2000. The company stumbled for many of the same reasons that Celera did, as the human genome story was out and there was a news vacuum. But while Celera began to branch out into other areas in order to reinvent itself, Affymetrix diversified its already-successful product line. As a result, stage 3 was short, and a recovery-reality stage followed. The message of the chart in figure 6.5 is clear: Yes, we like what you're doing. We don't expect great things for a while, but you are not going off the deep end, either.

The main difference between Celera and Affymetrix is that while Celera leases its database to its clients, Affymetrix is more for do-it-yourselfers. The company, which is 30 percent owned by Glaxo Wellcome, sells its GeneChip system and related products. GeneChip is a system of microarrays, or gene sequences. If you recall from chapter 2, DNA is composed of genes, which in turn are made up of smaller parts called bases. These bases are then arrayed on a microchip. The researcher then conducts tests on the compound being analyzed and tries to come up with base matches

Figure 6.5. *Affymetrix, a stage 4 company. Courtesy of Telescan.*

from its sample to the GeneChip. Once enough matches occur, a gene map could be made, and the research continues. This is aided by the company's software and analytical systems.

Of course, this means that the work is tedious. But it is better than it used to be. After all, this is genomics, which means that thousands of tests could be run simultaneously, thus creating a gene map in a fraction of the time that it used to take. Affymetrix recognized that its GeneChip system was only part of the answer, so it expanded through acquisition in order to round out its offerings to its customers by providing both high-cost and budget systems.

Perkin-Elmer (NYSE:PKI)

Perkin-Elmer *(www.perkinelmer.com)* was a science company before biotechnology became a buzzword. But the chart shown in figure 6.6 clearly shows that in the 1970s it was a stage 2 stock, as the dream of something special happening in the science world was being factored in. In the 1980s, the stock went into a stage 5 sideways move. Stage 5, what I call the reality stage, is where a company meets expectations and where the market decides whether management will be able to deliver the company to the next area of success.

As figure 6.6 shows, stage 5 could last for some time, but its resolution could be quite positive, as Perkin-Elmer emerged into a nice stage 2 move in the mid-1990s. As 2000 came to a close, the stock was within striking distance of its all-time highs, once again sending the message to investors that the market approved of management's plans and their ability to execute.

Perkin-Elmer is a centerpiece of the biotechnology sector, as its subsidiary companies, Celera Genomics and Applied Biosystems (NYSE:ABI), were crucial in the unraveling of the mystery of the human genome. But PKI is a well-rounded basic science products company that could make a long-term core portfolio holding based solely on its management's ability to discover significant trends and to develop sensible strategies while executing their

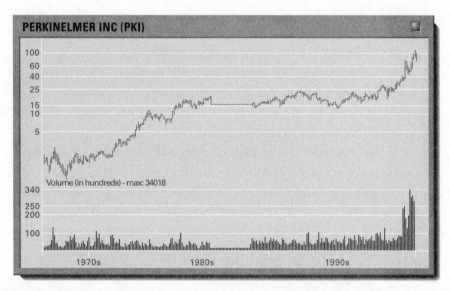

Figure 6.6. *Perkin-Elmer's multiple stages. Courtesy of Telescan.*

business plan. This is perfectly illustrated given the fact that the company expanded into genomics and used impressive strategies such as spinning off both Applied Biosciences and Celera Genomics to the public. By doing so, management showed a high degree of wisdom, as it recouped some of its initial investment and transferred risk to the public.

More important is the fact that Perkin-Elmer's stated goal is to help its clients speed up drug discovery. By stating this as its goal, management clearly encapsulates what it is trying to do and thus gives investors a clear direction and clear benchmarks by which to evaluate the company. This is an impressive bit of public relations by the company and a kudo for management, as it leaves no doubt as to what to look for from this company.

Perkin-Elmer has multiple divisions whose products and services it ensembles and coordinates in order to help its clients to discover new drugs. It is impressive that it has the resources of Celera Genomics from which to draw in this endeavor. But it also offers many other bench science products that help the nongenomics and nonproteomics aspects of research.

The companies that produce the products used in the basic science components of biotechnology tend to be limited investments. The problem is that these companies are only as good as their latest gadget or new twist on themes. The glamour of biotechnology, and most likely the money flow for the next few years, is likely to be directed toward companies that produce new drugs based on genomics and proteomics.

Thus, while Applied Biosystems, Affymetrix, and Celera Genomics are credible companies in their own right, Perkin-Elmer is a more complete way to invest in the basic science of biotechnology.

The Giants of Biotechnology

I have already discussed Genentech and Amgen at length in other parts of this book. But it's important to recognize their place in the biotechnology hierarchy. Genentech proved that biotechnology could produce drugs when it mass-manufactured human insulin produced by bacteria. Amgen proved that a biotechnology company could make money and become a pharmaceuticals company along the way.

But much of the story remains to be told on other companies, as the giant leap from research-based cash-flow-negative entities to revenue-producing and eventually profitable companies is not a guarantee.

Genentech was originally taken public in the 1970s, where the stock did little. In the 1980s, it rose but was taken private, only to be reintroduced to the markets in 1999. At this time, it went into a nice stage 2 move, as Wall Street rediscovered the dream, which in Genentech's case consists of the fact that this is a premier biotechnology company with a significant product line already in existence and deep corporate pockets behind it. This almost certainly means that a serious pipeline of drugs is under development. But the stock went into a stage 5 reality stall (see figure 6.7) after Wall Street decided that it could wait for the next major move from the company.

Genentech is a prime example of how tough it is to make money. The company, which is 58 percent owned by Swiss pharmaceuticals firm Roche Holdings, has eight very popular products and earns significant royalty income from its growth hormone, insulin, and hepatitis C vaccines. It also has significant entrants in the treatment of heart attacks and cancer chemotherapy. But a series of adverse reactions with a breast cancer treatment caused multiple deaths, and the company had to settle, leading to a major dilution of earnings in the year 2000.

There are a few points to be made here. First, this is a seminal biotechnology company. Second, it is partially owned by a large pharmaceuticals firm. Finally, despite generating $1.2 billion in revenue per quarter, the company still finds it difficult to make money. This may be a management problem, but it is also a suggestion that the intangibles of this sector could affect any company

Figure 6.7. *Genentech, a stage 5 company. Courtesy of Telescan.*

at any time. While Genentech and Amgen may survive, many other companies may find it difficult to continue if they have a run of bad luck. That is why a biotechnology stock should be part of a diversified portfolio of stocks and why I advocate active management of a portfolio, as I will discuss later.

As we look at the companies that follow, I suggest that you keep an open mind. There is no way I can cover all the companies in the biotechnology sector. Thus I have concentrated on those found in the popular AMEX Biotechnology Index (BTK) as well as others in the sector that show special qualities, although they are not in the index. Table 6.1 summarizes the stocks in the index. On my Web site, *www.wallstdet.com,* I have created research centers, or pages that feature sector news, and list the stocks in a particular index. These research centers make it easy for investors to check charts, quotes, news, and fundamental data on an entire sector and to apply some of the analysis concepts described in this book.

Table 6.1 *The AMEX Biotechnology Index*

Amgen (NASDAQ:AMGN)

Celera Genomics (NYSE:CRA)

Biotechnology General (NASDAQ:BTGC)

Biogen (NASDAQ:BGEN)

Cephalon (NASDAQ:CEPH)

Chiron (NASDAQ:CHIR)

Cor Therapeutics (NASDAQ:CORR)

Genzyme (NASDAQ:GENZ)

Gilead Sciences (NASDAQ:GILD)

Human Genome Sciences (NASDAQ:HGSI)

IDEC Pharmaceuticals (NASDAQ:IDPH)

Immunex (NASDAQ:IMNX)

MedImmune (NASDAQ:MEDI)

Millennium Pharmaceuticals (NASDAQ:MLNM)

Organogenesis (NYSE:ORG)

Protein Design Labs (NASDAQ:PDLI)

Vertex Pharmaceuticals (NASDAQ:VRTX)

Courtesy of Market Sentiment Central *(www.wallstdet.com)*.

Biotechnology General (NASDAQ:BTGC)

Biotechnology General *(www.btgc.com)* is a perfect example of a very volatile stock in the biotechnology sector and is best avoided by nonprofessional investors. The stock's volatility is compounded by heavy insider selling, which is illustrated by the dark bars below the stock chart in figure 6.8. Note that the selling began shortly after the initial public offering and that it continued unabated, whether the stock price rose or fell. This is often a sign

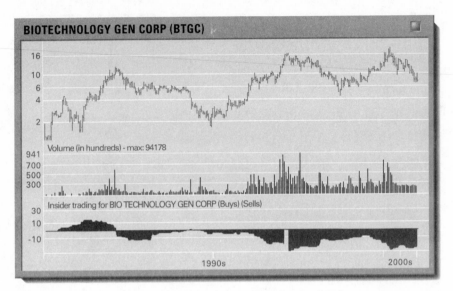

Figure 6.8. *Biotechnology General, a volatile multiple-stage company with a long history of insider selling.*

that management has little confidence in the company's prospects, although in all fairness stock sales can also be a significant source of income for management and employees in a publicly held company, especially in the first few years after a stock goes public.

But the chart pattern is not reassuring. When I did a news search on the company preparing this section, there were only two news items of any significance at the time. First, I noted that the chief operating officer had resigned and was heading back to California to spend time with his family, according to the news release. Second, the company had announced the European approval of BioHy, a product that is similar to Biomatrix's Synvisc product already on the market. Both BioHy and Synvisc are products aimed at the growing osteoarthritis market, a type of arthritis that is caused by the aging process's natural wear and tear of joints, especially the knees. Here is another example of the company's late-to-the-market strategy, as its product already faces serious competition in the marketplace.

While I have been somewhat critical here, I'm trying to provide balance to the investor, who should be concentrating on buying the best stock for the right reasons. Biotechnology General is a company with a great deal of potential.

This is another grandfather of the sector, as the company was established in 1980. It is a profitable stand-alone company. But it is not one that is a poster child for management execution or one that is known for endearing itself to the stock market. The company is headquartered in New Jersey, where administration, licensing, human clinical studies, marketing activities, quality assurance, and regulatory affairs are primarily coordinated. Research and development are performed in Israel.

Biotechnology General has done many things right, or it wouldn't have lasted as long as it has. The company's leading drug is Oxandrin, which is a steroid used to increase appetite and muscle mass in seriously ill patients, such as those suffering from AIDS or those who have had severe trauma or surgery.

But the company's pipeline is not particularly strong compared to other companies in the field, and therein lies the potential for this company to break out of its negative cycle, as it looks to be heading into the production of generic biotechnology products in a joint venture with Teva Pharmaceuticals (NASDAQ: TEVA), an Israeli pharmaceuticals company with a significant share of the generic pharmaceuticals market.

Generics are drugs that are marketed under the chemical name as opposed to the brand name. This is largely unexplored territory for the biotechnology industry. Therefore, Biotechnology General could well position itself as a leader in the industry. This is a good sign coming from management, and it is the kind of move that leverages the company's already existing infrastructure and expertise.

In my opinion, Biotechnology General is a stock to keep an eye on, as it has managed to make money despite facing several setbacks along the way. But there are companies that are better at executing their business plan in this sector.

Biogen (NASDAQ:BGEN)

Biogen *(www.biogen.com)* is another stalwart of the sector, as it is a profitable company with a highly regarded scientific tradition that includes two Nobel Prize winners among its founders. Like many of the stocks I've already mentioned, this is an older biotechnology company, having been founded in 1978.

Biogen has made its mark with protein-derived drugs, most notably interferon, the immune or defense system protein I discussed earlier. There are many kinds of interferon, and Biogen has harnessed much of the power of the diverse molecule for treating hepatitis C as well as a debilitating nerve-related disease called multiple sclerosis. Multiple sclerosis has the knack for attacking the young, especially women. Both actress Annette Funicello and comedian Richard Pryor are afflicted by the disease, as are 2.5 million others between the ages of 12 and 55.

Multiple sclerosis is not hereditary, but it is genetically influenced, being caused by the inflammation of the outer covering of nerves, which leads to scars and causes symptoms ranging from fatigue to severe impairment. There is no cure, but patients can achieve remissions with treatments like steroids.

Biogen has four major products in the market. Avonex is a form of interferon produced by Biogen that treats the resistant cases of multiple sclerosis and is the leading treatment for the disease in the world with over 93,000 patients under treatment, according to biogen.com. Avonex is significant because it is a drug that is both produced and marketed by Biogen.

A Biogen blockbuster is intron, another form of interferon used to treat hepatitis B and C, which is a product of recombinant DNA techniques. As I noted earlier, these viral diseases are fairly common and can respond to treatment by interferon. Biogen was the first company to use interferon to treat hepatitis. The drug was originally approved by the FDA to treat only a rare form of cancer called hairy cell leukemia. But, as a good company does, Biogen expanded the use of the drug to include other forms of cancer as well as hepatitis. Intron is the leading interferon preparation in the world, in a $2 billion market.

Biogen also produces the leading recombinant DNA vaccines against hepatitis B, placing it in a leading position in another billion-dollar market. Engerix-B and Recombivax are the brand names under which SmithKline Becham and Merck market the vaccines. Here again, we note that Biogen acted well in its early days, licensing its first products to large pharmaceutical firms with large sales forces. In return, the company formed a stable revenue stream with which to fund further research.

The company also produces Angiomax, a compound that breaks down blood clots in the coronary arteries of patients that are having potential heart attacks. This is a very competitive marketplace, with Centocor and Cor Therapeutics already having a significant presence in place. Thus, it is no wonder that Biogen licensed the drug to The Medicines Company (NASDAQ:MDCO) for marketing.

The Medicines Company is an interesting company on its own, as Angiomax is its leading contender for blockbuster status. The drug, as I write, is in phase 3 trials for treatment of heart attacks. Angiomax is aimed at a huge market where, under emergency situations, patients who are suffering with chest pain as a result of blocked coronary arteries are rushed to the heart catheterization suite, much as what happened to Vice President Dick Cheney.

Heart catheterization is a procedure in which x-ray dye is injected into the arteries in order to show blockages. Angiomax is used to thin the blood and dissolve the blood clot that is blocking the artery. A balloon is then inserted to open the artery, and this is often followed by the placement of a stent, or a small bridge with a hollow middle. The stent keeps the artery open while letting blood through.

Yes, I know, why do you need to know all this? Besides the fact that it is interesting and downright beautiful from a scientific standpoint, this kind of procedure is performed up to 680,000 times per day in the United States alone, where heart disease is still the number one killer. More important is that the procedure itself can cause the formation of blood clots, so that some intravenous blood thinner is required, whether the procedure is elective or an emergency. Thus, Angiomax has a huge potential market if it can gain favor over the products from Centocor and Cor Therapeutics. If the FDA approves Angiomax for the treatment of heart attacks, it could even be a more popular drug.

Biogen is a well-rounded, well-positioned company that is appropriate for a long-term aggressive portfolio.

The next members of the BTK are Celera Genomics and Cephalon. Celera has been detailed earlier in this chapter, and Cephalon (www.cephalon.com) is a company that I used in the early part of the book to illustrate the potential volatility of the sector in response to news.

Chiron (NASDAQ:CHIR)

Chiron (www.Chiron.com) is a stage 2 company, where it is a dream in discovery. The company is not a home-run hitter, but it hits lots of base hits, steals bases, hits sacrifice flies, and bunts the runner over. In other words, it has no real blockbusters, but it has many products on the market, including many vaccines, such as those against rabies, hepatitis, and meningitis. While these are not huge winners, they are high-profit products that the company sells to global health agencies in many cases, thus having long-term market and cash flow. Figure 6.9 clearly shows that the company's low-frills, two-yards-and-a-cloud-of-dust strategy of moving slowly and steadily forward is appreciated by Wall Street. The company's ability to be profitable is also reassuring, suggesting that it can deliver the goods.

Its most promising recent product is a collaboration with Ort-McNeil, a division of Johnson & Johnson, which once again brings up the collaboration aspect of the drug industry. The product is called Regranex, and it is a treatment for diabetic foot ulcers, a market with huge potential. Regranex is a recombinant DNA product produced by yeast, which stimulates cell growth and can heal the skin ulcers more rapidly. The product beat Human Genome Science's entry into the market, giving Chiron a slight advantage.

Chiron got its name from a Greek mythology character, the half-man, half-horse centaur with healing powers whose name the company bears. Another of the old wave of biotechnology companies, Chiron was formed in 1981, when three San Francisco–area professors decided to try their hand in the private sector. The story remains familiar, as Chiron's first product was a key ingredient in Recombivax, Merck's hepatitis B vaccine. Chiron also developed a key test for hepatitis C by cloning the virus that causes the disease and creating a diagnostic test that has improved the quality of the blood supply. The company is 45 percent owned by the large European pharmaceutical company Novartis, which explains why the company has a significant market share of the vaccine market in Europe.

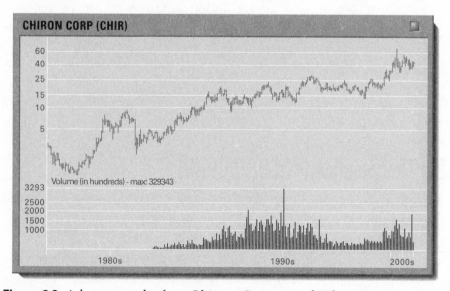

Figure 6.9. *A long-term look at Chiron. Courtesy of Telescan.*

Perhaps the most important achievement as a company thus far was its deciphering of the HIV virus genome. HIV causes AIDS, and Chiron's work was crucial in the fight against the deadly plague. Chiron also offers treatments for multiple sclerosis and cancer, where its Proleukin drug is a leader in kidney cancer and the deadly skin cancer melanoma.

Chiron focuses on blood testing products, vaccines, and traditional pharmaceuticals. In blood testing, it faces competition from Baxter, and in vaccines, it faces competition from many biotechnology firms, although the company is a leader in the Italian and German markets through its majority owner Novartis.

So far, Chiron has been a familiar story, but it begins to differ from the pack in its willingness to produce products for other companies. In other words, Chiron will contract out to other drug companies to produce their products. This can be a profitable business, and it has worked well in the electronics industry, where companies like Sanmina (NASDAQ:SANM) and Solectron (NYSE:SLR) are responsible for producing many familiar products, like PCs, which carry brand names like Dell and Gateway.

Chiron is a unique biotechnology company, as it has successfully adapted key strategies not just from the drug industry but also from other industries that have successful business models. The company is profitable and shows that a biotechnology company does not have to have blockbuster products to be successful. It is a suitable long-term investment.

Cor Therapeutics (NASDAQ:CORR)

Cor Therapeutics *(www.cortherapeutics.com)* is a new kid on the block, being established in 1988 and going public in 1992 (see figure 6.10). In 1999, the dream was discovered, as the company's first product, Integrilin, became accepted in the marketplace. The company may be ready to enter stage 3, as it faces difficult competition. Integrilin is used to keep blood from clotting during coro-

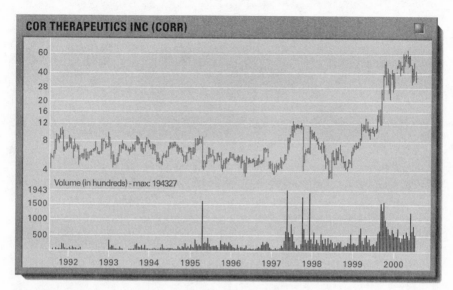

Figure 6.10. *Cor Therapeutics. Courtesy of Telescan.*

nary artery balloon procedures and is used in patients who have chest pain and are at high risk of having a heart attack. Integrilin is marketed by Schering Plough.

Cor is doing all the right things for a company at its stage. It is putting everything into research and trying to expand the label indications for Integrilin for the prevention of heart attacks, which would increase its earnings potential. The drug pipeline is along the same lines of action, with stroke and deep vein clot prevention products in different stages of testing.

Cor is an aggressive but encouraging portfolio component.

Gilead Sciences (NASDAQ:GILD)

Gilead Sciences *(www.gilead.com)* has the first flu pill, Tamiflu (see figure 6.11). The drug is the first in a new class of drugs to treat influenza viruses, and it is approved for use in the United States for children and adults as well as in 26 other countries. The stock remains in a nice stage 2 pattern, as the dream is being discovered,

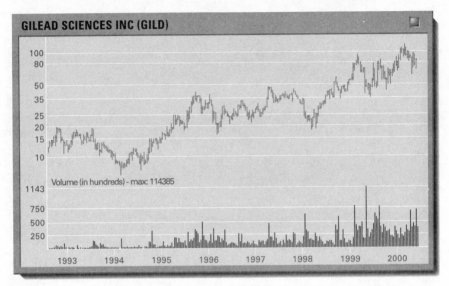

Figure 6.11. *A long-term look at Gilead Sciences. Courtesy of Telescan.*

albeit slowly. Tamiflu was developed in an alliance with Hoffman-La Roche, which is working on expanding the label.

The potential market in the United States alone is huge, as 40 million people develop flu symptoms every year, with 150,000 hospitalizations and 10,000 to 40,000 deaths per year. Tamiflu keeps the virus from reproducing by blocking a key enzyme in its replication pathway.

But Tamiflu is only part of the story. Gilead reworked an old drug called Amphotericin B into a new delivery system that uses fat droplets called liposomes to get the drug into the bloodstream. Amphotericin B is used to treat fungal infections, which are rising in frequency as a result of diseases such as AIDS that target the body's defense mechanisms. Liposomal delivery of Amphotericin B (AmbiSome) produces fewer side effects, is more efficient in reaching target areas, and increases the drug's stay at the infection site. The combination of AmbiSome and Tamiflu led to an increase in revenue and a decrease in losses, a fact that Wall Street likes. DaunoXome and Vistide are other drugs aimed at the AIDS population that are marketed by Gilead. The pipeline is focused on AIDS, hepatitis, and cancer treatments.

Gilead is well connected, well capitalized, and headed in the right direction. Its focus on problem solving and science is a sound practice. Like Cor Therapeutics, Gilead is a reasonable component of an aggressive biotechnology portfolio.

Human Genome Sciences (NASDAQ:HGSI)

Human Genome Sciences *(www.hgsi.com)* broke away from the pack and is a leader in genomics (see figure 6.12). The stock came a long way fast but remains in a consolidation pattern after making a huge splash in 2000 as the genomics craze caught on. The company chose to stay away from the race to unravel the human genome and focused on unraveling the mystery of which genes cause which diseases.

This strategy paid off, as it allowed the company to have a marketable database that it licenses to large drug companies like

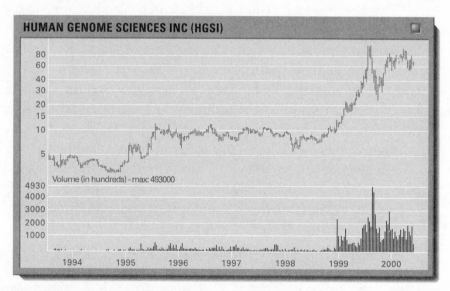

Figure 6.12. *Human Genome Sciences, a long-term view.*

Merck. This is a revenue-producing vehicle that the company then funnels into its research. The company has had great success in taking research into clinical trials and is on the verge of taking genomics-based drugs under the FDA microscope and into production as early as the 2002–2005 time frame.

Human Genome Sciences showed a nice bit of individual thinking, balancing laboratory and clinical research and thus becoming the first company with the potential to produce genomics-based drugs. This is the sign of leadership, as the revenue from its database made it possible to move into clinical trials involving four products with broad-ranging potential.

Again we can note that there is clear foresight and a great deal of problem solving involved in decision making, a sign of excellent management and leadership. This makes Human Genome Sciences a likely leader in the next wave of genomics- and proteomics-based biotechnology. In my opinion, this company has one of the best grasps on the future in the sector, and both its actions and its management decisions are worthy of note and likely to be copied in the future.

The key product in late-stage research for the company is called Repifermin. This is a protein that leads to cell growth. Unlike Chiron's product, which is meant for foot ulcers, Repifermin causes the growth of epithelial cells, which cover two-thirds of the body. This automatically broadens the potential uses for the drug, which is clearly stated by the company, as it is aiming the drug for the treatment of chronic wounds, such as diabetic ulcers, but also for the treatment of injuries to mucosal tissues as well as genetically influenced diseases such as ulcerative colitis, which causes ulcers in the intestines. Ulcerative colitis patients are usually treated with long-term steroids and often require multiple surgeries to remove affected sectors of bowel.

Mucosal tissues are the moist tissues that line the mouth, nose, throat, genitals, the digestive tract, and other areas of the body and can be harmed by chemotherapy. This is a nice leap from just skin ulcers and almost guarantees the potential for a wide label of indications to start with on FDA approval.

Human Genome Science's pipeline includes drugs to stimulate the defense system and to improve other side effects of chemotherapy. Most interesting is a drug called vascular endothelial growth factor, which has been shown to grow blood vessels and may allow patients with blocked blood vessels to grow new circulation. This would be critical for those who suffer from coronary artery disease as well as for those at risk for strokes.

Human Genome Sciences is an aggressive but well-focused company that has an excellent long-term strategy in place. The only fly in the ointment is that the company's pipeline needs to receive FDA approval with little room for disappointment.

IDEC Pharmaceuticals (NASDAQ:IDPH)

IDEC *(www.idecpharm.com)* is a leader in the use of monoclonal antibody therapy to treat cancer (see figure 6.13). Monoclonal antibodies are extremely efficient drug delivery systems since they function similarly to a lock-and-key mechanism, where the antibody is the key, and the target, in this case the cancer cell, is the lock. By attaching the drug to be delivered to the antibody, the drug has a higher chance of binding to a more specific target. This reduces the amount of drug necessary to reach the tumor and tends to reduce side effects.

IDEC's first drug, Rituxan, was approved by the FDA for use in high-grade lymphomas. Lymphoma is a cancer of the lymphatic system, a network of ducts and nodules located all over the body whose function is to be involved in the body's defense against disease. Rituxan is aimed at hard-to-treat forms of lymphoma and has been very successful. The antibody attaches to a specific marker, or receptor, that is highly specific for cancer cells. Once it attaches, it triggers a reaction that leads to the bursting of the tumor cell.

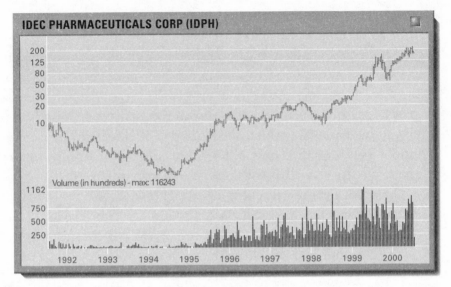

Figure 6.13. *IDEC Pharmaceuticals, a long-term view.*

IDEC is still in a long-term stage 2 pattern, as the potential for the drug and its offshoots, both in earnings and in product leverage, retains good prospects. This is no accident, as the company not only produces revenues but also is profitable.

The model is familiar but also well worth reviewing, as IDEC has multiple partnerships, including a major one with biotech kingpin Genentech, for the manufacture and distribution of Rituxan. More interesting is IDEC's partnership with Schering for a drug called Zevalin.

Zevalin is a great example of leveraging a successful product in what looks to be a hugely important drug delivery system. This drug attaches radiation-containing material to the monoclonal antibody and has already been proven effective with Rituxan. Lymphoma tumors are very sensitive to radiation. IDEC's goal is to treat the tumors with both Rituxan and Zevalin. This would theoretically allow higher amounts of tumor death with less dosage of either drug, thus reducing side effects while increasing chances of success.

IDEC has clinical trials with monoclonal antibody delivery systems for the treatment of rheumatoid arthritis, lupus (another, deadlier form of arthritis and autoimmune disorder), asthma, and the skin disorder psoriasis, which can also be associated with arthritis.

What I like about this company is that it is not trying to be all things to all people. It does one thing, monoclonal antibodies, and tries to do it better than anyone else. By the same token, it is taking its success and adapting it to high-volume areas, especially asthma, where treatment methods are still relying on technology and drug selection from the early 1990s.

In my opinion, any company that can design a once-a-day or once-a-week low-side-effect medication that can keep patients from going into breathing problems and return to a more normal lifestyle will have a blockbuster drug of huge impact. For this reason, I suggest keeping a very close eye on IDEC.

IDEC is another long-term holding for a diversified portfolio. As usual, I caution investors that long-term holdings need to be evaluated periodically. The questions to ask are whether the company is on target for delivering on its promise and whether the market is happy with the results.

Immunex (NASDAQ:IMNX)

I featured Immunex earlier when I outlined the mechanism of action of monoclonal antibodies. But the company, which remains in a nice stage 2 chart pattern, is worth mentioning again (see figure 6.14). Just as IDEC has proven that monoclonal antibodies can be successful to treat cancer, Immunex, which is 40 percent owned by American Home Products, already has Embrel on the market.

As you may recall, Embrel is a very successful treatment for rheumatoid arthritis. More important, Immunex makes money and has strong corporate backing from American Home Products. That means more than money. It means guidance, and it means the potential for a broader focus on drug development. Immunex also

Figure 6.14. *Immunex, a long-term view.*

has ongoing research into asthma and has Novantrone, a newly approved treatment for multiple sclerosis.

The strength of this company is in its corporate partnership with American Home Products, which is not just a valuable asset in its own right because of all the obvious tangible and intangible benefits but also a vote of confidence.

More important for the future will be the company's ability to leverage the use of Embrel into other disease entities. Perhaps the most promising use of Embrel will be in congestive heart failure (CHF), a condition that affects five million Americans. CHF results when heart muscle dies, thus reducing the ability of the heart to pump enough blood to the body. CHF can result from many causes, the most common being heart attacks, coronary artery disease, heart valve disease, high blood pressure, and the effects of diabetes, which include the four previously mentioned entities.

CHF is a very expensive disease and can last for years. The condition is eventually fatal and requires constant medical monitoring. Severe cases can include the need for coronary artery bypass surgery, heart valve replacements, frequent intensive care hospitalizations, expensive medication, pacemaker placements, and even the potential for heart transplants.

Again, the sleeper here is asthma. Currently, Immunex is involved in large-scale clinical trials of a product called Nuvance. This is an inhaled drug that prevents or reduces the production of mucus in the lungs. Asthmatic patients suffer when their bronchi, the pipes inside the lungs, constrict or narrow. The constriction usually results when an external event, such as dust, cat hair, or even exercise and cold temperatures, triggers a complex chemical reaction in the lungs. Part of the condition is the release of mucus into the bronchi, increasing the narrowing of the pipes. If Nuvance can prove successful at reducing the amount of mucus produced, this would be a significant advance in current therapy, which is aimed mostly at opening the bronchi. The current mucus-drying medication is an inhaled version of an old drug that has some unpleasant side effects and is more commonly used in patients who suffer from emphysema.

MedImmune (NASDAQ:MEDI)

MedImmune *(www.medimmune.com)* is another profitable biotechnology company that focuses on the prevention of disease (see figure 6.15). Its major products, Synagis and Respigam, are niche products aimed at the pediatric population. Synagis is a monoclonal antibody, while Respigam is a product of pooled antibodies from human plasma. Both products are aimed at the respiratory syncytial virus (RSV), which is a leading cause of asthma-like symptoms in newborns and infants, especially those who are born premature or have other underlying lung problems. The products, which are administered as preventive measures, can be lifesavers in this high-risk population and can actually help keep health care costs down since they decrease the number of hospitalizations in those who receive the drugs and shorten the hospitalizations of those who have to be admitted to the hospital.

MedImmune's Web site has managed care and billing information, which is a very nice touch and shows that the company is very

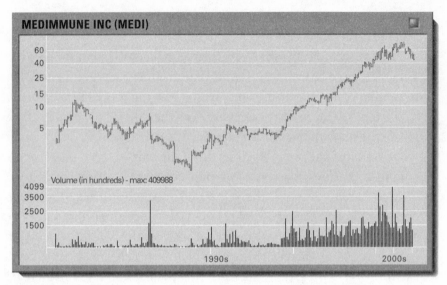

Figure 6.15. *MedImmune, a long-term view. Courtesy of Telescan.*

much in touch with the potential problems of reimbursement for its products in a managed care, aggressive cost-cutting environment.

MedImmune may prove to be a sleeper in its product pipeline, where it is developing a vaccine against cancer of the cervix and genital warts, both caused by a virus. This is a significant problem since the virus is sexually transmitted and is associated with early onset of sexual intercourse and multiple partners, both rising social trends. Cervical cancer affects women, but genital warts affect both sexes. If MedImmune is successful in this arena, it could have a blockbuster drug.

Even more exciting is the potential for a vaccine against urinary tract infections (UTIs), which affect women and children most often. UTIs are among the most frequent reasons for both doctor visits and hospitalizations. Medical costs associated with the condition are estimated at $1 billion per year. Here again is potential blockbuster material. Other interesting pipeline products are vaccines against Lyme disease and bacterial pneumonia.

MedImmune has alliances with Chiron, Alza, Human Genome Sciences, SmithKline Beecham, and multiple universities and is a solid niche player in the sector. The company acquired U.S. Biosciences, thus diversifying its product mix into the cancer treatment area, where its Ethyol product, a result of its Alza alliance, has shown promising results in the treatment of head and neck cancer.

This is a pure science play, as the chances of this company expanding into chewing gum and bandages to diversify its income stream are quite low. As a result, MedImmune is not likely to expand outside of biotechnology in the foreseeable future. It is, however, a serious player, one that remains focused in its niche and has shown foresight in its alliances as well as its acquisitions.

The stock began to show signs of weakness in early 2001 as a result of a general market downturn. But it is a bona fide major player in the business, and would be a prime takeover candidate for a very large biotechnology firm trying to expand into the vaccine market.

Millennium Pharmaceuticals (NASDAQ:MLNM)

Millennium Pharmaceuticals *(www.mlnm.com)* is one of my favorite concept companies in biotechnology, as it blends genomics with an ongoing review of the drug discovery process (see figure 6.16). The company's high throughput methodology screens high numbers of genes constantly, looking for those associated with diseases. The information is then turned into looking for molecules from which to produce drugs. But what I really like about the company is that its major goal is to be able to deliver custom-made medications based on the patient's genetic code as a guide to dosage, as stated in the company's mission, which is to provide "personalized and precise medicine."

Just as it shotguns research, Millennium also has more alliances than any other biotechnology company, with 20 described on its Web site as of January 2001. The alliances are a chief form

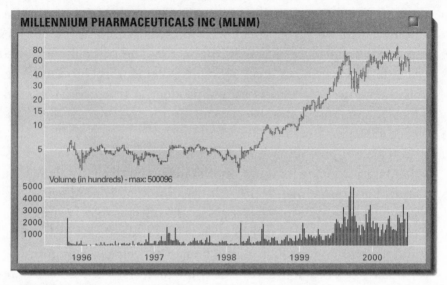

Figure 6.16. *Millennium Pharmaceuticals, a long-term view.*

of funding for operations and again show that Millennium has done its research and is implementing its business model.

Millennium focuses on cancer, immune diseases, and metabolic diseases, with a great deal of effort being focused on obesity, which could be a blockbuster sector on its own. Arthritis and asthma are also areas of focus, along with multiple sclerosis and other central nervous system disorders.

This is a highly innovative company that expects to have up to 10 products in the marketplace within the next five years. It is an aggressive and somewhat speculative stock at the preproduct stage but one with huge potential if it can deliver on even a modest portion of its expectations.

Organogenesis (AMEX:ORG)

Organogenesis *(www.organogenesis.com)* is an interesting concept stock with a long history (see figure 6.17). But the stock is

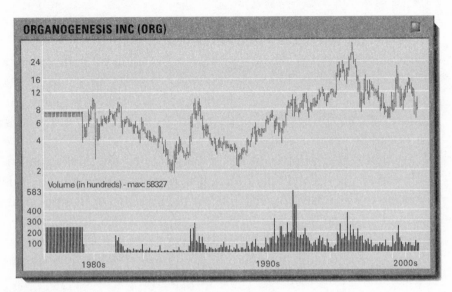

ORGANOGENESIS INC (ORG)

24
16
12
8
6
4
2

Volume (in hundreds) - max: 58327
583
400
300
200
100

1980s   1990s   2000s

Figure 6.17. *Organogenesis, a long-term view.*

not a particularly good performer. Its main product is Apligraf, a skin substitute from cell culture that has received FDA approval for use in diabetic foot ulcers. If this story sounds familiar, it is because there is plenty of competition in the diabetic foot ulcer business, with Human Genome Sciences and others either nearly in the market or already in the market with products that are not likely to require surgery. Organogenesis also produces Testskin II, which is a skin culture model preparation for use in the laboratory testing of drugs or of the effects of the environment on skin.

The company's pipeline consists of Vitrix, a substitute for a deeper layer of skin that is targeted at patients who have had very deep wounds through burns, surgery, or other trauma. Also in the pipeline is a synthetic liver that is aimed at keeping the patient alive until a transplant can be performed and a vascular graft aimed at the coronary artery bypass grafting market.

Organogenesis's products are good concepts. But the company is running against very serious challenges from companies that are on the verge of producing therapies that are less invasive. The technology may also be obsolete in the next decade if the promise of genomics is fulfilled. There may be some value in the company as a takeover candidate. But with a market capitalization of just under $400 million after a 20-year history of being traded publicly and no real profits or potential of profits in the near future, this is not a stock to be in the average investor's portfolio.

Organogenesis gives us the opportunity to use Intellectual Inclusion. I suggest making a mental note of this company's profile since it is obviously not well liked by the markets, or its stock price would be doing better. Perhaps the company's Web site is an excellent example of why Wall Street can't get excited. It is not very user friendly, and it lacks a modern look and feel. Thus it gives the impression that the company is out of step with the industry.

This impression is also clearly relayed by the company's products and niche, which have little to do with the dominant trends of genomics and molecular biology. It is not clear whether this is a management problem or a technology problem. But if Genzyme can deliver on its cell culture organ transplant technology, Organogenesis could be little more than a footnote.

Protein Design Labs (NASDAQ:PDLI)

Protein Design Labs *(www.pdl.com)* is at the forefront of the dominant trends of the future in the industry, as the company makes monoclonal antibodies (see figure 6.18). Its Zenapax product is a leader in the treatment of kidney rejection after transplantation. Rejection is a result of the body's defense mechanisms fighting a foreign body, in this case the new kidney. The market for antirejection medication is quite lucrative, as kidney failure continues to increase as a result of increasing incidence of diabetes and high blood pressure in the population. As with other companies, Protein Design Labs has allied itself with a profitable, large drug company, Hoffman-La Roche. Zenapax is being leveraged with clinical

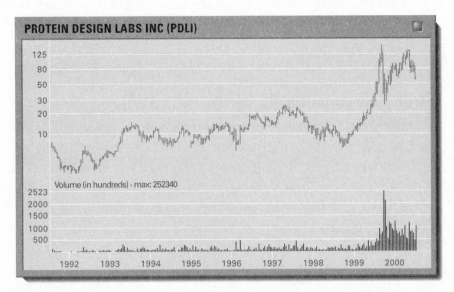

Figure 6.18. *Protein Design Labs, a long-term view.*

trials for eye inflammation, heart transplants, and psoriasis, a very common skin condition that is associated with a form of arthritis.

Protein Design Labs takes monoclonal antibodies to the next step by "humanizing" them, a process that cuts down on rejection. The company is also developing ways to leverage its antibody technology into the production of small-molecule antibiotics. This is a huge potential market, as there are an increasing number of bacteria that are becoming increasingly resistant to the currently available antibiotics. This antibiotic initiative is in cooperation with Eli Lilly, a leader in antibiotics. This is an excellent example of management's sound judgment in choosing a corporate partner since both companies have common interests.

More important is the fact that the company has shown that it can make money as well as increase its revenues. This is a solid company that is in the stage of being discovered by the market but one where the market's expectations are also rising. Thus the potential for a stumble is higher than most. For that reason, it is a more speculative stock than others in the field. Nevertheless, the company is likely to have a brighter future than most companies in the sector.

Vertex Pharmaceuticals (NASDAQ:VRTX)

Vertex Pharmaceuticals *(www.vpharm.com)* uses many branches of science to produce drugs (see figure 6.19). Its model includes computer analysis of protein structure, which is similar to the approach used by Pfizer's Auguron. Vertex takes a problem-solving approach and identifies the cause of the problem with its team working together from the beginning of the project. Computer analysis and information sharing are the rule, not the exception, at Vertex, resulting in constant communication and a more focused approach.

Vertex has created Agenerase, a drug that blocks a key enzyme in the viral reproductive cycle of the HIV virus. The drug, in combination with other anti-HIV drugs, keeps the virus from growing and making copies of itself, giving the body's defense system a po-

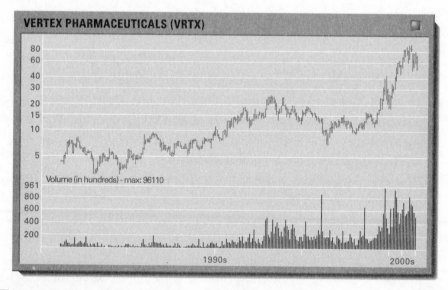

Figure 6.19. *Vertex Pharmaceuticals, a long-term view.*

tential chance to increase the infection-fighting cells that the virus targets and that make the patients with the disease susceptible to infection.

The key to Agenerase, and one that is a credit to Vertex's approach to designing instead of discovering drugs, is that it is taken twice a day and does not require food when it is taken. This gives the patient a bit more flexibility and makes it more convenient to go about day-to-day activities.

Vertex has had a spotty record of profitability and volatile revenues. The company has a great concept, and the market seems to have great faith in the company, having driven the price higher. But compared to other companies, it has a very narrow pipeline, concentrating on HIV for its first disease. While it is a noble cause and a potentially global drug in scope, HIV is not a particular moneymaker since no company has found a cure for it.

Thus this is a very speculative stock, especially when the specter of Pfizer's Auguron, with the deep pockets of the parent company behind it, is in a similar business. Vertex is an interesting concept stock at this point and one that may have trouble finding steady profitability in the future. This is not a core holding for a diversified biotechnology portfolio.

The Best of the Rest

The BTK is an excellent benchmark, as it highlights the key players in the industry and has allowed us insight into the strategies and business models that work and into some that don't work well at all. I hope this chapter has given you a feel for what the major players in the industry are, how they got there, and where they are likely to go next.

But there are many other companies in biotechnology that have interesting and successful business models as well. I can't describe them all. For a comprehensive summary of the industry, I recommend you consult appendix A, which was compiled by John Duke, whose research assistance was invaluable. The appendix provides company capsules and information about Web sites and other research sources. But before you get to the appendix, here are companies that I call the best of the rest.

Accredo Health (NASDAQ:ACDO)

Accredo Health *(www.accredohealth.com)* provides contract pharmacy services to the biotechnology industry. This is a company that goes the extra mile, including the provision of overnight delivery of medications for treating rare genetic disorders to patients and hospitals. Accredo's biggest client is Genzyme, which in my opinion is a sign of foresight in this small company to align itself with the potential emerging leader in the sector. Accredo also provides claim filing and consulting services.

As biotechnology drugs become the norm for most disease entities in the next 10 to 20 years, Accredo's business is likely to continue to grow and prosper since it will likely have the relationships and infrastructure in place for a significant distribution network.

Alexion Pharmaceuticals (NASDAQ:ALXN)

Alexion *(www.alexionpharmaceuticals.com)* is still a research-stage company, with a key alliance in Procter & Gamble. It is in late-stage clinical trials with drugs to treat allergic reactions that can occur after coronary artery disease. But perhaps its greatest potential is in the area of nerve regeneration. Alexion has successfully repaired spinal cord tissue in injured pigs. This is very early but has huge potential.

Aviron (NASDAQ:AVIR)

Aviron *(www.aviron.com)* is another development-stage company with great potential in the crowded vaccine production field. The company's Flu Mist, which currently is in front of the FDA, is a flu vaccine that is administered via a nasal inhaler. Because of such ease of administration, the potential for the vaccine to become a blockbuster, if approved by the FDA, is relatively high.

Biopure Corp. (NASDAQ:BPUR)

This is one of my favorite stories in biotechnology since it tackles a problem that has eluded giants like Baxter, which has searched for the key to synthetic blood for many year. Biopure *(www .biopure.com)* does not make synthetic blood but processes bovine (cattle) blood, changing it so that it can be administered to animals, primarily dogs and cats under the brand name Oxyglobin. When I discovered the company, I went to my vet and got a glowing report of the product, which is used for dogs with a rare anemia and for both dogs and cats that have had trauma.

Human use is expected to be approved by the FDA based on what the company described as "favorable" phase 3 trial data at the Hambrecht and Quist Biotechnology Conference on January 8, 2001. More interesting is the fact that the company, prior to submitting the product to FDA approval, announced that it was seeking financing in order to build a manufacturing plant for human blood.

Hemopure is not blood; rather, it is processed and sterilized cattle hemoglobin, the protein that carries oxygen in the blood. It is a potential blockbuster given the fact that it can be stored at room temperature for two years, requires no blood typing, and theoretically does not carry HIV or hepatitis C. On November 20, 2000, it was tested during surgery on a patient with a rare blood type and received glowing reviews.

Cerus Corp. (NASDAQ:CERS)

The hand of Baxter in the blood business extends far and wide, including a $22 million investment in Cerus Corp. *(www.ceruscorp.com)*. This company is in the late stages of developing an ingenious method to keep the blood supply clear of infection. The technology is simple and involves two steps.

Cerus has two small molecules that attach to the contaminant's DNA. When exposed to ultraviolet light, the attached molecule is turned on and does its job, which is to keep the bacteria or virus from reproducing. If it can't reproduce, it can't cause infection.

What I like here is that Baxter has put money into Cerus. This gives the company credibility. Second, I like the concept, as blood supply safety is a key public health issue and can translate into nice profits.

Cubist Pharmaceuticals (NASDAQ:CBST)

Cubist *(www.cubist.com)* is a pure research company with an aggressive plan for antibiotics discovery. Currently, its first drug, daptomycin, is in phase 3 clinical trials. The drug is aimed at bacteria that have become resistant to antibiotics that are currently available in the market.

Cubist has a patented drug discovery system that, through the use of genomics and aggressive database techniques known as bioinformatics, allows the company to find the most likely candidates for new drugs, cutting a great deal of the trial and error out of drug development. The company has focused its approach on finding naturally occurring substances that have antibiotic properties.

This is a powerful combination since nature provides most organisms with unique defense mechanisms against their enemies. In effect, Cubist has adapted biotechnology's most current methods to the old way of finding drugs, as was the case in the discovery of penicillin. This is an aggressive company that has formed strong alliances and has the potential to deliver many blockbusters in the coming decades.

Imclone Systems (NASDAQ:IMCL)

Finally, I suggest Imclone Systems *(www.imclone.com),* another unique idea company, as it combines mouse and human antibodies to produce anticancer treatments. One of its potential drugs is aimed at helping chemotherapy work better, a concept that is also being explored by Human Genome Sciences. But perhaps the blockbuster here can come if the company's platform for producing anticancer vaccines can deliver. This stock is highly speculative but worth keeping an eye on.

Summary

This has been a comprehensive chapter, one whose focus was not to give you a portfolio to invest in but to provide insights into which business models are likely to be successful or not in the coming 10 to 25 years. While that may seem somewhat nebulous, history clearly shows that companies that do the right thing at the right time are more likely to be successful.

This chapter focused on the companies featured in the AMEX Biotechnology Index, a well-recognized benchmark for the sector. Many of the companies in the index are profitable, and their methods should be carefully studied. Those companies that follow their lead are more likely to be successful than those that don't.

Several companies in the index are not profitable but do produce revenues. These are what I call bubble companies, which may or may not ever succeed in making money. The key to these companies is to study their technology and to figure out whether it is good enough for someone else to buy.

I recommend the use of Intellectual Inclusion while reading this chapter. If something sounds familiar, go back to the chapter on the large drug stocks and see which one of the giants is using a similar method. Remember, a successful biotechnology company is likely to have put in place the successful methods of the pharmaceuticals industry.

When in doubt, I suggest rereading the section on Genzyme, my prototype biotechnology company of the future. It is diversified and aggressive and employs the methods of giants like Johnson & Johnson to make money. While others have dazzling science behind them, they have a difficult time making money.

Finally, I hope that you are beginning to piece together the puzzle. Investing is an ever changing process, one that at the same time is full of familiar concepts. The key to success is to recognize similarities, not just between companies but also between events and situations. The constant study of the sector and its companies will lead you to making better decisions.

7

Technical and Fundamental Analysis

I f you've made it this far, congratulations. This has been a challenging and, I hope, exciting journey so far. Don't give up. You're almost there.

In the previous six chapters, I described the interactions among the science of biotechnology, the external market factors, the key companies in the sector, and the business practices and models that the successful companies use. Now it's time to put all that together in an applicable model that yields good stock picks, keeps you out of bad stock picks, and gets you out of trouble when you've made a mistake.

In my 12 years of investing, I've learned that using the best aspects of both technical and fundamental analysis is better than relying on either form alone. I've also learned that it is better to have a flexible outlook in going about my routine when looking for stocks. This means that being able to adapt to market conditions is a requirement in order to make money.

So rather than focusing on either value or growth investing or technical or fundamental analysis, I prefer to focus on the best of all approaches, with a great emphasis on what's working in the current market. Thus I combine value and growth analysis not just in my daily analysis but also when one form of philosophy is being used by the majority of players on Wall Street. Stay flexible, and you'll increase your chances of making money.

This chapter is much more hands-on. It will deal with chart reading, indicators, and oscillators, and it will use everything that I've discussed in the book so far. It will draw on everything that can make you a successful intermediate-term investor and will provide hints as to how to get started in shorter-term trading.

But, as I'll discuss a bit later, day trading and intermediate-term investing are two different worlds that are often confused by the public. To confuse an intermediate-term outlook of weeks to months, with a one-minute or even one-hour holding period is a guaranteed one-way ticket to big losses.

Day trading of biotechnology stocks requires no real knowledge of the sector, the nuances, or the history. It just requires a souped-up computer with a broadband connection and a good trading software package. When you add excellent instruction to that package and you develop experience, you are still at high risk of losing routinely. It is that risky. Instead, I recommend a more intermediate-term time frame with this sector since it is so volatile.

This chapter moves rapidly and has a great deal of information. I suggest that you set aside some time in a quiet place, with a nice beverage and a pencil and paper, and that you begin.

Analyzing Biotechnology Companies by Combining Growth and Value Criteria

A perfect example of a great opportunity to use my approach to the markets came in the year 2000. After the bear market in the NASDAQ hit, many stocks became quite inexpensive. Thus the market favored those investors who adhere to a value philosophy, which involves buying stocks when they are cheap relative to the market. Value players like to use ratios such as the price/earnings (P/E) ratio to estimate whether a stock is cheap or expensive.

The ratio is simple enough to calculate by dividing a stock's current price by the most recent earnings available. A ratio of 20 is traditionally thought to be average. A good general rule to keep in mind is that if the P/E ratio rises, then the stock becomes expensive, unless the rate of rising revenues and earnings also rises. That is the crux of a philosophy known as growth at a reasonable price (GARP), which is better at explaining why stocks with relatively high P/E ratios continue to rise.

A great example of GARP is a comparison between Genzyme and Amgen, whose revenues and earnings are illustrated in tables 7.1 and 7.2. This information was adapted from Market Guide *(www.marketguide.com)*, a premium service. There are other

Table 7.1 *Genzyme General Revenue and Earnings Summary (NASDAQ:GENZ)*

REVENUES (THOUSANDS OF U.S. DOLLARS)

Quarter	1997	1998	1999	2000
March	144,606	129,896	150,766	170,626
June	147,614	141,779	154,205	186,694
September	148,841	142,225	157,669	192,165
December	156,142	155,419	172,726	
Total	597,203	569,319	635,366	

EARNINGS PER SHARE

Quarter	1997	1998	1999	2000
March	0.270	0.420	0.380	0.570
June	0.300	0.500	0.280	0.770
September	0.310	0.640	0.430	0.640
December	0.110	0.490	0.620	
Total	0.990	2.050	1.710	

Courtesy of Market Guide.

places to get this form of data, but Market Guide's format is quite easy to follow.

The first thing to do is to note the P/E ratio, which on January 12, 2001, was at 29. This means that investors were paying $29 for every $1 in earnings. This is expensive when looked at from a pure fundamentals standpoint, as 20 times earnings is the mean P/E ratio. The next step is to compare this P/E ratio to that of a peer company and to compare the ratio to the earnings and revenue growth. Thus I looked up Amgen, the sector bellwether. It was selling at 54 times earnings, which is expensive. One point for Genzyme, a stock that was cheaper. Amgen's earnings and revenues are shown in table 7.2.

Table 7.2 *Amgen General Revenue and Earnings Summary (NASDAQ:AMGN)*

REVENUES (THOUSANDS OF U.S. DOLLARS)

Quarter	1997	1998	1999	2000
March	575,500	605,400	745,500	814,100
June	620,500	656,900	820,500	914,400
September	598,300	700,900	847,200	949,500
December	606,700	755,000	926,900	
Total	2,401,000	2,718,200	3,340,100	

EARNINGS PER SHARE

Quarter	1997	1998	1999	2000
March	0.160	0.180	0.230	0.250
June	0.180	0.210	0.250	0.280
September	0.075	0.210	0.280	0.330
December	0.165	0.220	0.260	
Total	0.580	0.820	1.020	

Courtesy of Market Guide.

When I look at earnings and revenue data, my first step is to identify the amount of time covered in the data. Market Guide provides up to four years of information per profile. In this case, the time covered for both companies is the same, making it a nice simple comparison. Next I look at the general trend in earnings. Both companies have made money in all the 1997 to 2000 quarters listed. This is an excellent sign, as it shows that both companies are able to show profits. For example, Amgen made 16 cents a share in March 1997 and 33 cents a share in September 2000, while Genzyme made 27 cents a share in December 1997 and 64 cents a share in September 2000. While profits are nice, it sometimes pays to read the fine print, as companies sell stock or other assets and count them as profits. This is a controversial practice and is something to keep an eye on, as a profitable quarter could occur, even if sales are falling.

That's why the revenue number is important. What we want to see is at least a favorable year-over-year comparison, meaning higher sales on a year-over-year basis. When companies can grow consistently on a year-over-year basis, their price tends to rise for longer. The champion of revenue and earnings growth was, until 2001, Cisco Systems (NADSAQ:CSCO), a stock that delivered tremendous growth for over a decade in the 1990s. In this comparison, it is here, in the earnings growth, that the fundamentals confirm what the charts suggested earlier. Both companies show healthy revenue growth over the three years covered. But we want to see what the most current numbers are doing.

Genzyme grew its September 2000 revenues by a 21.8 percent rate, while Amgen's year-over-year comparisons showed only 12 percent revenue growth over the same period. That suggests slowing sales. To arrive at this number, just subtract the latest revenue figure, which was 192,165 million for Genzyme, from the revenue a year earlier, 157, 669. The resulting figure is 34,439 million. This number is then divided by the prior year's revenue, 157,669, to get the percentage, which is expressed as a decimal, 0.218. To get the percentage, just multiply by 100. This is the simple method I use when I write my nightly columns at Market Sentiment Central, in which I frequently talk about revenue and earnings growth.

Amgen's figures show a nice 17 percent earnings growth on a year-over-year basis. But while Amgen's numbers are nice compared to Genzyme's 21.8 percent revenue growth and 48 percent earnings growth, the choice is clear: Buy the best stock in the best sector. In this case, it is Genzyme. A picture is worth a thousand words. Figure 7.1 clearly shows that Amgen, the thin lower line, was flat in the year measured by the chart, while Genzyme rose 75 percent. The market is very efficient, and the market likes to see sales and earnings growth together.

I previewed the basics of fundamental analysis in chapters 5 and 6 as we discussed business models and strategies. Along the way, there have also been plenty of charts to look at. Thus, much of the material in this chapter should be familiar. But that is only the beginning, as technical analysis involves much practice and the ability to look for sometimes very subtle signs that can make the difference between picking a winner or losing your shirt. Fun-

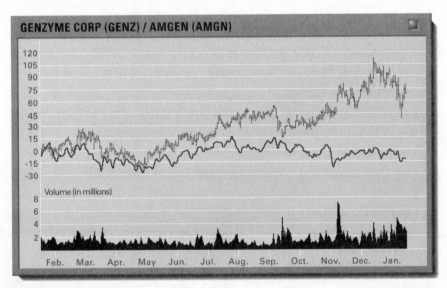

Figure 7.1. *Genzyme (upper bar graph) versus Amgen (lower line graph). A one-year comparison.*

damental analysis, as I described previously, involves looking at valuation, earnings and revenue growth, and the potential for the company to deliver on its promise in the future.

Technical analysis is the pure practice of looking at securities charts and predicting future performance based on price behavior exhibited in the past. The discipline is often misunderstood, as pure chart analysis is not particularly accurate without the use of moving averages and oscillators. Moving averages smooth out the price action, while oscillators are excellent tools used to measure momentum as well as tops and bottoms in securities.

Technical analysts work on the belief that in an efficient market, every up- or downtick in an asset takes into account the total sum of all the information and opinion available to the market at that instant in time as it pertains to that security, whether it is a commodity, a bond, a stock, a mutual fund, or something else. The caveat is that an efficient market is not always correct. Instead, an efficient market is one that is reacting to the information that it has available. In the current age of instant communications and blow-by-blow market coverage, markets make decisions (right or wrong) instantaneously, based on the information available. These decisions, especially when they are made as a news release is hitting the business wires, can often be reversed, creating volatility.

At the core of this decision-making process are the market makers and the specialists whose actions I discussed in detail earlier. Thus, in a volatile sector like biotechnology, a strong knowledge of technical analysis is not just useful but absolutely necessary.

Rather than spend a great deal of time on theories, I will take you through my daily routine of analyzing the markets as I write my daily columns. I don't expect you to duplicate every step. But this is a realistic illustration of what it takes to be a market analyst. The point is that you should develop and fine-tune a routine, and that you should be ready to make changes when necessary.

When I first started reading charts, I was a purist. Because of that, I lost a lot of opportunities and in some cases money. Here is where Intellectual Inclusion helped me. I review my results regularly by keeping a weekly diary where I summarize the markets and by keeping nightly notes on all the sectors I follow. As a result, I look at what works and doesn't work in a systematic and very frequent fashion. If it works, I keep it. If it doesn't work, I try to figure out why it's not working. If I can't figure that out, I'll stop using it. As a result, year after year, I become more familiar with the subtleties of chart reading, which I supplement with fundamentals, as I described previously, and my results are much better.

We could make technical analysis as simple or difficult as we want to. But I prefer to keep it very basic, concentrating on the fundamentals of chart reading, coupled with the basic understanding of indicators and oscillators. Finally, I note that the goal here is to take the information already presented and put it to good use by applying it to everyday decision-making situations.

Step 1: The Big Picture

My first step is to ask myself what interest rates, market sentiment, and money flow are doing. If the Federal Reserve is lowering rates, my chances of picking winning stocks in those sectors that are doing well are higher. Rising rates are eventually the kiss of death for most stocks. The key here is to pick the best stocks in the best sectors. I realize that this is a book about biotechnology investing, but if the biotechnology sector is falling, there is no reason to invest in it.

Interest Rates

Interest rates are easy to gauge. All the major newspapers carry them. Every major Internet financial commentary site devotes time to them, and the business networks are always talking about them. Learn the difference between them and develop the habit of buying more stocks when rates are falling and of selling more stocks when rates are rising. The general rule is to buy stocks when the Fed is lowering interest rates and to sell them when the Fed is raising interest rates. As I discussed earlier, there are some finer points to keep up with, but the basic principle is not to fight the Fed.

Market Sentiment

In *After-Hours Trading Made Easy*, I devoted a whole chapter to interpreting market sentiment, featuring my proprietary indicator the Super Seven Market Forecaster, which you can find updated on Market Sentiment Central. But you can visit the CBOE Web site on a nightly basis and calculate two ratios that will tell you a great deal about market sentiment.

The CBOE put/call ratio is already calculated on the site. This is a ratio of the number of put options, which are essentially bets that the underlying asset will fall, while calls are essentially bets that the underlying asset will rise. It measures sentiment on individual stocks, and it is a mixture of both retail and individual investor sentiment. When puts are placed over calls, the ratio creates a contrarian indicator. A ratio above 0.6 is bullish, as it signifies rising fear. Generally, as the ratio gets higher, it is more bullish, especially as the market is falling. Major market bottoms are usually marked when the ratio reaches above 1.0 at the market close. Put/call ratios below 0.40 are usually signs that the market is likely to, at the very least, slow its advance, as investors are getting too optimistic.

The second ratio is the CBOE put/call ratio for stock indexes, which is calculated by placing the number of put options on the CBOE over the number of call options. This is a measure of big-money sentiment, including big institutions, hedge funds, and large speculators. A ratio higher than 1.1 is bullish. Major bottoms often come when this indicator is greater than 1.5. A ratio below 0.7 is a bearish sign.

Other sentiment indicators include sentiment surveys from Investor's Intelligence and Market Vane. These are useful, but they work better in the context of the Super Seven Market Forecaster, which is beyond the scope of this chapter.

The key here is to watch what the market does when there are too many people acting in the same manner, either bullish or bearish. As a general rule, a reading of 40 percent bulls or less on Market Vane's Bullish Consensus is eventually bullish for the markets. Readings below 30 percent are extremely bullish. Tops or corrections usually come when the bullish number is over 60 percent. Readings over 70 percent are very cautionary and should be used as sell signals for non-long-term holdings, very profitable positions, or holdings that are not acting well. Too many extreme opinions on either side are usually signs that the major trend is about to change.

A perfect example came on July 31, 1997, when Market Vane's Bullish Consensus for stocks registered 70 percent bulls for stocks. On the same Friday, the CBOE put/call ratio was 0.49, a number leaning toward the danger zone. This was a sign that there was too much optimism in the markets and that vulnerability to bad news was very high. Thus, when the Asia currency crisis hit in August, by October the markets were crashing.

The opposite was true in December 1994, after a series of interest rate increases by the Fed. The broad market had gotten decimated, even if the major indexes had held up. On December 10, the put/call ratio was 1.19, while Market Vane's Bullish Consensus gave a reading of 34 percent bulls. Soon thereafter, the Fed began to lower interest rates, and 1995 was a fantastic year for stocks.

Money Flow

Money flow, in the context of the entire market, is more difficult to ascertain than it is with individual stocks, as I will discuss shortly. For the whole market's money flow, I recommend a visit to Trimtabs.com *(www.Trimtabs.com)* or Birinyi.com *(www .birinyi .com)*. Both offer premium services. Money flowing out of stocks and into money market funds will accompany a market sell-off. When it reaches a climactic level, which is usually accompanied by a sharp sell-off in stocks, this usually marks a bottom.

Mutual fund cash levels are a lagging indicator that can be useful in retrospect and can be seen weekly in print in *Barron's* or online at *www.barrons.com*. One of my favorite places to find the indicator is the General Markets & Sectors page of *Investor's Business Daily*. A quick scan will give you the most recent 21 months of data, which are released monthly by the Investment Company Institute *(www.ici.org)*.

When I looked at the data in the January 10, 2001, issue of *Investor's Business Daily*, it was easy to tell the story of the markets during the period, as mutual fund cash levels had been at 5 percent or below for 16 out of the 18 months covered. Levels below the 5 percent area are considered to be low by historical standards. In March 2000, levels fell to 4 percent. This coincided with the beginning of the bursting of the Internet bubble and began the huge NASDAQ bear market of the year 2000.

Incidentally, the put/call ratio on January 9 was 0.89. This coincided with mutual fund cash levels of 6.1 for the month of November 2000 since fund cash levels are a lagging indicator. Market Vane's Bullish Consensus for January 5, 2001, was a deliriously bullish 23 percent bulls. This triad of indicators lived up to its history in the month of January, but by March 2001, the bear was back.

Thus it was no surprise to me when the NASDAQ began to bottom in that period of time, despite the big fade in February and March. History will tell whether the analysis was eventually correct. But it most certainly got a good start.

Market Indexes and the 200-Day Moving Average

The best gauge of the overall market remains the Standard & Poor's (S&P) 500 index, which is the commonly used benchmark for investment returns and money manager performance. The best gauge of the overall long-term health of the market is the 200-day moving average. Figure 7.2 shows how the index rose above the 200-day moving average in late 1994 as the Fed began

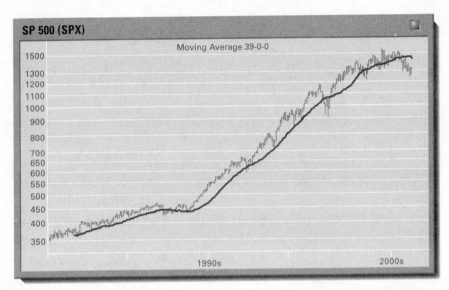

Figure 7.2. *The Standard & Poor's 500 index and the 200-day moving average. Courtesy of Telescan.*

to lower interest rates and remained above the average for most of the rest of the decade.

Note that each time the index fell below the average, it tended to show a period of weakness. Note also that the most notable period of weakness came in the year 2000.

The general rule is that the market is in a long-term uptrend when the S&P 500 is above its 200-day moving average. A fall below the average is usually a sign of weakness. I'll discuss moving averages in greater detail in the following pages, but for now remember that the 200-day moving average is a key gauge of the future of the market.

The New York Stock Exchange Advance Decline Line

The best measure of how the market is acting is the New York Stock Exchange (NYSE) advance decline line. This is the total obtained when you subtract the number of stocks declining from the number of stocks advancing. If you were plotting your own advance decline line, and the NYSE advances numbered 1,500 and decliners numbered 1,200, the number plotted on your graph would be 300, or 1,500–1,200.

The advance decline line measures something technicians call market breadth. A market that is acting right has a rising NYSE advance decline line, while a market that is not acting right will have a lagging advance decline line even if the indexes continue to rise.

A perfect example of a very difficult market came in 2000, when the technology stocks peaked in the spring and went into a tailspin, as higher interest rates in the early part of the year and political uncertainty as a result of the unusual presidential election led to a very negative climate for most stocks. The biotechnology sector held on much better than many stocks until early 2001, when it too collapsed. Instead, pharmaceutical, hospital, insurance, health insurance, and real estate investment trust stocks did well. Investors who did not look at the entire market missed the signs of danger as well as the opportunity to invest in sectors that did well despite an overall negative tone to the markets.

The advance decline's use as an early warning is perfectly illustrated in figure 7.3. The dark rising line is the NYSE Composite index ranging from 1991 to 2000. The thin line, which is initially going sideways and then falls off a cliff, is the NYSE advance decline line. I drew a line across the top of the advance decline line in the figure to illustrate the point that even though the indexes kept going higher, the broad market, which measures the average stock, failed to move higher. Purists would have sold as early as 1992. In reality, you want to see the advance decline line rise at least in the intermediate term, as it did in 1995, 1996, and 1997. In 1998, the line scored a nice move higher. But by 1999, things were looking a bit scary. Point A, in late 1999, is where the divergence, or the failure to confirm the new high on the NYSE, signaled that trouble was coming.

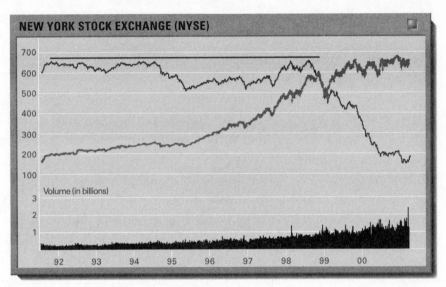

Figure 7.3. *The NYSE and the advance decline line. Courtesy of Big-charts.com.*

This dramatic representation of the health of the markets in what history shows is the greatest of all bull markets clearly illustrates why the year 2000 was the worst bear market since 1973–1974. Note how the failure of the advance decline line to move higher in 1999 than it had in 1994 led to the breakdown of the broad market despite the NYSE index remaining flat. Even more dramatic is how the breakdown in the NYSE advance decline line eventually translated itself into the NASDAQ's breakdown.

Note also how the NASDAQ Composite continued to advance until the early part of 2000 despite the clear indication from the NYSE advance decline line in 1998 that the market was in deep trouble (see figure 7.4). The point here is that by carefully looking at the market and at what some call out-of-date indicators, investors can stay out of trouble. Thus, when the fall came, it came harder than most expected since the NASDAQ was so clearly out of line with the average stock as measured by the advance decline line.

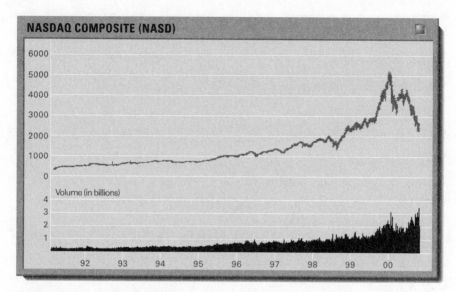

Figure 7.4. *The NASDAQ Composite. Courtesy of Bigcharts.com.*

During most of 1999 and into early 2000, investors were touting the usual line at major market tops: "This time is different." The battle cry was that Internet stocks would cure all the world's evils and that they could never fall in price. Of course, they fell, and most were very surprised, although as usual there had been plenty of warning signs that not all was well.

Sector Analysis

After looking at the big picture, I want to see which sectors are acting well and which are not. I analyze 21 indexes per day in order to understand what's working and what's not. Along with the major indexes, which are the Dow Jones Industrial Average, the S&P 500, the NASDAQ Composite, and the Russell 2000 Index of small stocks, I analyze 17 sectors on a daily basis. These are summarized in table 7.3.

Why do I look at so many indexes? Because the best markets are those in which a majority of sectors rise, a term that I will

Table 7.3 *Sector Indexes*

Index	Symbol	Sector
Philadelphia Bank Index	BKX	Banking
AMEX Biotechnology Index	BTK	Brokerage
AMEX Computer Technology	XCI	Technology
AMEX Computer Hardware Index	HWI	Technology
AMEX Morgan Stanley Health Care Provider Index	RXH	Hospitals
AMEX Morgan Stanley Health Care Payers Index	HMO	HMOs
Standard & Poor's Insurance Index	IUX	Insurance
AMEX Interactiveweek Internet Index	IIX	Internet
Philadelphia Oil Service Index	OSX	Oil service, drilling, transport
AMEX Natural Gas	XNG	Natural gas integrated
AMEX Networking Index	NWX	Network Communications
AMEX Oil and Gas Index	XOI	Diversified oil
AMEX Pharmaceuticals Index	DRG	Pharmaceuticals
Standard & Poor's Retailing Index	RLX	Retailing
Philadelphia Semiconductor Index	SOX	Semiconductors
CBOE Software Index	GSO	Software
Philadelphia Wireless Telecom Index	YLS	Wireless Communications

call technical harmony. Technical harmony is akin to musical harmony. If the market is acting right, just like if all the singers in the choir are singing the right notes, then the market will give more investors a better chance to pick winning stocks.

One of my favorite ways to compare how well a sector is doing is to chart it together with a major index, just as I did with

Genzyme and Amgen earlier. Since biotechnology stocks are traded mainly on the NASDAQ, it makes sense to compare AMEX Biotechnology Index (BTK) to the NASDAQ Composite. A great place to do this kind of exercise is BigCharts.com *(www.bigcharts.com)*, which offers the service free of charge.

In January 2000, the BTK got crushed, as panic selling hit. But a look at figure 7.5 shows that while the NASDAQ Composite was down nearly 45 percent during the period charted, the BTK was still up some 30 percent for the period. This is called relative strength, which means that the biotechnology stocks were stronger than the overall NASDAQ during the period. Relative strength is important because those stocks that perform best in a rising or a falling market are the leaders. From a technical standpoint, we want the best stocks in the best sector.

Taking the analysis to the next step, and following up on what we discussed in the previous paragraphs, we now compare two blue-chip biotechnology stocks, Genzyme and Amgen, in figure

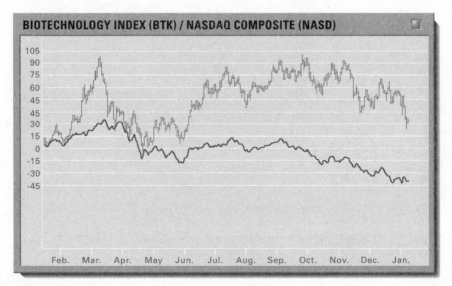

Figure 7.5 *Comparison of the AMEX Biotechnology Index (upper, bar graph) with the NASDAQ Composite (lower, line chart). Courtesy of BigCharts.com.*

7.6. As I described earlier, Amgen is the sector bellwether, but in my opinion Genzyme is the heir to the throne. This chart proves that during this time period, the market agreed with my analysis.

Even after Genzyme fell in the early part of 2001, along with the sector, the stock was still up over 60 percent from a year earlier while Amgen was flat. This again proves the point that a picture is worth a thousand words. A pure technician would be avoiding both stocks since they are clearly weak. But a long-term investor would be better served by thinking seriously about a buying opportunity in Genzyme versus Amgen. This is based on our analysis of earnings and revenue growth, which is more reassuring with Genzyme than with Amgen.

The same type of top-down analysis can be performed with any sector. An easy tool that I use is on Market Sentiment Central *(www.wallstdet.com)*, where I have my custom quotes page set with the stocks in the BTK. To access the custom quotes, just click on any custom quote link on the site and set up your own list of stocks to watch. For more details, you can set up and track your own portfolio, another interactive feature on my Web site.

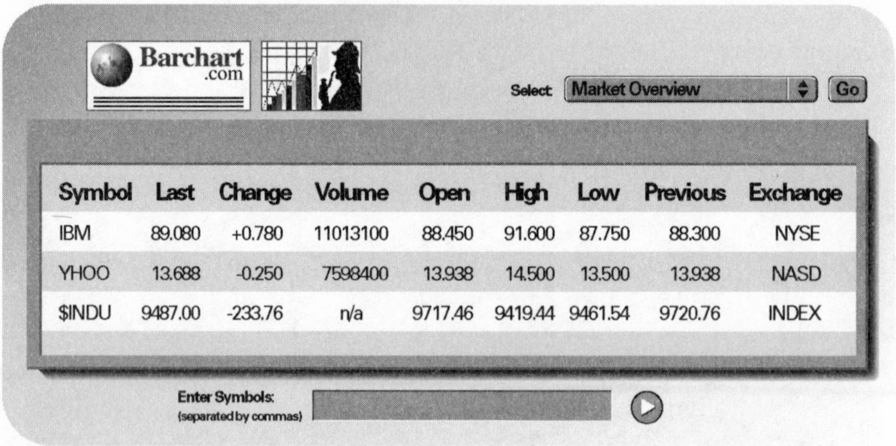
Barchart
.com
Select
Market Overview
Go
Symbol Last Change Volume Open High Low Previous Exchange
IBM 89.080 +0.780 11013100 88.450 91.600 87.750 88.300 NYSE
YHOO 13.688 -0.250 7598400 13.938 14.500 13.500 13.938 NASD
$INDU 9487.00 -233.76 n/a 9717.46 9419.44 9461.54 9720.76 INDEX
Enter Symbols:
(separated by commas)

Figure 7.6. *Custom quotes page on Market Sentiment Central. Courtesy of Barchart.com.*

Overview of Technical Analysis

Now that we have the big picture and sector analysis under control, it's time to learn the basics of technical analysis and chart reading.

Technical analysis is visual, as it is composed of looking at charts and graphically represented indicators. The more charts you look at, the better you will become at spotting winners. Again, I note that technical analysis works best when combined with fundamental analysis of the markets and companies.

Basic Chart Reading Techniques

New chart readers should settle on a routine that follows some basic principles. As figure 7.4 clearly points out, we want to be in the best stocks; thus, the first impression is the key to the rest of the analysis.

The First Impression

The most important principle of technical analysis is the first impression. A chart should always be carefully examined from left to right. You should always know at first glance if the stock is in an uptrend or downtrend. Stocks in uptrends are always worth researching.

Figure 7.7 is a chart of a defense company called Engineered Support Systems. There is no doubt about this stock. It is in an uptrend, and it has excellent relative strength. I included the stock to make two important points. First, this is a stock we want to know more about and may want to own. Second, it is not a biotechnology stock. The point here is that if biotechnology stocks are not rising along with the market, we want to avoid them. Always own strength.

Moving Averages

A moving average is the simplest of all technical indicators. To calculate it by hand, just add the closing prices of a stock for any number of days and divide it by the same number of days. Thus,

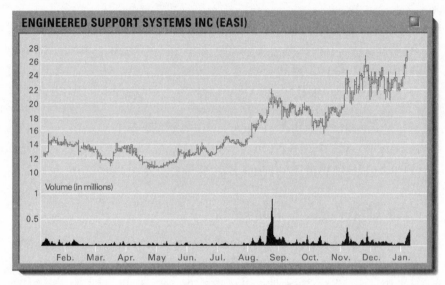

Figure 7.7. *Engineered Support Systems Inc. (NASDAQ:EASI).*

to calculate the 50-day moving average of EASI, as shown in the chart in figure 7.8, just add the prices for the prior 50 days and divide by 50. As you do this on a daily basis and plot the points on the chart, you get a line above or below the price of the stock. Moving-average buy and sell signals are triggered when the price crosses over or under the moving average. A rise by the stock above the moving average is generally bullish. A fall below the moving average is generally bearish. EASI, in figure 7.8, is above its 50-day moving average.

The most commonly used moving averages for intermediate-term trading are the 20-, 50-, and 200-day moving averages. The 20-day moving average is often coupled with Bollinger bands, whose purpose is to measure volatility and provide a dynamic trading range for the stock or index.

Bollinger bands were first described by master technician John Bollinger on the now defunct Financial News Network and later on CNBC. Most software and online services calculate the Bollinger bands automatically. The bands are derived by calculating two standard deviations above and below the moving average

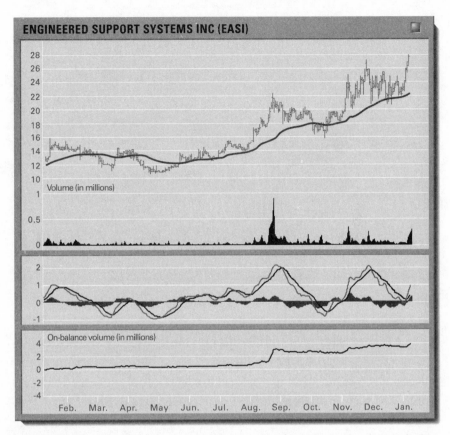

Figure 7.8. EASI *with 50-day moving average, MACD, volume, on-balance volume, and money flow oscillators.*

being used and are calculated as standard parts of just about every major online or other charting program. This is nice since calculating standard deviations takes a long time. I suggest trying it once, if you have time—but I bet you'll never do it again.

Figure 7.9 shows a chart for Genzyme. The 20-day moving average is the middle line, while the other two lines are the upper and lower Bollinger bands. The chart in figure 7.8 illustrates classic Bollinger band behavior, as it shows a buy and a sell signal.

The moving average is used as a trend indicator. A rising stock above the moving average is said to be in an uptrend. A falling stock below the moving average is said to be in a downtrend.

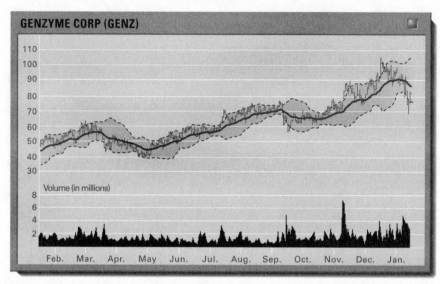

Figure 7.9. *Genzyme's 20-day moving average and Bollinger bands.*

Moving averages and Bollinger bands also provide areas of price resistance and price support in the short-term time frame. Resistance is an area above which prices often have difficulty rising, while support is an area where stocks usually hold their price and often build a base and subsequently rally. Moving averages and Bollinger bands have the advantage of providing a picture of dynamic support and resistance. Appendix A illustrates the basics of support and resistance as well as some basic chart formations.

Bollinger bands illustrate that as the price of the stock fluctuates, so does support and resistance. This allows traders to adjust their buy and sell stops as the stocks rise and fall, using the three lines as guidelines as to where the stock is and where it may be going. This dynamic quality of the Bollinger bands becomes useful when the price of the stock stalls. As the chart shows, the bands expand and constrict as the stock moves. Thus, a unique use of the Bollinger bands is as a predictor of an upcoming big move.

When the Bollinger bands constrict around the 20-day moving average, it signifies that volatility is decreasing. This often means that one side, either sellers or buyers, is becoming exhausted and that the opposite side is about to take control of the stock. Shrinking Bollinger bands, as happened with Genzyme in April 2000, preceded a big move up. In late December, when the bands constricted after the big move in the stock, they preceded a price breakdown.

Note also that the stock eventually dropped to the 70 to 80 area and bounced higher. This is no coincidence, as it illustrates support, provided by both the Bollinger band and an area where the stock had found buyers in November.

Next we note that volume during the December sell-off was very robust as the stock broke down. That is a negative sign. We also note that as the stock found support, the selling stopped. That is a potential positive. We want to see stocks sell off on low volume, as it usually means that it is more profit taking than real selling.

Returning to the chart for EASI, we note that as the stock started its advance in July 2000, it rallied with swelling volume. The pullback in September and October came on light volume, and the subsequent rallies all came on big volume. That is a textbook technical example of a stock in a bull market, and that is what we always want to strive for: to buy stocks that act right technically. A stock with excellent fundamentals that goes nowhere is useless.

MACD, On-Balance Volume, and Money Flow

Moving averages and Bollinger bands work best when coupled with oscillators. My three favorites are MACD (moving average convergence divergence), on-balance volume, and money flow.

MACD

MACD was developed by Gerald Appel and is derived by using a complex mathematical formula, as are on-balance volume and money flow (the formulas are beyond our scope here). Most technical software packages on the Internet and elsewhere will calculate the indicators automatically. But the curious reader is referred to an excellent treatise by Dr. Alexander Elder called *Trading for a Living*. We will focus on the interpretation of these indicators and use them to confirm our chart analysis.

MACD is summarized as a momentum oscillator that is derived from the relationship among three moving averages of prices. The default numbers are 26, 12, and 9 periods. This means that MACD can be measured in minutes, days, weeks, or months. Most traders use what is called a crossover method, which is highlighted in figure 7.10. The two thin lines illustrate the crossover method. The more jagged line is the MACD, which is calculated by using the relationship between the 12- and 26-period moving averages. The 9-period moving average is the smoother line above which the MACD line crosses.

When the MACD rises above the signal line, it's a buy signal. When it falls below the signal line, it's a sell signal. Note the buy signals in May and mid-September and the sell signals in March, September, and December.

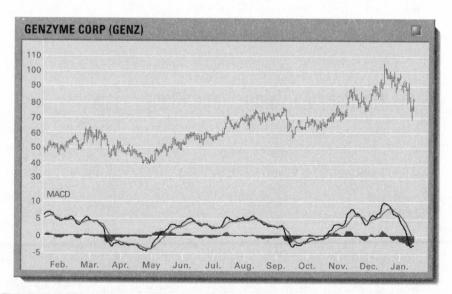

Figure 7.10. *Genzyme and the MACD and the MACD histogram. Lower graph illustrates both MACD crossover and histogram methods.*

The black bars moving along with the MACD make up the MACD histogram. This indicator is best for picking significant market bottoms. Note the double bottom in Genzyme in April and March. The stock fell to a lower low in April. But the MACD histogram did not fall to a new low. This is a positive divergence, which means that the new low in the stock came with much less conviction and told us that the stock was sold out. In May, the crossover method gave a buy signal, and the stock rallied.

That was the buy signal to go long and stay long. The first bottom was the left side of the W and is commonly referred to as the momentum bottom. At that time, just about anyone who wanted to get out did so. The second bottom is the panic bottom. During this sell-off, investors who thought that they bought at the bottom and were unsure of themselves sold because they panicked, thus the name panic bottom.

On-Balance Volume

On-balance volume (OBV) is a trend indicator that is calculated by adding the day's volume in a stock to a running total when the stock closes up for the day and subtracting it from the running total when the stock closes to the down side. It was developed by Joe Granville and is designed to be a gauge of the so-called smart money.

I use this indicator in two ways. First, I like to see it rise when stocks are going up. That tells me that there are more buyers than sellers. Second, when a stock rises and OBV fails to keep up, it is often a sign that money is actually coming out or at least that the buying is less energetic. This second case is clear in figure 7.11, where Sun Microsystems (NASDAQ:SUNW) rallied from June until August. OBV was flat throughout the entire advance. This was a sign of caution. The indicator remained in a negative trend on every reflex rally after the stock broke down, also confirming that this was a true sell-off and not a bout of profit taking.

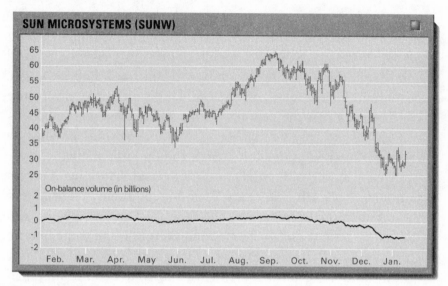

Figure 7.11. *On-balance volume and Sun Microsystems.*

Money Flow

Money flow is a momentum oscillator that is calculated in three stages and involves the use of both price and money (the calculation is again beyond our scope here). It is a measure of whether advances are sustainable. A downtrend in money flow is a signal that money is leaving and that the price of the stock will fall eventually.

Figure 7.12 shows how money continued to flow out of Amgen after the May bottom. Despite a slight improvement in July, the sellers were using strength to lighten up on their positions. Notice how the stock's actual top in August was preceded by falling money flow that began in July.

Summary of Oscillators

I like to trade by combining moving averages, Bollinger bands, MACD, OBV, and money flow, as it helps me arrive at much bet-

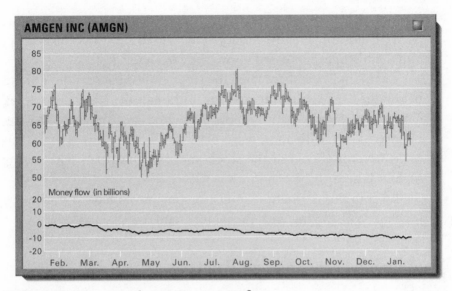

Figure 7.12. *Amgen and negative money flow.*

ter decisions than by just looking at naked charts. When I add simple fundamental analysis in order to fill in the gaps, the system works well.

Figure 7.8 shows how the indicators work together to provide a complete picture of what's really happening in the stock. EASI rallied beginning in May. MACD confirmed the rally and gave a nice enough sell signal just after the stock rolled over in August. Note how the MACD crossover in early May preceded the stock rising after the 50-day moving average.

But the key point was what happened after August, and this is a point I make often on Market Sentiment Central. Money flow turned negative along with MACD, but OBV remained very steady. This is the tiebreaker in most occasions and should be interpreted as a situation in which a stock is consolidating in an ongoing bull market.

This was confirmed in October, when the MACD gave a crossover buy signal. The MACD histogram also confirmed the bottom, when the stock fell beyond its September low but the MACD did not. Finally, money flow turned up, OBV turned up, and the histogram crossed above the zero line.

Again, in December, when the stock pulled back, it did not fall below the 50-day moving average, although the MACD complex gave a sell signal. Money flow remained steady, and OBV remained steady with an upward bias. The net result was that a patient investor stayed in the stock and was rewarded with a new high in January.

By combining multiple indicators, investors have a much better chance of staying with the major trend.

Fine-Tuning Entry and Exit Points

One of my favorite techniques when trying to enter or exit an intermediate-term trade is to see what the stock is doing in the short term. I like to look at multiple time frames in succession. This technique was taught to me by Mark Seleznov of TrendTrader.com *(www.trendtrader.com)*. The technique is used by day traders with a very short-term time horizon. These traders will use charts where each bar is five minutes long (see figure 7.13) as opposed to the one-year charts I have used in this chapter previously, where each bar is a day's worth of trading. By using the shorter-term charts, I can see whether a stock is working well right now or whether I should wait in order to make the trade.

Note that each large block of time with bars in it corresponds to one hour of trading. Thus this five-minute chart gives you an inside look at what happened with a stock during the day and spreads it out for you to see the action in greater detail. This is the same action that a one-year chart shows you in one bar. On January 11, 2001, a trader using this chart could have had several opportunities to execute short-term trades by using a simple moving-average crossover method. But the chart also gives the feeling that this stock is in a well-controlled trading range and that the market itself is fairly quiet.

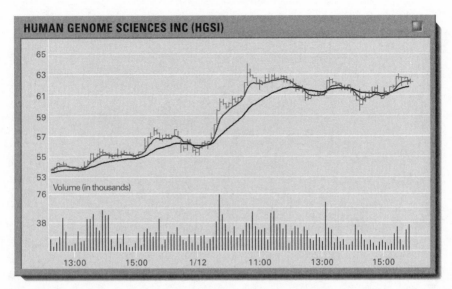

Figure 7.13. *Human Genome Sciences. A five-minute chart. Courtesy of siliconinvestor.com.*

Figure 7.14 gives an even more bullish picture of the stock, as it is giving the impression that a nice consolidation pattern was forming at the end of the day. This kind of pattern suggests that there is accumulation, as the stock is rising when volume is rising. The stock is also well above both moving averages. Based on this chart, I would be looking to get into HGSI at the beginning of the next trading day if the action continued or, more specifically, if the stock moved above the 64 to 65 area.

But thank goodness for daily charts, as this one clearly shows that HGSI is up against a tough resistance area with its 20-day moving average providing the impedance to higher prices. A quick look at volume shows that the stock has been rallying on lower volume as well. Finally, when we look at the daily chart (figure 7.15), the first impression is of a stock that is in a down-trend.

If you were trading this stock for the intermediate term of weeks to months, this is not a stock you would enter at this point. If you were a day trader, the best thing to do would be to see if the

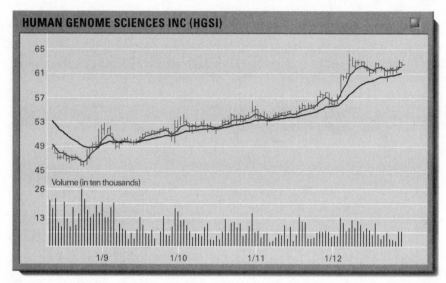

Figure 7.14. *Human Genome Sciences. A 15-minute chart. Courtesy of siliconinvestor.com.*

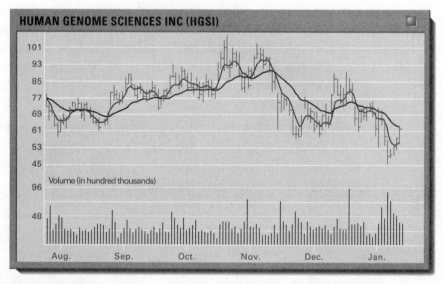

Figure 7.15. *Human Genome Sciences. The daily chart. Courtesy of siliconinvestor.com.*

stock rose above the 63 to 64 area. The stock could be owned for a short-term period. The charts also suggest that there is selling pressure above the 69 area.

When to Buy a Biotechnology Stock

As the charts in the previous section clearly illustrate, when to buy depends on your time frame. The key is to buy on strength. That means that I try to catch the stocks when they are accelerating their uptrend after a pause or when they are breaking a downtrend. I usually trade with a weeks-to-months outlook. This makes me an intermediate-term trader. It suits my personality, and it allows me to manage money for my clients without having to move large sums of money on a daily basis, which, aside from being difficult, can create tax consequences for the clients in their nonretirement accounts. Therefore, this section will deal with intermediate-term trading principles. But these chart reading and entry and exit points can also be used for short-term trading.

As I screen stocks, I look for stocks that are rising for that day. I look in *Investor's Business Daily* before the market opens. I especially like its market summary page, where it gives a nice snapshot of the big trend. I listen to news on CNBC as I write my morning columns. I look at what's happening in the premarket ticker, and I check what the overnight futures are doing. I look for everything to be in good order. If it is not, then I plan not to trade that day, unless I have to sell something or the market turns around. But even if I don't plan to trade, I still look for ideas.

When I've compiled my list, I go look at charts. I will look at 50 to 100 charts per day and sometimes more. When I see a good-looking chart, I start looking for earnings and revenue growth, as I described earlier in this chapter. If the market is acting right and the Fed is on my side, I look for an entry point by using the 5- and 15-minute charts, after I've looked at the longer-term charts, to make sure that I'm not getting into a stock that is in a long-term downtrend and that I won't be able to hold for weeks to months.

If you are day trading, you won't have time to look for earnings or revenue growth, and you will have to trade the chart. If you trade the chart, you should not be doing it without professional real-time software, or you are asking for big trouble. If you are looking for the best performance, don't use grandma's 486 PC with Windows 3.1 and a 14K modem.

You should really have at least Windows 95 or 98, a Pentium or equivalent microprocessor with either DSL, wireless broadband, or an equivalent system with good reliability and high speed. You should also consider direct access trading versus the usual online discount brokers for the best execution. In addition, you will have to learn about Level II quotes and other day trading tools.

In *After-Hours Trading Made Easy,* I devoted several chapters to connectivity, equipment, Level II quotes, trading terms, and direct access trading. There are many places on the Internet to access these tools, but a good reference point is TrendTrader.com, where Mark Seleznov offers a very nice comprehensive package that includes tutorials and both online and phone support. Mark is a sponsor of my Web site, but he is also a great source of information for anyone interested in short-term trading.

The two best times to buy a stock are when it is reversing a trend and when it is taking off after a consolidation. Figures 7.16 and 7.17 are two excellent examples.

Figure 7.16 shows Human Genome Sciences, during a better time, rising above a downtrend line and rallying impressively for the next three months. Note that the MACD histogram made a double bottom, when the stock bottomed at 25 and 35, respectively. The second MACD bottom was less deep, signifying that momentum to the down side was finished.

An equally potent buying opportunity is called a breakout. That happens when the stock has been forming a base, or moving sideways, and then erupts. A true breakout comes when volume rises impressively as the stock breaks out of the base. Carreker Corp. is a financial services software firm. The three bold lines on

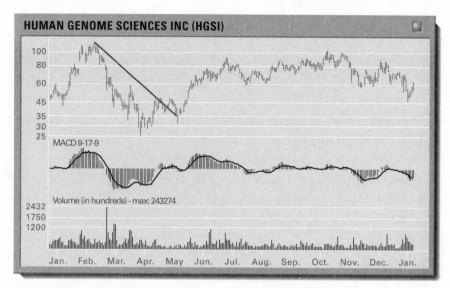

Figure 7.16. *Human Genome Sciences with MACD and a trend reversal. Courtesy of Telescan.*

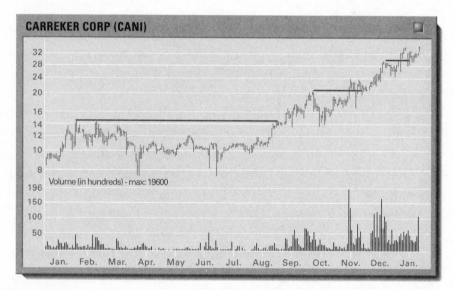

Figure 7.17. *Carreker Corp. (NASDAQ:CANI) shows how to buy on the breakout.*

the chart show resistance points above which the stock has risen and successfully broken out above.

Note the rise in volume on the breakout and how the stock came back to the breakout point after each breakout. That is called a successful retesting of the breakout. It is also highlighting the concept of support, as buyers who had missed the breakout took their chance to buy.

CANI scored three chart breakouts in the year covered by the chart. The latter two came after the stock consolidated, or rested. Consolidation patterns are usually best sorted out by using the oscillators, as I described earlier.

When to Sell

The best time to sell a stock is when you think you are the smartest person in the world for having bought it, when you brag to your significant other or your friends, and when you lie awake at night thinking about what the overnight session is doing with it. Because if you are doing it, then so are a majority of the others who own it. When too many people believe one thing on Wall Street, it usually means that the trend is about to reverse.

A more quantitative way of selling is when the stock begins to show signs of weakness, such as when the price is rising on low volume and when the oscillators are not making new highs along with the price of the stock or trending down as the stock rises.

A simple strategy is to use moving averages as selling points. For example, if you've held a stock that has doubled and is consolidating, you may want to sell any time it falls below the 20- or 50-day moving average. One way to avoid major trouble is to sell a stock that falls below a shorter moving average than the one used as the buying point. For example, if you bought using the 50-day moving average and the stock has done well, you can protect your gains by using the 20-day average, which is usually above the 50-day average in a rising trend.

Another way to protect yourself is to use sell stops. These are automatic sell orders that are triggered when your stock falls below a certain point. A common place to set stops is 8 percent below the purchase price. This method was initially described by William O'Neil, the guru of momentum investing and founder of *Investor's Business Daily*. I can tell you that if you put 8 percent sell stops below biotechnology stocks, you are going to get stopped out a lot.

For biotech stocks, I prefer to use the 50-day moving average. These are very volatile companies, and you want to give them a little more room to move than insurance or banking stocks. Biotechnology stocks have intraday trading ranges of more than 10 percent on some occasions.

It is also important to keep changing your stop as it rises. But use the same parameter all the way up. In other words, if you buy it at 50 and place your stop at 45, when the stock goes up to 55, move the stop to 50 and so on. If you get stopped out, it is best to take your hit or your profit and go trade somewhere else for a while. A stock that stops you out is often sending a signal that something bad may be about to happen.

In figure 7.18, we see that Organogenesis crossed above its 20- and 50-day moving averages in May. The 20-day average is the line that hugs the stock closer, while the 50-day average is the straighter, more distant line. The stock could have been bought when it crossed above the 50-day average since it is an intermediate-term signal. It rallied nicely and should have been sold when it crossed below the 20-day average. The point here is that when you buy, you want to be sure that you are giving yourself the best chance to succeed as possible. The 50-day moving average is better for intermediate-term trading. By using the 20-day average to sell, you save yourself a little heartburn and come out with more money.

Finally, you could sell by drawing a trend line and watching for the stock to break below it, as shown in figure 7.19. I used

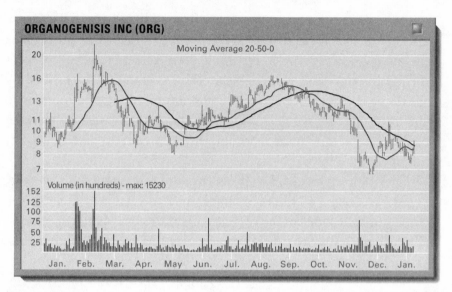

Figure 7.18. *Organogenesis and its 20- and 50-day moving averages. Courtesy of Telescan.*

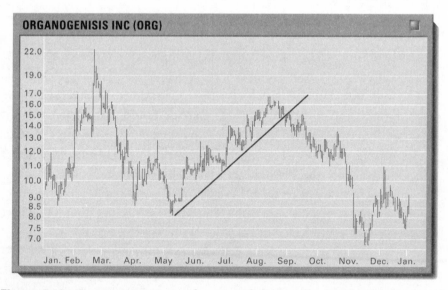

Figure 7.19. *Organogenesis and a trend line sell signal. Courtesy of Telescan.*

these simple examples to illustrate the simple principles of technical analysis for when to sell. In real trading, I suggest using oscillators, Bollinger bands, moving averages, and trend lines to make buying and selling decisions. Look for both confirmation, such as moving averages and trend lines being broken, and divergences, as I showed earlier with the oscillators.

I suggest that you carefully review the charts of Amgen and Genzyme shown earlier in this chapter, as they provide plenty of information on when to sell as a result of oscillator sell signals. Finally, it is important to know when not to buy. I hope that this chapter has provided adequate insight into analysis in order to keep most traders out of trouble in that respect.

But just in case I didn't make my point, don't buy stocks that have not crossed important resistance levels. Don't double up if you buy and your stock drops like a rock, and don't buy stocks that are going down, because chances are that they are going to go down some more.

Summary

In order to maximize the chances for success in investing, I begin my day with interest rate and general market analysis. Once I have decided that interest rates and the broad market trend are on my side, I like to look at many sectors and see which ones are acting best in the market.

In the best sectors, I look for the best stocks—those that are near the point of breaking out, are breaking downtrends or are already in rising trends, and are about to break above a consolidation area. I use comparison charts when I have any doubts. In the example cited, Genzyme was the clear winner on the charts when I used the chart comparison strategy.

Technical analysis is as important as fundamental analysis. A chart is indeed worth a thousand words. Time frame analysis, such as that I performed with Human Genome Sciences, is good for day trading and to pick exit and entry points for longer-term trading. Don't trade for the long term using five-minute charts without looking at the big picture. If you make a potential two-month decision on a five-minute chart, you're asking for trouble.

Moving averages smooth out the trend, and I like to use the 20-, 50-, and 200-day moving averages. Day traders use period averages customized to their trading time frame. Bollinger bands give you trading limits by providing support and resistance levels as well as forecasting big price movements. Oscillators either confirm or deny what the price action is telling you. A divergence, or a situation in which the oscillator is saying the opposite of the price, is a reason to double-check a trade by using more oscillators and to sell or buy a stock based on the message of the oscillator. MACD, money flow, and on-balance volume are three useful oscillators that work well together. Recall the money flow sell signal on Amgen discussed earlier this chapter.

I like to confirm what the charts are telling me by looking at the rate of revenue and earnings growth and evaluate a stock on the basis of valuation. A stock with a low P/E ratio is not enough to entice me into buying. I like to see earnings and revenue growth for several quarters and to see evidence that the growth is sustainable. This kind of analysis is not adequate for day trading. Day trading requires an expert level of knowledge of technical analysis, and nothing else matters. Do not day trade on fundamentals. That is a sure one-way ticket to the poorhouse.

I like to perform systematic analysis of the markets. That way I tend to miss fewer opportunities. There is no substitute in trading, investing, or any successful endeavor for doing the task as often as possible. Therefore, I do my rounds the same way each day. This became clear to me when I began writing daily commentary for my Web site. The deadline pressure helped me develop a system of analysis that is efficient and has served me well. I continue to add new wrinkles, such as looking at intraday charts before I enter a position, regardless of what my time frame is, whether several weeks to months or day trading.

Day trading (which I now do regularly compared to a few years ago, when the notion was foreign to me) has really sharpened my tape reading skills. By keeping tabs on the hot stocks of the day, I have learned to recognize what makes a stock work as well as what makes a stock underperform. This in turn helps me make better long-term trades.

When this kind of hands-on analysis is combined with an excellent knowledge of what a company does and how well it can deliver on its promise, you have a complete analysis model that works for biotechnology and any other sector.

Next, we'll look at how to invest in the entire sector of biotechnology or pharmaceuticals by using mutual funds and exchange-traded funds.

8

The Sector Plays

B iotechnology is a very volatile and labor-intensive sector. Thus stock picking is not for everyone who is interested in investing in the area. But thanks to Wall Street's never-ending need for fees, there are many vehicles with which to invest in the sector without having to directly pick your own stocks.

The two basic vehicles are sector mutual funds and exchange-traded mutual funds. Generally, the latter carry names like HOL-DRS and i-shares. The one characteristic that they all share is that they invest only in health, biotechnology, or both. The advantage is that you have a much smaller amount of homework to do when choosing one of these vehicles, especially the leading funds in the sector. There is also the advantage of knowing that the mutual funds have expert analyst staffs that will tend to find the best of the emerging companies.

The disadvantages is that these are volatile trading vehicles and that they offer no protection through diversification, although this is a fleeting concept on Wall Street, as most mutual funds tend to rise and fall with the market, with only very few exceptions. Thus sector funds are best used as timing vehicles in a well-diversified investment program of funds, stocks, or both.

Another characteristic is that sector funds tend to carry fees, although there are several no-load funds in the health care sector.

The two most well known of the no-load families are Invesco and Vanguard. They offer many sector funds that will rise and fall with the major trend in the sector that they invest in. The drawback is that they frown on frequent switching. From this vantage point, if I want to switch, I will, especially if the fund is dropping like a rock.

This attitude from the fund companies is exasperating but does have some reason behind it. Their operating expenses can increase if there are many frequent switchers in the fund. That is the main reason why Fidelity, Rydex, and other families that offer sector funds tack on loads both to enter and to exit. But that aspect will be fully explained later.

HOLDRS and i-shares trade like stocks. This means that as long as you pay your commission, you can day trade them if you want. I don't recommend this to the average person, as I stated in the prior chapter, but it is an option.

The goal of this chapter is to give you a well-balanced alternative to stocks in the biotechnology sector. I also want to show you that mutual funds are excellent vehicles for intermediate-term market timing and that, in some cases, they are a much better vehicle than some of the stocks in the sector.

What Is a Sector Mutual Fund?

A sector mutual fund is a mutual fund that invests in a single area of the market. Thus it is an investment company that sells shares to the public. These shares give the shareholder the opportunity to participate in the fund's fortunes. Mutual funds charge fees, which are usually calculated before the net asset value is reported at the end of the trading day.

The net asset value (NAV) is the price of the fund that most people see in their newspaper or on their Internet quotes page. The NAV is the sum of all the fund's assets minus all its liabilities divided by the number of outstanding shares at the end of the day. For example, if the Duarte fund had $1 million in assets but owed

$100,000 because of operations, short sales, pending stock settlements, salaries, management fees, and so on, and there were 1,000 shares outstanding, the NAV would be calculated as follows:

Assets – Expenses: $1,0000,000 – $100,0000 = $900,000 = Net assets
Net assets/outstanding shares = $900,000/1,000 shares = NAV
NAV = 1,000

I should note that the fees are calculated and removed on a daily basis before the NAV is calculated. This allows the fund company to get paid on a daily basis, thus removing the risk of your cashing out and not paying their management fee.

Load Versus No-Load Funds

A load fund is one that charges you a fee on top of their management fee. Loads are used to pay sales commissions and other fees. Loads are separate charges from the daily management fees that get taken out of the NAV daily. Many people refuse to pay loads, and they really don't have to anymore, given the number of mutual funds available as well as the opportunities to trade sector vehicles like stocks and the availability and ease of online trading.

A no-load fund charges just their management fee. Fees are found in the fund prospectus, which is easier to read now than it was a few years ago.

Loaded funds don't necessarily perform better than no-load funds, but neither do no-load funds necessarily perform better than load funds. There are also commission fees to consider if you buy the fund through a discount broker like Fidelity or Schwab.

A great place to learn about sector funds is donoghue.com (*www.donoghue.com*), which is owned by Bill Donoghue, a money manager who is a pioneer in sector fund investment.

My opinion is that if you are going to own a fund for the next 10 years, then why pay a load? But if you are going to trade with the trend, then the load is worthwhile.

I use Fidelity sector funds for my managed accounts and my own accounts regularly. Once you pay the load for a certain amount of money, you are done. For example, I want to buy $10,000 worth of Fidelity Select Biotechnology. The front load is 3 percent. That means that it cost me $300 to enter the fund. On a good day, I could have my load and then some back by the day's end. That's how much this fund could go up in a day.

Fidelity also charges 0.75 percent to get out if you hold the fund for less than 30 days. So don't get in, unless you expect to be in for 30 days. If you sell after 30 days but sell online on their Web site, it costs you only $7.50. If you call their toll-free number and sell by talking to a representative, it costs $15.00. My advice? If you decide to trade Fidelity sector funds, do it online and time your entry and exit according to the rules barring a true emergency.

The beauty of the system is that once you've paid the fee for that $10,000, you never have to pay it again. Here's how it works. You bought the shares, and you held them for two months. You made 20 percent, which means that you got out with $12,000. Now you have $12,000, which has paid the load. That means that if you play it right, you only have to pay a maximum of $7.50 every time you get out. If your fund does well for a year or more, you've made much more than the fees.

Other fund companies have different rules based on the principle that long-term holders get a better break when they sell their shares. I suggest checking appendix B for details on just about every active health and biotechnology fund available.

Another caveat is to be careful when you buy through a funds network. For example, Schwab and Fidelity make it hard to buy each other's funds through their networks, and Fidelity will begin to charge high fees for those who use mutual funds to day trade through their online account.

Funds will also have class B and C shares. This is usually a way to change fee structures. As a rule, I avoid fund families that use class B shares. It's usually a way to charge more and have more loopholes.

Finally, stay away from funds with a 12B-1 fee. This is a fee that the funds charge the shareholders so that they can pay for advertisement. The fund is required to disclose that they have this kind of fee. But why should we pay for their advertisement when they have all our money?

My best advice is that if you decide to buy sector funds, pick a single company and make all your sector bets through that company. That way you have lower fees and fewer hassles.

Comparing Funds

Two great ways to compare load versus no-load funds is by their return and by their expense ratios, which is how much they spend to conduct business but does not include commissions or investment-related expenses. While there are many places on the Internet to look for information related to mutual funds, it's hard to beat Morningstar.

Tables 8.1 and 8.2 are adapted from morningstar.com screens. There are several more informative views that I recommend aside

Table 8.1 *Fund Comparisons Based on Return*

Mutual Fund	Year-to-Date Return	One-Year Return
Rydex Biotechnology Investment	−9.16	+11.77
Munder Framlington Health	−10.39	+52.17
GenomicsFund.com	−14.46	
Invesco Health Sciences	−12.40	+8.06
Fidelity Select Health Care	−10.14	+18.01
Fidelity Select Biotechnology	−11.81	+12.10
All Funds Average Return	−0.08	+1.59
S&P 500	−0.13	−6.88

Data featured are from January 1 to January 12, 2001. Courtesy of morningstar.com.

Table 8.2 *Fund Comparisons Based on Return (Data Ends 12/31/00)*

Mutual Fund (Load)	Three-Year Return	Five-Year Return	Expense Ratio
Rydex Biotechnology Investment (NL)	—	—	1.41
Munder Framlington Health (5.5 percent, 0 percent)	+34.81	—	1.61
Invesco Health Sciences (NL)	+17.46	+15.64	1.22
GenomicsFund.com (NL)	—	—	
Fidelity Select Health Care (3 percent, 0.75 percent)	+19.26	+21.17	1.15
Fidelity Select Biotechnology (3 percent, 0.75)	+40.90	+27.49	1.05
All Funds Average Return	+8.82	+9.50	
S&P 500	+13.44	+18.84	
All Funds Expense Ratio*			1.38

Courtesy of morningstar.com. NL = no load (first number is front, second number is back end).

*Expense ratio refers to the percentage of assets deducted each fiscal year for fund expenses, including 12b-1 fees, management fees, administrative fees, operating costs, and all other asset-based costs incurred by the fund.

from just the return screens. For example, the Portfolio View allows you to screen funds based on the average price-to-earnings (P/E) ratio of the stocks in the portfolio as well as the three-year earnings growth. If those criteria sound familiar, they should, for they are similar to what I described in the last chapter. For example, on January 11, 2001, Fidelity Select Biotechnology held stocks that sported an average P/E ratio of 48, with a three-year earnings growth of 33 percent. By comparison, Invesco's Health Sciences fund held stocks with an average P/E ratio of 48, with only an 18 percent ratio of three-year growth.

The expense ratio, when combined with the one-, three-, and five-year return, gives a great picture of where you get the most for your money. In this group, the best all-around fund, based on this criteria, is Fidelity Select Health Care, whose 1.05 percent expense ratio, combined with 18 percent, 19.2 percent, and 27.4 percent one-, three-, and five-year returns, is excellent.

When we look at the return table, we see that Invesco lagged Fidelity in one-, three-, and five-year return. We also note that Invesco's fund fell farther in the first 11 days of 2001 than either Fidelity fund. Yet they want investors to leave their money with them indefinitely. This analysis is not particularly flattering to no-load funds, but it is meant to illustrate that investors should do a full analysis before going with a fund. Whether or not the fund is loaded should not be the deciding factor.

This is not about loads but about the best return for your money, and this analysis suggests that with the six funds I studied for this example, you get what you pay for.

A Sampling of Health and Biotechnology Sector Funds

My goal for this section is to give you a wide cross section of the funds that are available, how they stack up against each other, and their advantages and disadvantages based on their investment strategies. For more detail, I suggest a visit to appendix B or to *www.morningstar.com*, where there is more information about funds than anyone could ever hope for. For illustration's sake and for background information, I have condensed and adapted the fund capsules from the appendix. Again, thanks to John Duke for his assistance.

Fidelity Select Biotechnology Fund (www.fidelity.com)

Fund: Fidelity Select Biotechnology

Symbol: FBIOX

Description: The fund seeks capital appreciation with investments in the companies engaged in research and development of biotechnological or biomedical products, services, and processes. The fund also invests in related manufacturing or distributing companies.

It is more volatile than the typical health care fund. The fund buys bigger, more established biotech names, so it can be more stable than some of its biotech rivals.

Morningstar Rating: Five stars

Net Assets as of December 2000: $4,118 million

2000 Return as of December 31: 32.8 percent

Fund Inception: 12/16/85

This is my favorite biotechnology fund. It isn't necessarily the best during every period when the sector rises, but it is very consistent. Fidelity trains its young managers through their sector funds before moving them to larger, more well-known funds, such as Magellan. The fund's performance is outstanding for the long term, as the chart in figure 8.1 clearly shows. This fund is very aggressive, as it remains no less than 80 percent to 90 percent invested in biotechnology regardless of the market climate.

As the chart shows, the fund went through a multiyear consolidation in the mid-1990s. But long-term investors with patience were well rewarded.

Fidelity Select Health Care (www.fidelity.com)

Fund: Fidelity Select Health Care

Symbol: FSPHX

Description: Seeking capital appreciation, the fund invests at least 80 percent of assets in equity securities of companies in the health care industry. Companies include those engaged in the design, manufacture, or sale of products or services used for or in connection with health care or medicine.

The fund is one of the best in the health care category. Its drug, biotech, and health care services stocks annually yield great returns thanks to Fidelity's research team.

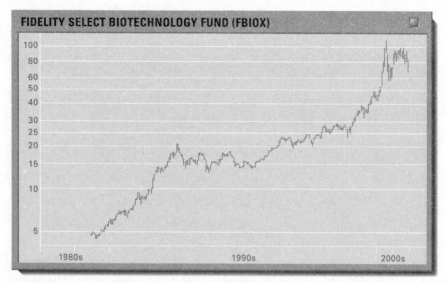

Figure 8.1. *Fidelity Select Biotechnology Fund (FBIOX), a long-term view.*

Morningstar Rating: Five stars

Net Assets as of December 2000: $2,990 million

2000 Return as of December 31: 36.7 percent

Fund Inception: 7/14/81

Fidelity Select Health Care is as reliable a health care fund as there is (see figure 8.2). It can sometimes get very aggressive and lean heavily on biotechnology. But it invests mostly in the old, reliable, blue-chip pharmaceuticals and related businesses. Interestingly, as of August 31, 2000, both Fidelity Select Biotechnology and Select Health Care were managed by Yolanda McGettigan, who became their manager on June 1, 2000.

As of August 31, 2001, Select Health Care, according to its prospectus, had 57.5 percent of its portfolio in pharmaceutical stocks, with Bristol Myers-Squibb, Pfizer, and Johnson & Johnson making up the top three holdings and 21.3 percent of the portfolio. The only biotechnology stock in the top 10 was Genentech, which was 3.1 percent of the portfolio.

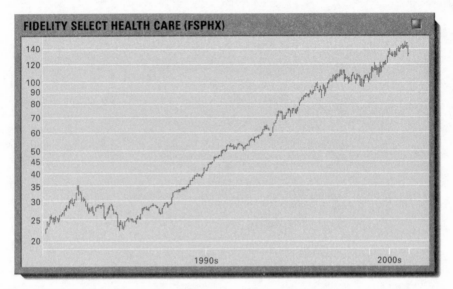

Figure 8.2. *Fidelity Select Health Care, a long-term view.*

By contrast, Fidelity Select Biotechnology held Genentech, MedImmune, and Immunex as the top three stocks, which made up 18 percent of the portfolio. Nontraditional biotechnology stocks made up a large portion of the top 10, with Merck, Schering Plough, and Alza, all stocks that we discussed earlier as having biotechnology connections, making up 14.5 percent of the portfolio. This is more proof of the inevitable blurring between the lines that used to separate the two sectors.

Invesco Health Sciences (www.invesco.com)

Fund: INVESCO Health Sciences Inv

Symbol: FHLSX

Description: This growth fund invests primarily in equity securities of companies that develop, produce, or distribute products or services related to health care. The fund may invest up to 25 percent of assets in securities of foreign companies.

Morningstar Rating: Four stars

Net Assets as of December, 2000: $1,990 million

2000 Return as of December 31: 25.8 percent

Fund Inception: 1/19/84

Invesco Health Sciences is included here because it is a no-load fund. The chart in figure 8.3 also shows that the fund has done well. But a closer inspection at Morningstar reveals that the fund gets four stars and a below-average rating compared to the sector. This is important because it once again goes to the same advice used to buy stocks. In this case, get the best fund in the best sector and don't be afraid to pay a load. Sometimes it may be worth it.

The Genomics Fund (www.genomicsfund.com)

Fund: Genomics Fund

Symbol: GENEX

Description: GenomicsFund.com is the world's first and only mutual fund specializing in investing in the rapidly emerging ge-

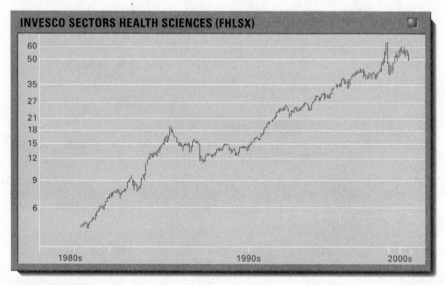

Figure 8.3. *Invesco Sectors Health Sciences.*

nomics industry. The principal objective of the fund is capital appreciation.

It was the current investment strategy of the fund in January 2001 to maintain a fully invested position in a diversified portfolio of genomics-related securities. It can, however, diversify into other investment areas.

Morningstar Rating: Not rated

Net Assets as of December 2000: $23 million

2000 Return as of December 31: N.A.

Fund Inception: 3/1/00

The Genomics Fund is among the newest in the field. As the chart in figure 8.4 clearly shows, the subsector did not have a sterling period after the fund's start date. This is the reason why a very narrow focus does not lend itself to the long-term holding of a fund. This is a very aggressive fund and should be viewed carefully. As the capsule shows, the fund had $23 million under management in De-

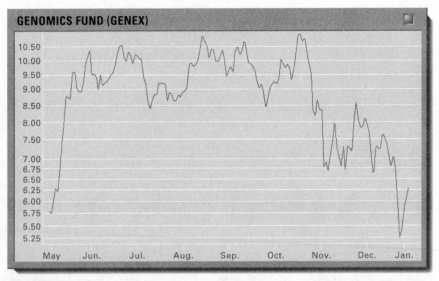

Figure 8.4. *The Genomics Fund, the only view available at the present time. Courtesy of Telescan.*

cember 2000. It will be interesting to watch the performance of this fund over the next few years if it can survive its stormy beginning.

Rydex Trust Biotechnology

Fund: Rydex Biotechnology Investments

Symbol: RYOIX

Description: The fund normally invests at least 80 percent of its assets in equity securities issued by biotechnology companies that are traded in the United States as well as in futures and options contracts. Biotechnology companies include those engaged in the research, development, and manufacture of various biotechnological and biomedical products.

Morningstar Rating: Not rated

Net Assets as of December 2000: $476 million

2000 Return as of December 31: 28.6 percent

Fund Inception: 4/1/98

Rydex is for heavy hitters, as its minimal investment is $25,000. The fees are high as well, with a 1.41 expense ratio, second only to Framlington in that department. Another distinguishing characteristic is that the fund, as most of the Rydex funds do, also invests in futures and options, either leveraging or protecting the portfolio against risk.

The fund doubled in 1999, which shows that a little leverage can go a long way (see figure 8.5). But as the early days of 2001 show, either management didn't see the decline coming and forgot to hedge, or their hedging strategies are not particularly helpful.

Technical Analysis

Mutual funds lend themselves to technical analysis, including the use of oscillators and moving averages. The same techniques that I described in the previous chapter are applicable here.

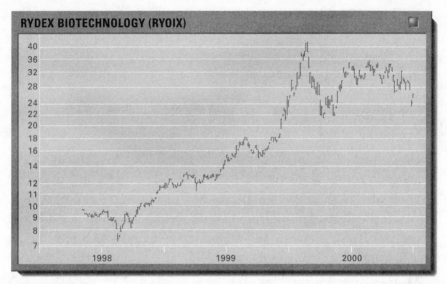

Figure 8.5. *Rydex Biotechnology, a long-term view. Courtesy of Telescan.*

Figure 8.6 is a perfect example of how to apply technical analysis to mutual funds. The fund fell below its 50-day moving average in July and October. But the MACD (moving average convergence divergence) did not totally break down, and the fund remained above a rising trend line. But in November, the fund broke below all support provided by the indicators. By January, it had fallen over 30 percent. Although the fund bounced in early January, MACD and the 50-day moving average were still suggesting that it was not time to buy.

Also note that each attempt at a new high by the fund met with a lower high in the MACD. This is a clear divergence and a sign that bad things were on the way.

Exchange-Traded Sector Funds

A HOLDRS trust is traded on the American Stock Exchange like any other stock (see figure 8.7). HOLDRS stands for "holding company depository receipts." The HOLDRS trust concept was

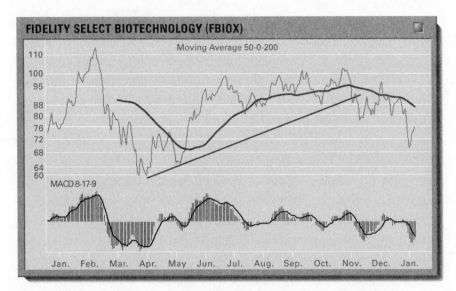

Figure 8.6. *Fidelity Select Biotechnology breaking an uptrend. Note the lack of confirmation from the MACD. Courtesy of Telescan.*

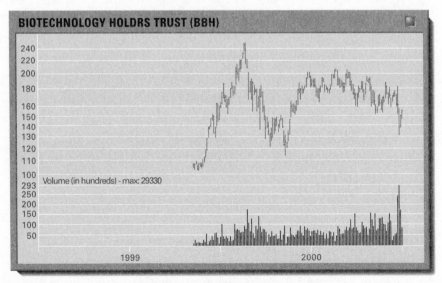

Figure 8.7. *The Biotechnology HOLDRS trust (BBH). Courtesy of Telescan.*

created by Merrill Lynch. HOLDRS are not mutual funds, but they are based on the concept that a basket of stocks representing a sector can be easily bought and sold on an exchange like a stock.

HOLDRS can be bought only in lots of 100 shares. The custodian, the Bank of New York, charges a $2.00 custodian fee per quarter. So if you trade online and you pay your $14.95 commission fee and hold the trust for a year, the whole transaction cost you $37.90. That's not bad considering the following: If you bought the same amount of Fidelity Select Biotechnology on January 10, 2001, at the close, it would have cost you $15,300 just to get into the fund since the closing price for BBH was $153.00. Add the 3 percent fee, if you hadn't paid it before, and it would have cost you another $459.

The HOLDRS trust has many of the same shares represented in it as the fund. When you buy 100 shares, you are actually owning 268 shares of the stocks that it holds. The beauty of the HOLDRS is that they move along with the market. If biotechnology goes up, it's almost a no-brainer that the HOLDRS will rise as well. In a sense, you are buying an index. HOLDRS are also ideal for short-term trading as opposed to mutual funds. As with stocks, the same rules of technical analysis apply. HOLDRS pass on dividends from the companies they hold. Thus, your account is likely to have odd lots of all kinds of shares sprinkled in it, as long as you hold the trust.

Table 8.3 shows the components of the biotechnology HOLDRS trust. Table 8.4 shows the components of the pharmaceuticals HOLDRS trust. There are HOLDRS for many sectors, including semiconductors (SMH), Internet (HHH), software (SWH), and B2B (BHH).

Summary

For investors who wish to own a sector and not individual stocks, there are plenty of options, beginning with mutual funds and extending to HOLDRS trusts. Technical and fundamental analysis can be performed on both instruments.

Table 8.3 *Components of the Biotechnology HOLDRS Trust*

Stock	Number of Shares in the HOLDRS Trust
Amgen Inc. (AMGN)	46
IDEC Pharmaceuticals Corp. (IDPH)	4
Genentech, Inc. (DNA)	44
QLT Inc. (QLTI)	5
Biogen, Inc. (BGEN)	13
Millennium Pharmaceuticals, Inc. (MLNM)	12
Immunex Corporation (IMNX)	42
BioChem Pharmaceuticals Inc. (BCHE)	9
Applera Corp.—Applied Biosystems Group (ABI)	18
Affymetrix, Inc. (AFFX)	4
MedImmune, Inc. (MEDI)	15
Human Genome Sciences, Inc. (HGSI)	8
Chiron Corporation (CHIR)	16
ICOS Corporation (ICOS)	4
Genzyme Corporation (GENZ)	7
Enzon, Inc. (ENZN)	3
Gilead Sciences, Inc. (GILD)	4
Applera Corp.—Celera Genomics Group (CRA)	4
Sepracor Inc. (SEPR)	6
Alkermes, Inc. (ALKS)	4

Adapted from *www.amex.com*.

No-load mutual funds are not always the best options when costs and returns are carefully studied. Both load mutual funds and the HOLDRS trusts can be more economical in the long run.

In the next chapter, we wrap everything up with a look at what the future holds.

Table 8.4 *Components of the Pharmaceuticals HOLDRS Trust*

Stock	Number of Shares in the HOLDRS Trust
Merck & Co., Inc. (MRK)	22
King Pharmaceuticals, Inc. (KG)	3.187
Pfizer Inc. (PFE)	58
Forest Laboratories, Inc. (FRX)	1
Johnson & Johnson (JNJ)	13
Andrx Corporation (ADRX)	2
Bristol Myers-Squibb Co. (BMY)	18
Allergan, Inc. (AGN)	1
Eli Lilly & Company (LLY)	10
Watson Pharmaceuticals, Inc. (WPI)	1
Schering Plough Corporation (SGP)	14
ICN Pharmaceuticals, Inc. (ICN)	1
American Home Products Corp. (AHP)	12
Mylan Laboratories, Inc. (MYL)	1
Abbott Laboratories (ABT)	14
IVAX Corporation (IVX)	1.5
Biovail Corporation International (BVF)	4

Adapted from *www.amex.com.*

CHAPTER

9

Conclusion

There are two ways of looking at the future of the biotechnology sector. From the human standpoint, the potential advances are staggering. From the market's standpoint, they are still huge. But investors, health care practitioners, and those who suffer from illnesses that may be cured by the wonders of this branch of science should be cautious. Disappointment is a rule, not an exception.

More important is how we define disappointment. For investors, it comes when the Food and Drug Administration (FDA) denies a drug application and the stock falls. But for patients and doctors, the promise of a cure that fails to materialize is even worse.

Thus the future is brighter than ever, but not without the potential for an occasional setback. For investors, if the company has a good record and meets the criteria I discussed earlier, a huge fall is often an opportunity to reevaluate the stock and the company using the methods I have outlined. If the analysis comes up with no major changes, then the market's knee-jerk reaction is an opportunity to buy.

For the ill who placed their hopes on a drug that did not deliver, there is little I can say.

I started this book in the late spring of 2000. More than a year has passed, and much has changed. Yet much has stayed the same as well. Politics is as ugly and as predictable as ever, with the 2000 presidential election being decided by the courts instead of the voters. The Federal Reserve has the final say on whether most of America is happy by controlling interest rates, and scientists have discovered one of the secrets to life itself with the unraveling of the human genome.

This confluence of events and its significance can only be magnified by the speed of communications (brought on by DSL, fiberoptics, and the Internet), which, when combined with blow-by-blow television commentary, can be overwhelming. At the center of it all is Wall Street, assessing, postulating, and always questioning whether the event has any significance to the financial markets and eventually our portfolios.

As we enter the 21st century, one thing is clear: This time is different. There will always be bull and bear markets, but the speed with which information travels will magnify the highs and the lows in the markets, in politics, and maybe in life itself. This constant analysis of events on CNBC, CNNfn, and Bloomberg, often by the same analyst who climbs into a cab only to appear on the next network in a little while, can lead only to confusion—a confusion that I hope to help you deal with effectively as it pertains to biotechnology and drug stocks.

When I started writing this book, I wanted to give the reader a tool. I said it many times in the text. I wanted to teach you to fish instead of giving you a fish to eat. That is somewhat against the grain in our society. After all, as the older President Bush told an audience after the 2000 election, "I thought our boy did all right. But I thought I'd better turn on CNN, just to make sure."

Of course he was joking. But he was also trying to make a point. This book is not flashy, and it is not hype. Even if I had wanted to make it a bit flamboyant, my trusty and very level-headed editor at Prima Publishing, David Richardson, wouldn't let me. I'm glad for this because I can stand behind this book as I could stand behind my last one, *After-Hours Trading Made Easy.* I'm glad to be going somewhat against the grain in my usual contrarian fashion, and I think I have accomplished my goal.

But, as often happens, I may have given myself a few tools. As I conducted my research, I learned a great deal. Much of what is in this book came as a result of conclusions that I reached while doing the research, not out of knowledge that I had possessed and repackaged. I would like to think that my wonder in what I discovered came across. Of course, you will be the judge of that.

The chapters about the business practices of the health care companies and how biotechnology companies are trying not to be mavericks but to become the next Merck and Pfizer all came to me as I wrote. The history of the science, as well as the research into how the FDA and other agencies go about drug approval, was an incredible experience, as I learned much more than I already knew.

It is that same kind of revelation and learning that I hope you experience. If, as a professional, I added to my knowledge and became elated with my new discoveries, then the casual investor should find this a treasure trove, one that I hope will turn you into a former casual investor and a newly born expert. If you learn something by studying it and coming to your own conclusions, it is likely to become part of your DNA. Discovery is the essence of growth.

I started with the idea that I would write 70,000 words. But as I worked on the manuscript, it became clear that the scope of this work would be much larger. I ended with much more. I had intended one appendix and got four times that number. I had intended a few charts but needed to use many more. Of course, it's not *War and Peace.* But, as probably the first of its kind, this book will likely be highly scrutinized, and nasty things will be said about it as well as good things. But, as P.T. Barnum said, "Publicity is good."

By the time this book hits the bookstores, there may have been even more earth-shattering news in the biotechnology sector and in the world. For example, several drugs may have finished their phase 3 clinical trials and may be on the verge of approval, and many others may fall by the wayside. But no matter what happens, the biotechnology juggernaut will move on. I strongly believe that this book offers a strong foundation from which to build a reliable method of analyzing the markets and the biotechnology sector.

I discussed the concept of Intellectual Inclusion, which I derived myself, as I thought about what a gift we have been given with the ability to think. But it is more than that. It is the ability to recognize patterns and to organize them into a system that is easy to access and that is readily accessible, for thought is what makes us human. But the ability to see something special before the crowd and to put our money in that something special before it becomes readily evident is what makes us rich. If biotechnology seems like a difficult sector, then it means that you have to think a little harder.

Of course, I'm not trying to be patronizing. All I'm saying is that we have been spoon-fed too long by being surrounded by analysts on radio, television, and now the Internet. Therefore, this book is about becoming your own analyst. We all have the capacity. We all can make intelligent decisions about our money, and this book is about increasing your confidence and your knowledge not just about biotechnology, but also about Wall Street and the world in general.

Wall Street is the center of our culture, whether we like it or not. It is here that the world puts its money where its mouth is. The efficient market discounts all the possibilities based on the information it has available. As I said earlier, that information is not always immediately correct. But Wall Street's job is not to think but to act, to discount, and to make things happen.

The market maker will move the price up and down based on what he or she knows at that instant. The day traders will buy and sell based on what the market maker does. Somewhere in that chaos lies the truth. This book is about giving you the tools to find your own truth, one that gives you the courage to be prudent and to not always take the bait, one that lets you be patient and pick your spot, and, I hope, one that will help you make more profitable trades and investments.

As we enter the 21st century, never have Americans depended more on the markets for their future, and never has there been more information available about investment and trading. Yet many people started 2001 down 40 percent to 50 percent because there was a bear market and few saw it coming. This book offers you an opportunity to see both good and bad things before they cause terminal damage.

The majority of workers have some sort of retirement plan, and much of that retirement money is self-directed through 401(k) plans and IRAs. Those plans are affected by what happens on Wall Street with every tick, and those plans and the futures they serve deserve the opportunity to perform better.

The 2000 presidential election and the intense scrutiny by the media showed us that news does matter. Never was this more clear than on those volatile trading days when Al Gore would speak and the market would fall, only to rise when George W. Bush or Dick Cheney came back with an answer. No, I'm not saying Gore worsened the NASDAQ's bear market. I'm saying that the premise that an election of the president of the most powerful country in the world was filled with what seemed like never-ending uncertainty was more than a market-moving event.

It was clear unedited notice of our own vulnerability as a nation and perhaps as individuals, and that is the crux of human experience. We are going along just fine, until something comes out of the blue and knocks the heck out of us.

But once in a generation, an intangible arises and we evolve. We rise to another level, which in and of itself comes fully equipped with its own set of problems to solve. But the progression is clearly higher.

That is what I think is the impact of biotechnology. When the new drugs hit the street, bad hearts will beat better. Alzheimer's sufferers may recover their memories, and those with injured spinal cords will have a great chance to walk again and to move their hands and breathe without tubes in their throats. We may live long enough to see more of those places we want to see but don't have the time to visit now.

Okay, stop the music, douse the film. It comes down to this: Big bucks are possible for those who can see beyond the short-term setbacks in biotechnology. Those companies with the best management and the ability to execute their business plans are going to be the winners, and that is what this book is about. It is about seeing beyond the obvious and learning to recognize the patterns that lead to success. If I can make you think about making a stock transaction for one second longer because you remember something I wrote, and that extra second helps you make a better decision, I will have done my job.

For me, it has been a full circle. I went to medical school because I wanted a great challenge. I became an anesthesiologist because the mystery was appealing. I became an investment adviser because I enjoyed investing and the excitement of the contest. And I wrote this book because I could bring all the things I know to bear on one set of pages. I understand the science better than I ever did as a student, and I can see a much better connection between health care and the world. More important, the Wall Street connection is clearer for me than when I started.

As an investor, I began as a pure chartist. And although I am not a fundamentalist, I have come to appreciate that there are many areas of fundamental analysis that can help anyone make a better decision. It's never too late to learn something new, and right now, I'm learning that my next book project may be even more challenging. That makes me happy.

Finally, I would like to leave you with the following. Among the biggest killers and the most common stealers of humanity are cancer, heart disease, Alzheimer's disease, diabetes, asthma, and organ failure. While not all these conditions are lethal, they can kill us slowly. If they don't rob us of life itself, they rob us of our memories and our ability to interact with a wonderful world and those whom we love. Biotechnology can change much of that, and that is a wonderful gift to be treasured, even if you are not an investor.

I hope that this book makes you rich—if not in money, then maybe in spirit. Happy hunting.

A

Technical Analysis

A s I said earlier, a picture is worth a thousand words. Thus, in this appendix, I will give more examples of key technical analysis concepts. This appendix is designed to expand on the topics introduced in chapter 7.

Support and Resistance

Support is a chart point below which the stock does not fall. It means that there are buyers that are coming in at that price. Support can be seen either at a bottom or as part of a consolidation pattern or even in a rising trend, as it is often seen when a moving average or a trend line provides support.

Resistance is a chart point that keeps a stock from rising. That means that sellers are waiting for the stock to get there in order to unload. Resistance can happen at a top or when a stock is in a downtrend as well. Figure A1 is a diagram of both support and resistance. Figure A2 is of the pharmaceuticals HOLDRS trust, with the 50-day moving average and several trend lines indicating both support and resistance.

The rising trend line provided support for nearly a year, as did the 50-day moving average in the intermediate term. But when the stock broke below the 105 area, it broke below support. That

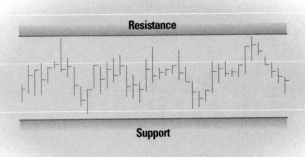

Figure A1. *Support and resistance lines in a trading range.*

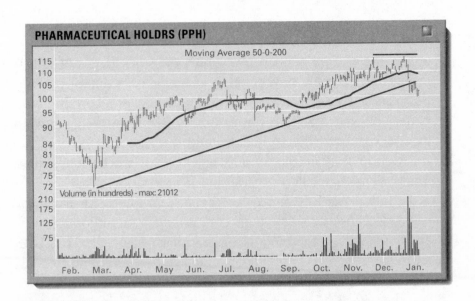

Figure A2. *PPH with suport and resistance. Courtesy of Telescan.*

same 105 area will turn into resistance in the future. The figure also shows that the 115 area was a crucial resistance area above which the trust could not rise.

Drawing Trend Lines

As the chart of PPH shows, a trend line is a useful tool in making buy and sell decisions. There are two ways of drawing them. Some technicians draw them through the middle of the trading range, while others use them to connect support and resistance levels. I prefer to use the trend line to connect support levels, as I show in figure A3.

In figure A3, the stock can be held as long as it remains above the trend line. At the top right-hand corner, the stock has broken below the trend line and should be sold. Trend lines can be used when day trading, as they can be drawn or plotted automatically by most technical software. It's just as easy to draw a trend line on

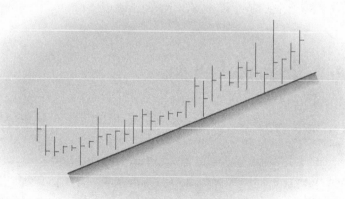

Figure A3. *Drawing trend lines.*

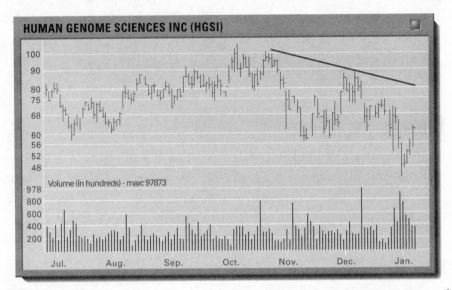

Figure A4. *Human Genome Sciences and a downtrend line. Courtesy of Telescan.*

an intraday chart as it is on a one-year chart. Downtrend lines should be drawn using the same principles.

Figure A4 shows a correctly drawn trend line. Note how it does not cross through any of the price bars. This trend line says that the 80 price area is one of resistance.

Head-and-Shoulders Patterns

The head-and-shoulders patterns are the most recognized, misused, and misquoted of all patterns in technical analysis. As figure A5 shows, head-and-shoulders bottoms are composed of three parts: the left shoulder, the head, and the right shoulder. The formation got the name from its resemblance to a person shrugging his shoulders. The stock of Charter Communications in figure A6 shows a classic head-and-shoulders bottom. March and April formed the left shoulder. The apex of the head came in May, and

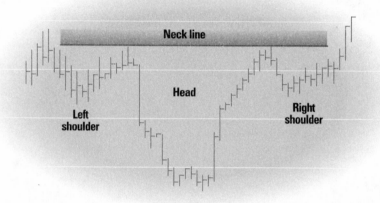

Figure A5. *The head-and-shoulders bottom.*

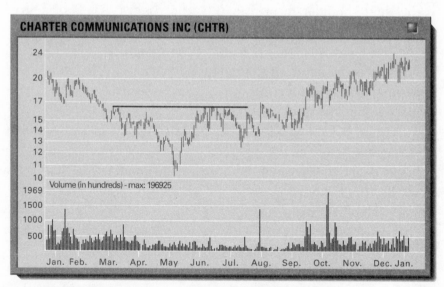

Figure A6. *Charter Communications (NASDAQ:CHTR) and a nice real-life head-and-shoulders bottom pattern. Courtesy of Telescan.*

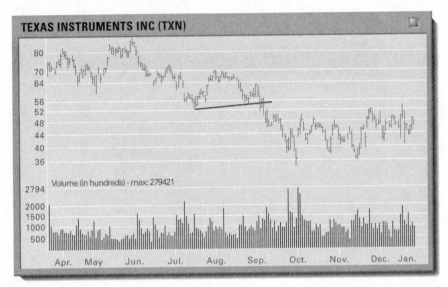

Figure A7. *Texas Instruments (NYSE:TXN) and a short-term head-and-shoulders top. Courtesy of Telescan.*

the right shoulder formed in July and August. The stock broke out soon thereafter. Note that the breakout came on huge volume.

The line connecting the top of the pattern is called the neck line and is the important part of the formation. A breakout, such as in Charter Communications, above the neck line is a great place to buy the stock.

Figure A7 shows a clear head-and-shoulders top in Texas Instruments before it fell 35 percent in mid-2000. The neck line break came at 56, while the bottom was made at 36, just a few weeks after the break.

The Upside Reversal

An upside reversal is a key technical pattern that often reveals unusually strong characteristics in a stock. The imaginary stock in figure A8 has been in a sustained downtrend. The descending trend line has provided resistance all along the way. This pattern

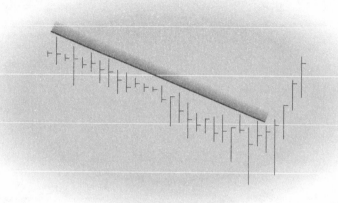

Figure A8. *The upside reversal.*

is often seen when a stock has been very beaten up and unusually good news comes out. I really like to see a stock reverse trend when there is insider buying.

The bars in the lower part of figure A9 show that insiders were very bullish on the shares of Humana. The HMO was beaten mercilessly by the market because it was very inefficient in controlling costs, and there were lawsuits pending against the industry. Note the trend reversal in mid-2000. This came when Aetna settled some lawsuits and restructured, signaling that managed care had thrown in the towel and was going to change the way it did business. Note also how insider buying accelerated when the trend reversed.

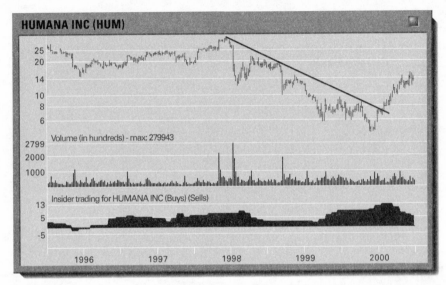

Figure A9. *Humana (NYSE:HUM) shows a very dramatic upside reversal, including insider buying.*

B

Mutual Funds Index

Fund Family: AIM Family of Funds

Address: 11 Greenway Plaza, Houston, TX 77046-1173
Phone: (800) 959-4246
Web site: www.aimfunds.com

Fund: AIM Global Health Care A
Symbol: GGHCX
Description: AIM Funds is one of the nation's largest and most successful mutual fund companies. AIM funds are sold through financial advisers.
Morningstar Rating: Four stars
Net Assets as of December 2000: $493 million
2000 Return as of December 31: 52.08 percent
Fund Inception: 8-7-89
Fees: Maximum Sales Fees Total Cost Projections ($10,000)
    Initial: 4.75 percent
    3-Year: $1,026
    Deferred: None
    5-Year: $1,423
    Redemption: None
    10-Year: $2,531

Fund: AIM Global Health Care B
Symbol: GTHBX
Morningstar Rating: Five stars
Net Assets as of December 2000: $158 million
2000 Return as of December 31: 51.34 percent
Fund Inception: 4-1-93
Fees: Maximum Sales Fees Total Cost Projections ($10,000)
  Initial: None
  3-Year: $1,030
  Deferred: 5.00 percent
  5-Year: $1,450
  Redemption: None
  10-Year: $2,552

Fund: AIM Global Health Care C
Symbol: GTHCX
Morningstar Rating: Not rated
Net Assets as of December 2000: $14 million
2000 Return as of December 31: 51.34 percent
Fund Inception: 3-1-99
Fees: Maximum Sales Fees Total Cost Projections ($10,000)
  Initial: None
  3-Year: $730
  Deferred: 1.00 percent
  5-Year: $1,250
  Redemption: None
  10 Year: $2,676

Fund Family: Alliance Funds

Address: P.O. Box 1520, Secaucus, NJ 07096
Phone: (800) 221-7672
Web site: www.alliancecapital.com

Fund: Alliance Health Care A
Symbol: AHLAX
Description: The fund's investment objective is long-term growth of capital through equity securities of domestic and foreign health care companies. These companies (1) derive at least 50 percent of their revenues or earnings from health care activities or (2) devote at least 50 percent of their assets to such activities based on their most recent fiscal year.

Typical companies include pharmaceutical companies, biotechnology research firms, companies that sell medical products, and companies that own or operate health care facilities. The fund also invests in debt securities issued by health care companies or in equity and debt securities of other companies.
Morningstar Rating: Not rated
Net Assets as of December 2000: $86 million
2000 Return as of December 31: 31.40 percent
Fund Inception: 8-27-99
Fees: Maximum Sales Fees Total Cost Projections ($10,000)
   Initial: 4.25 percent
   3-Year: $1,200
   Deferred: None
   5-Year: $1,758
   Redemption: None
   10-Year: $3,271

Fund: Alliance Health Care B
Symbol: AHLBX
Morningstar Rating: Not rated
Net Assets as of December 2000: $235 million
2000 Return as of December 31: 30.68 percent
Fund Inception: 8-27-99
Fees: Maximum Sales Fees Total Cost Projections ($10,000)
   Initial: None
   3-Year: $1,216

Deferred: 4.00 percent
5-Year: $1,733
Redemption: None
10-Year: $3,472

Fund: Alliance Health Care C
Symbol: AHLCX
Morningstar Rating: Not rated
Net Assets as of December 2000: $72 million
2000 Return as of December 31: 30.4 percent
Fund Inception: 8-28-99
Fees: Maximum Sales Fees Total Cost Projections ($10,000)
Initial: None
3-Year: $1,016
Deferred: 1.00 percent
5-Year: $1,733
Redemption: None
10-Year: $3,630

Fund Family: American Century Investments

Address: 4500 Main Street, Kansas City, MO 64141-6200
Phone: (800) 345-2021
Web site: www.americancentury.com

Fund: American Century Life Sciences Institutional
Symbol: M$-EBAH
Description: This aggressive fund invests in U.S. and foreign companies of any size in the life sciences sector. It invests in stocks of companies with earnings and revenues that are growing at an accelerating pace or companies that experience a change in their business that may stimulate future revenue and earnings acceleration.
Morningstar Rating: Not rated
Net Assets as of December 2000: $3 million

2000 Return as of December 31: N.A.
Fund Inception: 7-17-00
Fees: Maximum Sales Fees Total Cost Projections ($10,000)
   Initial: None
   3-Year: $410
   Deferred: None
   5-Year: N.A.
   Redemption: None
   10-Year: N.A.

Fund: American Century Life Sciences Investments
Symbol: ALSIX
Description: The fund focuses on capital growth, primarily investing in U.S. and foreign equity securities of companies in the life sciences sector. It may invest in companies of any size. It may invest in derivative instruments, such as stock index futures and options. The fund looks for companies with accelerating earnings and sales growth.
Morningstar Rating: Not rated
Net Assets as of December 2000: $234 million
2000 Return as of December 31: N.A.
Fund Inception: 6-30-00
Fees: Maximum Sales Fees Total Cost Projections ($10,000)
   Initial: None
   3-Year: $472
   Deferred: None
   5-Year: N.A.
   Redemption: None
   10-Year: N.A.

Fund Family: Dresdner RCM Global Investors

Address: Four Embarcadero Center, San Francisco, CA 94111
Phone: (800) 726-7240
Web site: www.dresdnerrcm.com

Fund: Dresdner RCM Biotechnology
Symbol: DRBNX
Description: The fund invests in the biotechnology sector that is expected to generate superior returns over time. The fund focuses on companies engaged in the research, development, provision, and/or manufacture of biotechnological products, services, and processes. Such companies generally employ genetic engineering to develop new drugs and apply new and innovative processes to discover and develop diagnostic products and services.
Morningstar Rating: Not rated
Net Assets as of December 2000: $803 million
2000 Return as of December 31: 81.9 percent
Fund Inception: 12-30-97
Fees: Maximum Sales Fees Total Cost Projections ($10,000)
   Initial: None
   3-Year: $1,162
   Deferred: None
   5-Year: $2,174
   Redemption: None
   10-Year: $4,716

Fund: Dresdner RCM Global Health Care
Symbol: DGHCX
Description: The fund believes that the health care sector is one of the most dynamic sectors in the world's economy. The fund's health care equity approach combines the firm's bottom-up, growth stock investing style with a top-down look at global economic policies. The fund manager then utilizes proprietary analytical tools in the search for reasonable valuations.
Morningstar Rating: Five stars
Net Assets as of December 2000: $219 million
2000 Return as of December 31: 73.4 percent
Fund Inception: 12-31-96
Fees: Maximum Sales Fees Total Cost Projections ($10,000)
   Initial: None
   3-Year: $918

Deferred: None
5-Year: $1,705
Redemption: None
10-Year: $3,766

Fund Family: Eaton Vance Group

Address: 255 State Street, Boston, MA 02109
Phone: (800) 225-6265
Web site: www.eatonvance.com

Fund: Eaton Vance Worldwide Health Sciences A
Symbol: ETHSX
Description: This fund forges its own path. It owns some big drug stocks, but it also holds lots of foreign issues and the shares of tiny firms. This eclectic portfolio produces variable returns. It is best for those who want a health care fund with some small-cap focus.

The fund's investment objective is to seek long-term capital growth by investing in a global and diversified portfolio of health sciences companies. The fund invests primarily in companies engaged in the development, production, or distribution of products related to scientific advances in health care. The fund has significant investments in foreign securities and the shares of many tiny firms.
Morningstar Rating: Five stars
Net Assets as of December 2000: $530 million
2000 Return as of December 31: 81.6 percent
Fund Inception: 7-26-85
Fees: Maximum Sales Fees Total Cost Projections ($10,000)
    Initial: 5.75 percent
    3-Year: $1,080
    Deferred: None
    5-Year: $1,445
    Redemption: None
    10-Year: $2,468

Fund: Eaton Vance Worldwide Health Sciences B
Symbol: EMHSX
Morningstar Rating: Five stars
Net Assets as of December 2000: $482 million
2000 Return as of December 31: 80.4 percent
Fund Inception: 9-26-96
Fees: Maximum Sales Fees Total Cost Projections ($10,000)
   Initial: None
   3-Year: $1,164
   Deferred: 5.00 percent
   5-Year: $1,506
   Redemption: None
   10-Year: $2,786

Fund: Eaton Vance Worldwide Health Sciences C
Symbol: ECHSX
Morningstar Rating: Not rated
Net Assets as of December 2000: $169 million
2000 Return as of December 31: 80.4 percent
Fund Inception: 1-5-98
Fees: Maximum Sales Fees Total Cost Projections ($10,000)
   Initial: None
   3-Year: $764
   Deferred: 1.00 percent
   5-Year: $1,306
   Redemption: None
   10-Year: $2,786

Fund Family: Evergreen Funds

Address: 401 South Tryon Street, Charlotte, NC 28288-1195
Phone: (800) 225-2618
Web site: www.evergreen-funds.com

Fund: Evergreen Health Care A
Symbol: EHABX
Description: The fund seeks long-term capital growth investing in equity securities of health care companies. This includes companies that develop, produce, or distribute products or services related to the health care or medical industries and derive more than 50 percent of their sales from products and services in health care. The fund may invest in securities of relatively well known and large companies as well as small and medium-size companies. It may invest in securities of both domestic and foreign issuers.
Morningstar Rating: Not rated
Net Assets as of December 2000: $12 million
2000 Return as of December 31: 119.0 percent
Fund Inception: 12-22-99
Fees: Maximum Sales Fees Total Cost Projections ($10,000)
  Initial: 4.75 percent
  3-Year: $997
  Deferred: None
  5-Year: N.A.
  Redemption: None
  10-Year: N.A.

Fund: Evergreen Health Care B
Symbol: EHCBX
Morningstar Rating: Not rated
Net Assets as of December 2000: $28 million
2000 Return as of December 31: 117.6 percent
Fund Inception: 12-22-99
Fees: Maximum Sales Fees Total Cost Projections ($10,000)
  Initial: None
  3-Year: $1,076
  Deferred: 5.00 percent
  5-Year: N.A.

Redemption: None
10-Year: N.A.

Fund: Evergreen Health Care C
Symbol: M$-DCCC
Morningstar Rating: Not rated
Net Assets as of December 2000: $12 million
2000 Return as of December 31: 117.6 percent
Fund Inception: 12-22-99
Fees: Maximum Sales Fees Total Cost Projections ($10,000)
    Initial: None
    3-Year: $776
    Deferred: 2.00 percent
    5-Year: N.A.
    Redemption: None
    10-Year: N.A.

Fund: Evergreen Health Care Y
Symbol: M$-DCCG
Morningstar Rating: Not rated
Net Assets as of December 2000: $1 million
2000 Return as of December 31: 110.7 percent
Fund Inception: 12-22-99
Fees: Maximum Sales Fees Total Cost Projections ($10,000)
    Initial: None
    3-Year: $471
    Deferred: None
    5-Year: N.A.
    Redemption: None
    10-Year: N.A.

Fund Family: Fidelity Advisor Funds

Address: 82 Devonshire Street, Boston, MA 02109
Phone: (800) 522-7297
Web site: www.fidelity.com

Fund: Fidelity Advisor Health Care A
Symbol: FACDX
Description: This fund looks for capital appreciation, investing at least 80 percent of assets in companies engaged in the design, manufacture, or sale of products or services used for or in connection with health care or medicine. These may include pharmaceutical companies, companies involved in research and development, and companies involved in health care facilities.
Morningstar Rating: Five stars
Net Assets as of December 2000: $143 million
2000 Return as of December 31: 36.2 percent
Fund Inception: 9-3-96
Fees: Maximum Sales Fees Total Cost Projections ($10,000)
 Initial: 5.75 percent
 3-Year: $943
 Deferred: None
 5-Year: $1,212
 Redemption: 1.00 percent
 10-Year: $1,978

Fund: Fidelity Advisor Health Care B
Symbol: FAHTX
Morningstar Rating: Five stars
Net Assets as of December 2000: $462 million
2000 Return as of December 31: 35.2 percent
Fund Inception: 3-3-97
Fees: Maximum Sales Fees Total Cost Projections ($10,000)
 Initial: None
 3-Year: $921
 Deferred: 5.00 percent
 5-Year: $1,268
 Redemption: 1.00 percent
 10-Year: $2,022

Fund: Fidelity Advisor Health Care C
Symbol: FHCCX

Morningstar Rating: Five stars
Net Assets as of December 2000: $236 million
2000 Return as of December 31: 35.2 percent
Fund Inception: 11-3-97
Fees: Maximum Sales Fees Total Cost Projections ($10,000)
  Initial: None
  3-Year: $612
  Deferred: 1.00 percent
  5-Year: $1,052
  Redemption: 1.00 percent
  10-Year: $2,275

Fund: Fidelity Advisor Health Care Institutional
Symbol: FHCIX
Description: The fund invests at least 80 percent of assets in companies engaged in the design, manufacture, or sale of products or services used for or in connection with health care or medicine, seeking capital appreciation. Investments include pharmaceutical companies, companies involved in research and development, and companies involved in health care facilities.
Morningstar Rating: Five stars
Net Assets as of December 2000: $46 million
2000 Return as of December 31: 36 percent
Fund Inception: 9-3-96
Fees: Maximum Sales Fees Total Cost Projections ($10,000)
  Initial: None
  3-Year: $309
  Deferred: None
  5-Year: $536
  Redemption: 1.00 percent
  10-Year: $1,190

Fund: Fidelity Advisor Health Care T
Symbol: FACTX

Description: A capital appreciation fund that invests at least 80 percent of assets in companies engaged in the design, manufacture, or sale of products or services used for or in connection with health care or medicine. Companies include pharmaceuticals, companies involved in research and development, and companies involved in health care facilities.

Morningstar Rating: Five stars

Net Assets as of December 2000: $430 million

2000 Return as of December 31: 35.9 percent

Fund Inception: 9-3-96

Fees: Maximum Sales Fees Total Cost Projections ($10,000)

Initial: 3.50 percent

3-Year: $796

Deferred: None

5-Year: $1,120

Redemption: 1.00 percent

10-Year: $2,035

Fund: Fidelity Select Biotechnology

Symbol: FBIOX

Description: The fund seeks capital appreciation with investments in companies engaged in research and development of biotechnological or biomedical products, services, and processes. The fund also invests in related manufacturing or distributing companies.

It is more volatile than the typical health care fund. The fund buys bigger, more established biotech names, so it can be more stable than some of its biotech rivals.

Morningstar Rating: Five stars

Net Assets as of December 2000: $4,118 million

2000 Return as of December 31: 32.8 percent

Fund Inception: 12-16-85

Fees: Maximum Sales Fees Total Cost Projections ($10,000)

Initial: 3.00 percent

3-Year: $665

Deferred: None
5-Year: $927
Redemption: 0.75 percent
10-Year: $1,674

Fund: Fidelity Select Health Care
Symbol: FSPHX
Description: Seeking capital appreciation, the fund invests at least 80 percent of assets in equity securities of companies in the health care industry. Companies include those engaged in the design, manufacture, or sale of products or services used for or in connection with health care or medicine.

The fund is one of the best in the health care category. Its drug, biotech, and health care services stocks annually yield great returns thanks to Fidelity's research team.
Morningstar Rating: Five stars
Net Assets as of December 2000: $2,990 million
2000 Return as of December 31: 36.7 percent
Fund Inception: 7-14-81
Fees: Maximum Sales Fees Total Cost Projections ($10,000)
Initial: 3.00 percent
3-Year: $638
Deferred: None
5-Year: $880
Redemption: 0.75 percent
10-Year: $1,574

Fund: Fidelity Select Medical Equipment/Systems
Symbol: FSMEX
Description: This fund seeks capital appreciation with investments in companies engaged in research, development, manufacture, distribution, supply, or sale of medical equipment, devices, and related technologies. It may also invest a small portion of its portfolio in lower-quality debt. The fund may invest a significant portion of assets in foreign issues.
Morningstar Rating: Not rated

Net Assets as of December 2000: $133 million
2000 Return as of December 31: 50.4 percent
Fund Inception: 4-28-98
Fees: Maximum Sales Fees Total Cost Projections ($10,000)
Initial: 3.00 percent
3-Year: $815
Deferred: None
5-Year: $1,183
Redemption: 0.75 percent
10-Year: $2,214

Fund: Fidelity Select Medical Delivery
Symbol: FSHCX
Description: This fund is focused on capital appreciation with investments in securities of companies engaged in the ownership or management of hospitals, nursing homes, health maintenance organizations, and other companies specializing in the delivery of health care services.
Morningstar Rating: One star
Net Assets as of December 2000: $252 million
2000 Return as of December 31: 67.8 percent
Fund Inception: 6-30-86
Fees: Maximum Sales Fees Total Cost Projections ($10,000)
Initial: 3.00 percent
3-Year: $836
Deferred: None
5-Year: $1,218
Redemption: 0.75 percent
10-Year: $2,287

Fund Family: First American Investment Funds

Address: One Freedom Valley Drive, Oaks, PA 19456
Phone: (800) 637-2548
Web site: www.usbank.com/invest/mutual/firstam

Fund: First American Health Sciences A
Symbol: FHSAX
Description: The fund invests primarily in common stocks of companies that develop, produce, or distribute products or services connected with health care or medicine and that derive at least 50 percent of their assets, revenues, or profits from these products or services at the time of investment. This includes products or services connected with health care or medicine, such as pharmaceuticals, health care services and administration, diagnostics, medical equipment and supplies, medical technology, and medical research and development.

The fund's investments may include development stage companies and small- and mid-capitalization companies. The fund may also invest in real estate investment trusts (REITs) that finance medical care facilities. Under certain market conditions, the fund may frequently invest in companies at the time of their initial public offering (IPO).
Morningstar Rating: Three stars
Net Assets as of December 2000: $6 million
2000 Return as of December 31: 46.9 percent
Fund Inception: 1-31-96
Fees: Maximum Sales Fees Total Cost Projections ($10,000)
    Initial: 5.25 percent
    3-Year: $915
    Deferred: None
    5-Year: $1,200
    Redemption: None
    10-Year: $2,010

Fund: First American Health Sciences B
Symbol: FHSBX
Morningstar Rating: Three stars
Net Assets as of December 2000: $4 million
2000 Return as of December 31: 45.7 percent
Fund Inception: 1-31-96

Fees: Maximum Sales Fees Total Cost Projections ($10,000)
  Initial: None
  3-Year: $1,043
  Deferred: 5.00 percent
  5-Year: $1,303
  Redemption: None
  10-Year: $2,187

Fund: First American Health Sciences Y
Symbol: FHSHX
Morningstar Rating: Three stars
Net Assets as of December 2000: $20 million
2000 Return as of December 31: 47.1 percent
Fund Inception: 1-31-96
Fees: Maximum Sales Fees Total Cost Projections ($10,000)
  Initial: None
  3-Year: $334
  Deferred: None
  5-Year: $579
  Redemption: None
  10-Year: $1,283

Fund Family: Franklin Group of Funds

Address: 777 Mariners Island Boulevard, San Mateo, CA 94404
Phone: (800) 342-5236
Web site: www.franklintempleton.com

Fund: Franklin Biotechnology Discovery A
Symbol: FBDIX
Description: This is an aggressive fund that avoids big-cap drug stocks in favor of biotech firms exclusively. Such a narrow focus has thus far led to dismal returns, as many biotech stocks have struggled. It is a commendable fund for investors who are sure they need a strong position in biotechs.

Morningstar Rating: Five stars
Net Assets as of December 2000: $1,274 million
2000 Return as of December 31: 46.6 percent
Fund Inception: 9-15-97
Fees: Maximum Sales Fees Total Cost Projections ($10,000)
    Initial: Closed
    3-Year: $1,054
    Deferred: Closed
    5-Year: $1,401
    Redemption: Closed
    10-Year: $2,376

Fund: Franklin Global Health Care A
Symbol: FKGHX
Description: The fund invests in smaller companies, making it more aggressive than most of its health care peers. It carries higher-than-normal risk but can bring good returns, as it did in 2000.
Morningstar Rating: Two stars
Net Assets as of December 2000: $175 million
2000 Return as of December 31: 69.3 percent
Fund Inception: 2-14-92
Fees: Maximum Sales Fees Total Cost Projections ($10,000)
    Initial: 5.75 percent
    3-Year: $919
    Deferred: None
    5-Year: $1,172
    Redemption: None
    10-Year: $1,892

Fund: Franklin Global Health Care C
Symbol: FGIIX
Morningstar Rating: Five stars
Net Assets as of December 2000: $33 million
2000 Return as of December 31: 68 percent

Fund Inception: 9-3-96
Fees: Maximum Sales Fees Total Cost Projections ($10,000)
    Initial: 1.00 percent
    3-Year: N.A.
    Deferred: 1.00 percent
    5-Year: N.A.
    Redemption: None
    10-Year: N.A.

Fund Family: World Funds

Address: 1500 Forest Avenue, Richmond, VA 23229
Phone: (877) 433-4363
Web site: www.genomicsfund.com

Fund: Genomics Fund
Symbol: GENEX
Description: GenomicsFund.com is the world's first and only mutual fund specializing in investing in the rapidly emerging genomics industry. The principal objective of the fund is capital appreciation.

It is the current investment strategy of the fund to maintain a fully invested position in a diversified portfolio of genomics-related securities. The fund does not presently have any holdings in nongenomics securities, although it has the flexibility to do so in the future.
Morningstar Rating: Not rated
Net Assets as of December 2000: $23 million
2000 Return as of December 31: N.A.
Fund Inception: 3-1-00
Fees: Maximum Sales Fees Total Cost Projections ($10,000)
    Initial: None
    3-Year: $596
    Deferred: None

5-Year: N.A.
Redemption: 2.00 percent
10-Year: N.A.

Fund Family: John Hancock Funds

Address: 101 Huntington Avenue, Boston, MA 02199-7603
Phone: (800) 225-5291
Web site: www.johnhancock.com

Fund: Hancock Health Sciences A
Symbol: JHGRX
Description: The fund invests in health care companies that are attractive in terms of earnings stability, growth potential, and valuation. The managers study economic trends to identify promising industries within pharmaceuticals and biotechnology, medical devices, and health care services.

A unique independent advisory board composed of scientific and medical experts provides advice and consultation on health care developments.
Morningstar Rating: Three stars
Net Assets as of December 2000: $186 million
2000 Return as of December 31: 38.2 percent
Fund Inception: 10-1-91
Fees: Maximum Sales Fees Total Cost Projections ($10,000)
  Initial: 5.00 percent
  3-Year: N.A.
  Deferred: None
  5-Year: N.A.
  Redemption: None
  10-Year: N.A.

Fund: Hancock Health Sciences B
Symbol: JHRBX
Morningstar Rating: Three stars

Net Assets as of December 2000: $305 million
2000 Return as of December 31: 37.3 percent
Fund Inception: 3-7-94
Fees: Maximum Sales Fees Total Cost Projections ($10,000)
    Initial: None
    3-Year: N.A.
    Deferred: 5.00 percent
    5-Year: N.A.
    Redemption: None
    10-Year: N.A.

Fund: John Hancock Health Sciences C
Symbol: JHRCX
Morningstar Rating: Not rated
Net Assets as of December 2000: $15 million
2000 Return as of December 31: 37.3 percent
Fund Inception: 3-1-99
Fees: Maximum Sales Fees Total Cost Projections ($10,000)
    Initial: 1.00 percent
    3-Year: $721
    Deferred: 1.00 percent
    5-Year: $1,235
    Redemption: None
    10-Year: $2,646

Fund Family: Hartford Mutual Funds

Address: P.O. Box 8416, Boston, MA 02266-8416
Phone: (888) 843-7824
Web site: www.thehartford.com

Fund: Hartford Global Health A
Symbol: HGHAX
Description: The fund seeks long-term capital appreciation
through investments in equity securities issued by domestic and

foreign health care companies. The fund is allocated across the major subsectors of the health care sector, including pharmaceuticals, medical products, managed health care, and health information services. The fund uses the fundamental analysis approach in its stock selection and seeks companies with attractive entry valuation.

Morningstar Rating: Not rated
Net Assets as of December 2000: $66 million
2000 Return as of December 31: N.A.
Fund Inception: 5-1-00
Fees: Maximum Sales Fees Total Cost Projections ($10,000)
    Initial: 5.50 percent
    3-Year: $1,068
    Deferred: None
    5-Year: $1,449
    Redemption: 1.00 percent
    10-Year: $2,513

Fund: Hartford Global Health B
Symbol: HGHBX
Morningstar Rating: Not rated
Net Assets as of December 2000: $29 million
2000 Return as of December 31: N.A.
Fund Inception: 5-1-00
Fees: Maximum Sales Fees Total Cost Projections ($10,000)
    Initial: None
    3-Year: $1,054
    Deferred: 5.00 percent
    5-Year: $1,494
    Redemption: 1.00 percent
    10-Year: $2,767

Fund: Hartford Global Health C
Symbol: HGHCX
Morningstar Rating: Not rated

Net Assets as of December 2000: $35 million
2000 Return as of December 31: N.A.
Fund Inception: 5-1-00
Fees: Maximum Sales Fees Total Cost Projections ($10,000)
    Initial: 1.00 percent
    3-Year: $840
    Deferred: None
    5-Year: $1,368
    Redemption: 1.00 percent
    10-Year: $2,811

Fund: Hartford Global Health Y
Symbol: HGHYX
Morningstar Rating: Not rated
Net Assets as of December 2000: $4 million
2000 Return as of December 31: N.A.
Fund Inception: 5-1-00
Fees: Maximum Sales Fees Total Cost Projections ($10,000)
    Initial: None
    3-Year: $392
    Deferred: None
    5-Year: $681
    Redemption: 1.00 percent
    10-Year: $1,503

Fund Family: INVESCO Family of Funds

Address: P.O. Box 173706, Denver, CO 80217-3706
Phone: (800) 525-8085
Web site: www.invescofunds.com

Fund: INVESCO Health Sciences Inv
Symbol: FHLSX
Description: This growth fund invests primarily in equity securities of companies that develop, produce, or distribute products or

services related to health care. The fund may invest up to 25 percent of assets in securities of foreign companies.
Morningstar Rating: Four stars
Net Assets as of December 2000: $1,990 million
2000 Return as of December 31: 25.8 percent
Fund Inception: 1-19-84
Fees: Maximum Sales Fees Total Cost Projections ($10,000)
    Initial: None
    3-Year: $399
    Deferred: None
    5-Year: $690
    Redemption: None
    10-Year: $1,518

Fund: INVESCO Health Sciences C
Symbol: M$-CHIJ
Morningstar Rating: Not rated
Net Assets as of December 2000: $8 million
2000 Return as of December 31: N.A.
Fund Inception: 2-14-00
Fees: Maximum Sales Fees Total Cost Projections ($10,000)
    Initial: None
    3-Year: $523
    Deferred: None
    5-Year: $902
    Redemption: 1.00 percent
    10-Year: $1,965

Fund Family: Icon Funds

Address: 12835 East Arapahoe Road, Englewood, CO 80112
Phone: (800) 764-0442
Web site: www.iconfunds.com

Fund: Icon Health Care
Symbol: ICHCX
Description: The fund normally invests at least 65 percent of assets in securities of companies principally engaged in the health care industry for long-term capital appreciation. This industry includes but is not limited to biotechnology, health care delivery, health care drugs, and medical equipment and devices.
Morningstar Rating: Four stars
Net Assets as of December 2000: $62 million
2000 Return as of December 31: 43 percent
Fund Inception: 2-21-97
Fees: Maximum Sales Fees Total Cost Projections ($10,000)
  Initial: None
  3-Year: $523
  Deferred: None
  5-Year: $902
  Redemption: 1.00 percent
  10-Year: $1,965

Fund Family: Janus

Address: 100 Fillmore Street, Denver, CO 80206-4923
Phone: (800) 525-8983
Web site: www.Janus.com

Fund: Janus Global Life Sciences
Symbol: JAGLX
Description: A long-term growth fund that invests at least 65 percent of assets in foreign and domestic securities of companies with a life sciences orientation. These companies generally consist of those related to maintaining or improving the quality of life, such as health care, nutrition, personal hygiene, medical diagnostics, and nuclear and biochemical research. Management utilizes a bottom-up investment approach and looks at companies

without regard to size, country allocation, place of principal business activity, or other similar criteria.

Morningstar Rating: Not rated
Net Assets as of December 2000: $3.992 million
2000 Return as of December 31: 33.3 percent
Fund Inception: 12-31-98
Fees: Maximum Sales Fees Total Cost Projections ($10,000)
  Initial: Closed
  3-Year: $353
  Deferred: Closed
  5-Year: $612
  Redemption: Closed
  10-Year: $1,352

Fund Family: Kinetics Mutual Funds

Address: 1311 Mamaroneck Avenue, White Plains, NY 10605
Phone: (800) 930-3828
Web site: www.kineticsfund.com

Fund: Kinetics Medical Fund
Symbol: MEDRX
Description: The Medical Fund invests all its investable assets in the Medical Portfolio. The fund normally invests at least 65 percent of its assets in common stocks, convertible securities, warrants, and other equities, such as ADRs and IDRs of U.S. and foreign companies engaged in the medical research, pharmaceutical and technology industries, and related medical technology industries.

Generally, the fund has an emphasis toward companies engaged in cancer research and drug development. The Medical Portfolio may also write and sell options on securities in which it invests for hedging purposes and/or direct investment. The fund sees favorable investment opportunities in companies that are developing technology, products, and/or services for cancer research and treatment and related medical activities.

Morningstar Rating: Not rated
Net Assets as of December 2000: $64 million
2000 Return as of December 31: 57 percent
Fund Inception: 10-1-99
Fees: Maximum Sales Fees Total Cost Projections ($10,000)
  Initial: None
  3-Year: $627
  Deferred: None
  5-Year: $1,078
  Redemption: None
  10-Year: $2,327

Fund Family: Morgan Stanley Dean Witter Funds

Address: Two World Trade Center, Suite 72, New York, NY 10048
Phone: (800) 869-3863
Web site: http//msdwonline.stockpoint.com

Fund: MSDW Health Sciences A
Symbol: HCRAX
Description: The fund normally invests at least 65 percent of its total assets in common stock of health science companies throughout the world. Companies include those that derive at least 50 percent of their earnings or revenues or devote at least 50 percent of their assets to health sciences activities.

Health sciences companies include hospitals, clinical test laboratories, convalescent and mental health care facilities, and home care businesses; pharmaceutical, biotechnology, medical diagnostics, biochemical, and nuclear research and development; and manufacturers of medical, dental, and optical supplies and equipment.

Morningstar Rating: Five stars
Net Assets as of December 2000: $14 million

2000 Return as of December 31: 58.3 percent
Fund Inception: 7-28-97
Fees: Maximum Sales Fees Total Cost Projections ($10,000)
    Initial: 5.25 percent
    3-Year: N.A.
    Deferred: None
    5-Year: N.A.
    Redemption: None
    10-Year: N.A.

Fund: MSDW Health Sciences B
Symbol: HCRBX
Morningstar Rating: Four stars
Net Assets as of December 2000: $670 million
2000 Return as of December 31: 57 percent
Fund Inception: 10-30-92
Fees: Maximum Sales Fees Total Cost Projections ($10,000)
    Initial: None
    3-Year: N.A.
    Deferred: 5.00 percent
    5-Year: N.A.
    Redemption: None
    10-Year: N.A.

Fund: MSDW Health Sciences C
Symbol: HCRCX
Morningstar Rating: Five stars
Net Assets as of December 2000: $25 million
2000 Return as of December 31: 57 percent
Fund Inception: 7-28-97
Fees: Maximum Sales Fees Total Cost Projections ($10,000)
    Initial: None
    3-Year: N.A.
    Deferred: 1.00 percent
    5-Year: N.A.

Redemption: None
10-Year: N.A.

Fund: MSDW Health Sciences D
Symbol: HCRDX
Morningstar Rating: Five stars
Net Assets as of December 2000: $14 million
2000 Return as of December 31: 58.5 percent
Fund Inception: 7-28-97
Fees: Maximum Sales Fees Total Cost Projections ($10,000)
    Initial: None
    3-Year: N.A.
    Deferred: None
    5-Year: N.A.
    Redemption: None
    10-Year: N.A.

Fund Family: Merrill Lynch Investment Managers

Address: Box 9011, Princeton, NJ 08543-9011
Phone: (800) 995-6526
Web site: www.ml.com/mutual_funds.htm

Fund: Merrill Lynch Health Care A
Symbol: MAHCX
Description: The fund seeks long-term capital appreciation through worldwide investment in equity securities of companies that derive, or are expected to derive, a substantial portion of their sales from products and services in health care.

The fund tries to achieve its objective by investing primarily in securities of health care companies. These will range from very large corporations to small, "developmental stage" companies. The fund may invest up to 15 percent of its assets in venture capital investments in developmental-stage companies. The fund may invest without limit in foreign securities. The fund may seek to hedge all or a portion of its portfolio against interest rate, market, and currency risks by investing in certain kinds of derivative securities.

Morningstar Rating: Five stars
Net Assets as of December 2000: $296 million
2000 Return as of December 31: 39.9 percent
Fund Inception: 4-4-83
Fees: Maximum Sales Fees Total Cost Projections ($10,000)
  Initial: 5.25 percent
  3-Year: $904
  Deferred: None
  5-Year: $1,180
  Redemption: None
  10-Year: $1,968

Fund: Merrill Lynch Health Care B
Symbol: MBHCX
Morningstar Rating: Five stars
Net Assets as of December 2000: $351 million
2000 Return as of December 31: 38.3 percent
Fund Inception: 10-21-88
Fees: Maximum Sales Fees Total Cost Projections ($10,000)
  Initial: None
  3-Year: $912
  Deferred: 4.00 percent
  5-Year: $1,220
  Redemption: None
  10-Year: $2,427

Fund: Merrill Lynch Health Care C
Symbol: MCHCX
Morningstar Rating: Five stars
Net Assets as of December 2000: $63 million

2000 Return as of December 31: 38.4 percent
Fund Inception: 10-21-94
Fees: Maximum Sales Fees Total Cost Projections ($10,000)
Initial: None
3-Year: $718
Deferred: 1.00 percent
5-Year: $1,230
Redemption: None
10-Year: $2,636

Fund: Merrill Lynch Health Care D
Symbol: MDHCX
Morningstar Rating: Five stars
Net Assets as of December 2000: $101 million
2000 Return as of December 31: 39.6 percent
Fund Inception: 10-21-94
Fees: Maximum Sales Fees Total Cost Projections ($10,000)
Initial: 5.25 percent
3-Year: $977
Deferred: None
5-Year: $1,305
Redemption: None
10-Year: $2,232

Fund Family: Monterey Mutual Funds

Address: Monterey 1299 Ocean Ave, Suite 210, Santa Monica, CA 90401
Phone: (800) 251-1970
Web site: montereyfunds.com

Fund: Monterey Murphy New World Biotech
Symbol: MNWBX

Description: This biotechnology fund's objective is long-term growth of capital through investing primarily in equity securities of companies that it believes can produce products or services that provide or benefit from advances in biotechnology.
Morningstar Rating: Three stars
Net Assets as of December 2000: $21 million
2000 Return as of December 31: 64 percent
Fund Inception: 10-21-93
Fees: Maximum Sales Fees Total Cost Projections ($10,000)
   Initial: None
   3-Year: $1,158
   Deferred: None
   5-Year: $1,953
   Redemption: None
   10-Year: $4,027

Fund Family: Monument Funds Group

Address: 7920 Norfolk Avenue, Suite 500, Bethesda, MD 20814
Phone: (888) 420-9950
Web site: www.monumentfunds.com

Fund: Monument Medical Science A
Symbol: MFMAX
Description: The fund's objective is long-term appreciation of capital. The fund seeks to achieve its objective by investing, under normal circumstances, primarily in equity securities of companies principally engaged in research, development, and distribution of medical products and services.

The fund sees that the aging populations of most of the developed countries will be composed of people over 65. Better nutrition, more leisure, the availability of more powerful medicines, and better health care facilities are all contributing to a longer life expectancy. This population will require or demand more potent medicines and more effective health care. The medical sciences sector will likely experience a long period of sustained growth.

Morningstar Rating: Five stars
Net Assets as of December 2000: $24 million
2000 Return as of December 31: 34.1 percent
Fund Inception: 1-2-98
Fees: Maximum Sales Fees Total Cost Projections ($10,000)
  Initial: 4.75 percent
  3-Year: N.A.
  Deferred: None
  5-Year: N.A.
  Redemption: None
  10-Year: N.A.

Fund Family: The Munder Funds

Address: 480 Pierce Street, Birmingham, MI 48009
Phone: (800) 438-5789
Web site: www.munder.com

Fund: Munder Framlington Health
Symbol: MFHAX
Description: The fund invests in equity securities of companies
engaged in developing, producing, and marketing technologically
advanced solutions for the health care and medical fields. The
fund may invest in foreign companies; however, most of these
companies are currently located in the United States. The fund
will invest in biotechnology firms, medical device and instrumen-
tation manufacturers, pharmaceuticals companies, specialty
pharmaceuticals, health care information technologies firms, and
medical device and instrument manufacturers.

The fund may invest in small companies and may invest without limit in initial public offerings (IPOs). It is uncertain whether
IPOs will be available for investment by the fund or what impact,
if any, they will have on the fund's performance. The fund may
also purchase and sell futures, options, and forward currency exchange contracts.

Morningstar Rating: Five stars
Net Assets as of December 2000: $221 million
2000 Return as of December 31: 86.4 percent
Fund Inception: 2-14-97
Fees: Maximum Sales Fees Total Cost Projections ($10,000)
    Initial: 5.50 percent
    3-Year: N.A.
    Deferred: None
    5-Year: N.A.
    Redemption: None
    10-Year: N.A.

Fund: Munder Framlington Health B
Symbol: MFHBX
Morningstar Rating: Five stars
Net Assets as of December 2000: $253 million
2000 Return as of December 31: 85.2 percent
Fund Inception: 1-31-97
Fees: Maximum Sales Fees Total Cost Projections ($10,000)
    Initial: None
    3-Year: N.A.
    Deferred: 5.00 percent
    5-Year: N.A.
    Redemption: None
    10-Year: N.A.

Fund: Munder Framlington Healthcare C
Symbol: MFHCX
Morningstar Rating: Five stars
Net Assets as of December 2000: $150 million
2000 Return as of December 31: 85.10 percent
Fund Inception: 1-13-97
Fees: Maximum Sales Fees Total Cost Projections ($10,000)
    Initial: None
    3-Year: N.A.
    Deferred: 1.00 percent

5-Year: N.A.
Redemption: None
10-Year: N.A.

Fund: Munder Framlington Health K
Symbol: MFHKX
Morningstar Rating: Five stars
Net Assets as of December 2000: $1 million
2000 Return as of December 31: 86.6 percent
Fund Inception: 4-1-97
Fees: Maximum Sales Fees Total Cost Projections ($10,000)
    Initial: None
    3-Year: N.A.
    Deferred: None
    5-Year: N.A.
    Redemption: None
    10-Year: N.A.

Fund: Munder Framlington Health Y
Symbol: MFHYX
Morningstar Rating: Five stars
Net Assets as of December 2000: $14 million
2000 Return as of December 31: 87 percent
Fund Inception: 12-31-96
Fees: Maximum Sales Fees Total Cost Projections ($10,000)
    Initial: None
    3-Year: N.A.
    Deferred: None
    5-Year: N.A.
    Redemption: None
    10-Year: N.A.

Fund Family: Nicolas Applegate Mutual Funds

Address: P.O. Box 82169, San Diego, CA 92138-2169
Phone: (800) 551-8643

Fund: Nicholas-Applegate Global Health I
Symbol: NAGHX
Description: The fund seeks long-term capital appreciation with investments in U.S. and foreign companies with business operations in the health care and health care–related industries. This includes any company that designs, manufactures, or sells products or services used for or in connection with health care or medicine.
Morningstar Rating: Not rated
Net Assets as of December 2000: $169 million
2000 Return as of December 31: 96.2 percent
Fund Inception: 9-1-99
Fees: Maximum Sales Fees Total Cost Projections ($10,000)
    Initial: None
    3-Year: $1,638
    Deferred: None
    5-Year: N.A.
    Redemption: None
    10-Year: N.A.

Fund Family: Orbitex

Address: 410 Park Avenue, 18th Floor, New York, NY 10022
Phone: (888) 672-4839
Web site: www.orbitexusa.com

Fund: Orbitex Health & Biotechnology A
Symbol: ORHAX
Description: The fund invests at least 65 percent of total assets in equity securities issued by health care companies and biotechnology companies and up to 25 percent of total assets in foreign companies. The fund also invests primarily in common stocks regardless of their market capitalization. The fund is designed for investors who want to capitalize on the long-term growth opportunities.

Morningstar Rating: Not rated
Net Assets as of December 2000: $102 million
2000 Return as of December 31: 56.2 percent
Fund Inception: 7-12-99
Fees: Maximum Sales Fees Total Cost Projections ($10,000)
    Initial: 5.75 percent
    3-Year: $1,410
    Deferred: None
    5-Year: N.A.
    Redemption: None
    10-Year: N.A.

Fund: Orbitex Health & Biotechnology B
Symbol: ORHBX
Morningstar Rating: Not rated
Net Assets as of December 2000: $113 million
2000 Return as of December 31: 55 percent
Fund Inception: 7-12-99
Fees: Maximum Sales Fees Total Cost Projections ($10,000)
    Initial: None
    3-Year: $1,363
    Deferred: 5.00 percent
    5-Year: N.A.
    Redemption: None
    10-Year: N.A.

Fund Family: Prudential Funds

Address: One Seaport Plaza, New York, NY 10292
Phone: (800) 225-1852
Web site: www.prudential.com/investing/mutualfunds/

Fund: Prudential Health Sciences A
Symbol: PHLAX

Description: The fund invests in equity securities of companies in the health sciences industry. It may invest in companies outside the health sciences industry and those located outside the United States. The fund may engage in short selling.
Morningstar Rating: Not rated
Net Assets as of December 2000: $108 million
2000 Return as of December 31: 75.5 percent
Fund Inception: 6-30-99
Fees: Maximum Sales Fees Total Cost Projections ($10,000)
   Initial: 5.00 percent
   3-Year: $1,017
   Deferred: None
   5-Year: N.A.
   Redemption: None
   10-Year: N.A.

Fund: Prudential Health Sciences B
Symbol: PHLBX
Morningstar Rating: Not rated
Net Assets as of December 2000: $234 million
2000 Return as of December 31: 74.1 percent
Fund Inception: 6-30-99
Fees: Maximum Sales Fees Total Cost Projections ($10,000)
   Initial: None
   3-Year: $1,061
   Deferred: 5.00 percent
   5-Year: N.A.
   Redemption: None
   10-Year: N.A.

Fund: Prudential Health Sciences C
Symbol: PHLCX
Morningstar Rating: Not rated
Net Assets as of December 2000: $99 million
2000 Return as of December 31: 74.1 percent

Fund Inception: 6-30-99
Fees: Maximum Sales Fees Total Cost Projections ($10,000)
    Initial: None
    3-Year: $854
    Deferred: 1.00 percent
    5-Year: N.A.
    Redemption: 1.00 percent
    10-Year: N.A.

Fund: Prudential Health Sciences Z
Symbol: M$-CAID
Morningstar Rating: Not rated
Net Assets as of December 2000: $36 million
2000 Return as of December 31: 75.9 percent
Fund Inception: 6-30-99
Fees: Maximum Sales Fees Total Cost Projections ($10,000)
    Initial: None
    3-Year: $456
    Deferred: None
    5-Year: N.A.
    Redemption: None
    10-Year: N.A.

Fund Family: Putnam Funds

Address: One Post Office Square, Boston, MA 02109
Phone: (800) 225-1581
Web site: www.putnaminv.com

Fund: Putnam Health Sciences A
Symbol: PHSTX
Description: This fund seeks capital appreciation with investments in common stocks and other securities of companies in the health sciences industries, including pharmaceuticals, health care services, research and development, and medical equipment and supplies. It may invest the remaining assets in other industries.

Morningstar Rating: Four stars
Net Assets as of December 2000: $4,228 million
2000 Return as of December 31: 40 percent
Fund Inception: 5-28-82
Fees: Maximum Sales Fees Total Cost Projections ($10,000)
  Initial: 5.75 percent
  3-Year: N.A.
  Deferred: None
  5-Year: N.A.
  Redemption: None
  10-Year: N.A.

Fund: Putnam Health Sciences B
Symbol: PHSBX
Morningstar Rating: Four stars
Net Assets as of December 2000: $3,075 million
2000 Return as of December 31: 39 percent
Fund Inception: 3-1-93
Fees: Maximum Sales Fees Total Cost Projections ($10,000)
  Initial: None
  3-Year: N.A.
  Deferred: 5.00 percent
  5-Year: N.A.
  Redemption: None
  10-Year: N.A.

Fund: Putnam Health Sciences C
Symbol: PCHSX
Morningstar Rating: Not rated
Net Assets as of December 2000: $107 million
2000 Return as of December 31: 39.1 percent
Fund Inception: 7-26-99
Fees: Maximum Sales Fees Total Cost Projections ($10,000)
  Initial: None
  3-Year: $536

Deferred: 1.00 percent
5-Year: $923
Redemption: None
10-Year: $2,009

Fund: Putnam Health Sciences M
Symbol: PHLMX
Morningstar Rating: Four stars
Net Assets as of December 2000: $128 million
2000 Return as of December 31: 39.3 percent
Fund Inception: 7-3-95
Fees: Maximum Sales Fees Total Cost Projections ($10,000)
   Initial: 3.50 percent
   3-Year: N.A.
   Deferred: None
   5-Year: N.A.
   Redemption: None
   10-Year: N.A.

Fund Family: Rydex Series Trust

Address: 6116 Executive Boulevard, Rockville, MD 20852
Phone: (800) 820-0888
Web site: www.rydexfunds.com

Fund: Rydex Biotechnology Adv
Symbol: RYOAX
Description: This capital appreciation fund invests mainly in common stocks and other securities of companies in the health sciences industries, including pharmaceuticals, health care services, research and development, and medical equipment and supplies. It may invest the remaining assets in other industries.
Morningstar Rating: Not rated
Net Assets as of December 2000: $74 million
2000 Return as of December 31: 28 percent

Fund Inception: 4-1-98
Fees: Maximum Sales Fees Total Cost Projections ($10,000)
    Initial: None
    3-Year: N.A.
    Deferred: None
    5-Year: N.A.
    Redemption: None
    10-Year: N.A.

Fund: Rydex Biotechnology Investments
Symbol: RYOIX
Description: The fund normally invests at least 80 percent of assets in equity securities issued by biotechnology companies that are traded in the United States as well as in futures and options contracts. Biotechnology companies include those engaged in the research, development, and manufacture of various biotechnological and biomedical products.
Morningstar Rating: Not rated
Net Assets as of December 2000: $476 million
2000 Return as of December 31: 28.6 percent
Fund Inception: 4-1-98
Fees: Maximum Sales Fees Total Cost Projections ($10,000)
    Initial: None
    3-Year: $490
    Deferred: None
    5-Year: $845
    Redemption: None
    10-Year: $1,845

Fund: Rydex Healthcare Adv
Symbol: RYHAX
Description: The fund seeks capital appreciation with investments in health care companies that are traded in the United States as well as in futures and options contracts. Health care

companies include pharmaceutical companies, companies involved in the research and development of pharmaceutical products and services, companies involved in the operations of health care facilities, and other health care–related issuers.
Morningstar Rating: Not rated
Net Assets as of December 2000: $42 million
2000 Return as of December 31: 30.3 percent
Fund Inception: 5-11-98
Fees: Maximum Sales Fees Total Cost Projections ($10,000)
    Initial: None
    3-Year: N.A.
    Deferred: None
    5-Year: N.A.
    Redemption: None
    10-Year: N.A.

Fund: Healthcare Inv
Symbol: RYHIX
Description: Another capital appreciation–oriented fund that normally invests at least 80 percent of assets in equity securities issued by health care companies that are traded in the United States as well as in futures and options contracts. Health care companies include pharmaceutical companies, companies involved in the research and development of pharmaceutical products and services, companies involved in the operations of health care facilities, and other health care–related issuers.
Morningstar Rating: Not rated
Net Assets as of December 2000: $91 million
2000 Return as of December 31: 31.07 percent
Fund Inception: 4-17-98
Fees: Maximum Sales Fees Total Cost Projections ($10,000)
    Initial: None
    3-Year: $452

Deferred: None
5-Year: $782
Redemption: None
10-Year: $1,713

Fund Family: Schwab Funds

Address: 101 Montgomery Street, San Francisco, CA 94104
Phone: (800) 435-4000
Web site: www.schwab.com

Fund: Schwab Health Care Focus
Symbol: SWHFX
Description: The fund invests at least 65 percent of assets in securities issued by U.S. health care companies, including drug and biotechnology companies, health care facilities, medical product manufacturers, medical providers, and medical services firms. It may also invest in futures contracts.
Morningstar Rating: Not rated
Net Assets as of December 2000: $33 million
2000 Return as of December 31: N.A.
Fund Inception: 7-30-00
Fees: Maximum Sales Fees Total Cost Projections ($10,000)
    Initial: None
    3-Year: $387
    Deferred: None
    5-Year: N.A.
    Redemption: 0.75 percent
    10-Year: N.A.

Fund Family: SunAmerica Funds

Address: 733 Third Avenue, New York, NY 10017-3204
Phone: (800) 858-8850
Web site: www.sunamerica.com

Fund: SunAmerica Biotech/Health
Symbol: SBHAX
Description: The fund invests in biotechnology companies and health care companies. The fund will invest in 30 to 50 biotechnology companies and health care companies, with the number of holdings varying from time to time.
Morningstar Rating: Not rated
Net Assets as of December 2000: $28 million
2000 Return as of December 31: N.A.
Fund Inception: 6-14-00
Fees: Maximum Sales Fees Total Cost Projections ($10,000)
    Initial: 5.75 percent
    3-Year: $1,036
    Deferred: None
    5-Year: $1,371
    Redemption: None
    10-Year: $2,314

Fund: SunAmerica Biotech/Health 30 B
Symbol: SHFBX
Morningstar Rating: Not rated
Net Assets as of December 2000: $25 million
2000 Return as of December 31: N.A.
Fund Inception: 6-14-00
Fees: Maximum Sales Fees Total Cost Projections ($10,000)
    Initial: None
    3-Year: $988
    Deferred: 4.00 percent
    5-Year: $1,380
    Redemption: None
    10-Year: $2,293

Fund: SunAmerica Biotech/Health 30 II
Symbol: SBHTX
Morningstar Rating: Not rated

Net Assets as of December 2000: $22 million
2000 Return as of December 31: N.A.
Fund Inception: 6-14-00
Fees: Maximum Sales Fees Total Cost Projections ($10,000)
    Initial: 1.00 percent
    3-Year: $781
    Deferred: 1.00 percent
    5-Year: $1,268
    Redemption: 1.00 percent
    10-Year: $2,609

Fund Family: T. Rowe Price Funds

Address: 100 East Pratt Street, Baltimore, MD 21202
Phone: (800) 638-5660
Web site: www.troweprice.com

Fund: T. Rowe Price Health Science
Symbol: PRHSX
Description: An aggressive stock fund seeking long-term capital growth. The majority of fund assets are invested in large- and mid-capitalization companies that are divided into four main areas of health science: pharmaceuticals, health care services companies, products and devices providers, and biotechnology firms.

The fund uses fundamental, bottom-up analysis that seeks to identify high-quality companies and the most compelling investment opportunities. In general, the fund will follow a growth investment strategy, seeking companies whose earnings are expected to grow faster than inflation and the economy in general.

Morningstar Rating: Five stars
Net Assets as of December 2000: $863 million
2000 Return as of December 31: 52.19 percent
Fees: Maximum Sales Fees Total Cost Projections ($10,000)

Fund Family: Vanguard Group

Address: Vanguard Financial Center, Valley Forge, PA 19482
Phone: (800) 662-7447
Web site: www.vanguard.com

Fund: Vanguard Health Care
Symbol: VGHCX
Description: The fund normally invests at least 80 percent of assets in companies that develop, produce, or distribute products and services related to the treatment or prevention of diseases and other medical conditions. This includes pharmaceutical firms, medical supply firms, and companies that operate hospitals and other health care facilities.
Morningstar Rating: Five stars
Net Assets as of December 2000: $17,508 million
2000 Return as of December 31: 60.6 percent
Fund Inception: 5-23-84
Fees: Maximum Sales Fees Total Cost Projections ($10,000)
> Initial: None
> 3-Year: $230
> Deferred: None
> 5-Year: $202
> Redemption: 1.00 percent
> 10-Year: $456

Fund Family: Warburg Pincus Funds

Address: P.O. Box 9030, Boston, MA 02205
Phone: (800) 927-2874
Web site: www.warburg.com

Fund: Warburg Pincus Global Health Science Cm
Symbol: WPHSX

Description: Invests mainly in equity securities of U.S. and foreign companies with an emphasis on the health services, pharmaceuticals, biotechnology, and medical devices industries.

The fund can invest in companies of any size and focuses on individual stock-picking risk assisted by a top-down approach to four sector concentration categories of health sciences companies: buyers, providers, suppliers, and producers.

Morningstar Rating: Five stars

Net Assets as of December 2000: $107 million

2000 Return as of December 31: 38.9 percent

Fund Inception: 12-31-96

Fees: Maximum Sales Fees Total Cost Projections ($10,000)

    Initial: None

    3-Year: $618

    Deferred: None

    5-Year: $1,062

    Redemption: None

    10-Year: $2,296

APPENDIX

C

Company Directory

Abgenix, Inc. (NASDAQ:ABGX)
7601 Dumbarton Circle
Fremont, CA 94555
Phone: (510) 608-6500
Fax: (510) 608-6511
Web site: www.abgenix.com
Business Summary: Abgenix develops antibody therapeutic products for the treatment of a variety of disease conditions, including transplant-related diseases, inflammatory and autoimmune disorders, cardiovascular disease, infectious diseases, and cancer. Its XenoMouse technology produces antibodies with human protein sequences and generates a diverse antibody response to essentially any disease target appropriate for antibody therapy and high-affinity antibodies that do not require further engineering.

Affymetrix, Inc. (NASDAQ:AFFX)
3380 Central Expressway
Santa Clara, CA 95051
Phone: (408) 731-5000
Fax: (408) 481-0422
Web site: www.affymetrix.com

Business Summary: Affymetrix develops DNA chip technology to acquire, analyze, and manage genetic information to improve the diagnosis, monitoring, and treatment of disease.

Alkermes, Inc. (NASDAQ:ALKS)
64 Sidney Street
Cambridge, MA 02139
Phone: (617) 494-0171
Fax: (617) 494-9263
Web site: www.alkermes.com
Business Summary: Alkermes works with partners and develops product candidates utilizing its drug delivery technologies. Their sustained-release injectable drugs last from as little as several days to as many as several weeks utilizing the company's Advanced Inhalation Research technology; the delivery of drugs into the brain past the blood-brain barrier utilizing the company's Cereport technology; and oral delivery of drugs utilizing the company's RingCap technology and dose-sipping technology.

Alliance Pharmaceutical Corporation (NASDAQ:ALLP)
3040 Science Park Road
San Diego, CA 92121
Phone: (858) 410-5200
Fax: (858) 410-5201
Web site: www.allp.com
Business Summary: Alliance Pharmaceutical is a pharmaceutical research and development company focused on developing scientific discoveries into medical products and licensing these products to multinational pharmaceutical companies. The company generates income through fixed payments and royalty or profit-sharing payments. Its products that are in clinical trials are Oxygent, an intravascular oxygen carrier to temporarily augment oxygen delivery in surgical and other patients at risk of acute oxygen deficiency; Liquivent, an intrapulmonary agent for use in

reducing a patient's exposure to the harmful effects of conventional mechanical ventilation; and Imavist, an intravenous contrast agent for enhancement of ultrasound images to assess cardiac function and organ lesions and to detect blood flow abnormalities.

Alteon Inc. (AMEX:ALT)
170 Williams Drive
Ramsey, NJ 07446
Phone: (201) 934-5000
Fax: (201) 934-8880
Web site: www.alteonpharma.com
Business Summary: Alteon develops pharmaceutical products for the treatment of cardiovascular and renal disease and other disorders of diabetes and aging. Its focus is on advanced glycosylation end products (AGEs), formed as a result of circulating blood glucose reacting with proteins.

Amgen, Inc. (NASDAQ:AMGN)
One Amgen Center Drive
Thousand Oaks, CA 91320
Phone: (805) 447-1000
Fax: (805) 447-1010
Web site: www.amgen.com
Business Summary: Amgen, Inc., is a vertically integrated biotechnology company that discovers, develops, manufactures, and markets human therapeutics based on advances in cellular and molecular biology. Its four human products are Epogen, Neupogen, Infergen, and Stemgen. Epogen is used in the treatment of anemia associated with chronic renal failure in patients on dialysis. Neupogen stimulates the production of neutrophils, a type of white blood cell. Infergen is an interferon that stimulates the immune system to fight viral infections such as chronic hepatitis. Stemgen is used in support of stem cell transplantation.

Amylin Pharmaceuticals (NASDAQ:AMLN)
9373 Towne Centre Drive
San Diego, CA 92121
Phone: (858) 552-2200
Fax: (858) 552-2212
Web site: www.amylin.com
Business Summary: Amylin develops drug candidates for the treatment of metabolic disorders. Current developments include Symlin (pramlintide acetate) for the treatment of insulin-dependent diabetics.

Antigenics, Inc. (NASDAQ:AGEN)
630 Fifth Avenue, Suite 2100
New York, NY 10111
Phone: (212) 332-4774
Fax: (212) 332-4778
Web site: www.antigenics.com
Business Summary: Antigenics develops immunotherapeutic drugs for the treatment of life-threatening and chronic medical conditions that work by modulating the immune system to fight disease. Other drugs in the pipeline include a variety of immunotherapeutics to treat infectious diseases, such as genital herpes, and autoimmune disorders, such as diabetes and multiple sclerosis.

Aphton Corporation (NASDAQ:APHT)
444 Brickell Avenue, Suite 51-507
Miami, FL 33131
Phone: (305) 374-7338
Fax: (305) 374-7615
Web site: www.aphton.com
Business Summary: Aphton Corporation develops products using its vaccine-like technology for neutralizing hormones involved in gastrointestinal system and reproductive system cancer and non-cancer diseases and the prevention of pregnancy. The company uses antihormone therapy that neutralizes or blocks targeted hor-

mones that play a critical role in diseases of the gastrointestinal and reproduction systems.

Applied Molecular Evolutions (NASDAQ:AMEV)
3520 Dunhill Street
San Diego, CA 92121
Phone: (858) 597-4990
Fax: (858) 597-4950
Web site: www.mevolution.com
Business Summary: Applied Molecular works in the field of directed evolution, a process that optimizes genes and proteins for specific commercial purposes. The company's primary focus is in the application of technology to human biotherapeutics. Applied Molecular uses directed evolution technology to develop improved versions of currently marketed, FDA-approved drugs and novel human therapeutics.

Arena Pharmaceuticals (NASDAQ:ARNA)
6166 Nancy Ridge Drive
San Diego, CA 92121
Phone: (858) 453-7200
Fax: (858) 453-7210
Web site: www.arenapharm.com
Business Summary: This biotechnology company developed CART, a new technology used to identify new drug candidates more efficiently than traditional techniques. Using CART, Arena has discovered new drug candidates in the areas of obesity and schizophrenia. With the success of CART, the company has established collaborative drug discovery programs with a number of pharmaceutical and biotechnology companies with a focus on drugs that target the IG protein-coupled receptors.

Avant Immunotherapeutics (NASDAQ:AVAN)
119 Fourth Avenue
Needham, MA 02494

Phone: (781) 433-0771
Fax: (781) 433-0262
Web site: www.avantimmune.com
Business Summary: Avant Immunotherapeutics, Inc., develops and markets products that harness the human immune response to prevent and treat disease. The company uses its technologies to develop vaccines and immunotherapeutics that prevent or treat disease caused by infectious organisms and drugs and treatment vaccines that modify undesirable activity by the body's own proteins or cells. Avant has pharmaceutical partners, including Novartis Pharma AG; AstraAB; Yamanouchi Pharmaceutical Co., Ltd.; Pasteur Merieux Connaught; and SmithKline Beecham.

AVAX Technologies, Inc. (NASDAQ:AVXT)
4520 Main Street, Suite 930
Kansas City, MO 64111
Phone: (816) 960-1333
Fax: (816) 960-1334
Web site: www.avax-tech.com
Business Summary: AVAX is engaged in the development and potential commercialization of products and technologies for the treatment of cancer and other life-threatening diseases. The company produces the autologous cell (AC) vaccine, designed to stimulate a patient's immune system to recognize, contain, and eliminate the cancer cells and is made using the patient's own tumor cells.

Avigen, Inc. (NASDAQ:AVGN)
1201 Harbor Bay Parkway, Suite 1000
Alameda, CA 94502
Phone: (510) 748-7150
Fax: (510) 748-7155
Web site: www.avigen.com
Business Summary: Avigen develops gene therapeutic products used in the treatment of inherited diseases. Current developments

include a broad-based proprietary gene delivery technology based on adeno-associated virus vector technology, known as AAV vectors. This technology delivers DNA to cells of patients with genetic diseases, such as hemophilia, Gaucher disease, Parkinson's disease, and beta-thalassemia.

Aviron (NASDAQ:AVIR)
297 North Bernardo Avenue
Mountain View, CA 94043
Phone: (650) 919-6500
Fax: (650) 919-6216
Web site: www.aviron.com
Business Summary: Aviron is focused on preventing disease through innovative vaccine technology. Its lead product candidate is FluMist, an investigational live virus vaccine for influenza delivered as a nasal spray. The company's strategy is to develop, manufacture, and market vaccines targeting the general population that are safe, effective, and economical enough to merit their use in immunization programs.

BioChem Pharma, Inc. (NASDAQ:BCHE)
275 Armand-Frappier Boulevard
Laval, Quebec H7V 4A7, Canada
Phone: (450) 978-7771
Fax: (450) 978-7755
Web site: www.biochempharma.com
Business Summary: BioChem develops and sells drugs to prevent and treat human diseases with a focus on infectious diseases and cancer.

BioMarin Pharmaceutical (NASDAQ:BMRN)
371 Bel Marin Keys Boulevard, Suite 210
Novato, CA 94949
Phone: (415) 884-6700
Fax: (415) 382-7427

Web site: www.biomarinpharm.com.
Business Summary: BioMarin develops carbohydrate enzyme therapies for debilitating, life-threatening, chronic genetic disorders and other diseases and conditions. The company's lead drug is Aldurazyme, useful in the treatment of a serious genetic disorder, mucopolysaccharidosis-I (MPS-I). An additional revenue source is its wholly owned subsidiary, Glyko, Inc. Glyko sells carbohydrate analysis products and services.

Biomatrix, Inc. (NYSE:BXM)
65 Railroad Avenue
Ridgefield, NJ 07657
Phone: (201) 945-9550
Fax: (201) 945-0363
Web site: www.biomatrix.com
Business Summary: Biomatrix develops, manufactures, markets, and sells a series of proprietary viscoelastic products called hylans. Hylans are the second generation of viscoelastics used in medicine. Their physical properties, including elasticity, viscosity, and pseudoplasticity, make them ideal for replicating body parts. Viscoelastic devices are ideally made from the body's own molecules found in the intercellular matrix that separates cells and integrates them into functional tissues.

Biopure Corporation (NASDAQ:BPUR)
11 Hurley Street
Cambridge, MA 02141
Phone: (617) 234-6500
Fax: (617) 234-6505
Web site: www.biopure.com
Business Summary: Biopure develops, manufactures, and markets oxygen therapeutics. Biopure's two products, Hemopure and Oxyglobin, are oxygen therapeutics. Hemopure, for human use, is currently in a U.S. pivotal phase 3 clinical trial as an alternative

to red blood cell transfusions before, during, or after elective orthopedic surgery.

Oxyglobin is a veterinary product for the treatment of anemia in dogs.

Bio-Technology General (NASDAQ:BTGC)
70 Wood Avenue South
Iselin, NJ 08830
Phone: (732) 632-8800
Fax: (732) 632-8844
Web site: www.btgc.com
Business Summary: Bio-Technology General manufactures and markets biopharmaceuticals. The company distributes its products through a direct sales force in the United States and primarily through third-party license and distribution relationships internationally.

Celgene Corporation (NASDAQ:CELG)
7 Powder Horn Drive
Warren, NJ 07059
Phone: (732) 271-1001
Fax: (732) 271-4184
Web site: www.celgene.com
Business Summary: Celgene discovers, develops, and commercializes orally administered, small-molecule drugs for the treatment of cancer and immunological diseases. The chief action of the company's drugs is inhibition of angiogenesis.

Cell Genesys, Inc. (NASDAQ:CEGE)
342 Lakeside Drive
Foster City, CA 94404
Phone: (650) 425-4400
Fax: (650) 358-0803
Web site: www.cellgenesys.com

Business Summary: Cell Genesys researches and develops human disease therapies based on gene modification technologies. The company emphasizes breakthrough therapies in vivo and/or ex vivo gene therapies to treat cancer and other major, life-threatening diseases, including hemophilia. It also has products under development for treatment of prostate cancer and lung cancer.

Celltech Group PLC (NYSE:CLL)
216 Bath Road, Slough
Berkshire, UK
Phone: (212) 333-3810
Fax: (212) 333-3811
Web site: www.celltech.co.uk
Business Summary: Celltech is the successor of the merger of Celltech with Medeva Plc as an international integrated biopharmaceutical group. The company combines Celltech's discovery and development portfolio with the development pipeline and marketing infrastructure of Medeva.

Cephalon, Inc. (NASDAQ:CEPH)
145 Brandywine Parkway
West Chester, PA 19380
Phone: (610) 344-0200
Fax: (610) 344-0065
Web site: www.cephalon.com
Business Summary: Cephalon markets Provigil (modafinil) tablets (C-IV), which treats the daytime sleepiness associated with narcolepsy. Provigil may also prove useful for patients with fatigue associated with multiple sclerosis and excessive daytime sleepiness due to obstructive sleep apnea. The company completed a merger with Anesta Corporation in the third quarter of 2000. Anesta develops therapies for management of pain associated with chronic diseases such as cancer.

Chiron Corporation (NASDAQ:CHIR)
4560 Horton Street
Emeryville, CA 94608
Phone: (510) 655-8730
Fax: (510) 655-9910
Web site: www.chiron.com
Business Summary: Chiron participates in three global health care businesses: biopharmaceuticals, vaccines, and blood testing. The company develops products for preventing and treating cancer, infectious diseases, and cardiovascular disease. Chiron's products include Proleukin, a treatment for metastatic renal cell carcinoma and metastatic melanoma, and Regranex Gel, a treatment for diabetic foot ulcers.

Ciphergen Biosystems (NASDAQ:CIPH)
6611 Dumbarton Circle
Fremont, CA 94555
Phone: (510) 505-2100
Fax: (510) 505-2101
Web site: www.ciphergen.com
Business Summary: Ciphergen manufactures and markets the ProteinChip System that enables protein-based biology research, known as proteomics. Proteomics enhances the researcher's understanding of gene function and the molecular basis of disease. The ProteinChip System is the platform for protein biomarker discovery and proteomics research in basic biological research, clinical research and diagnostics, and pharmaceutical drug discovery and development markets.

Collateral Therapeutics (NASDAQ:CLTX)
11622 El Camino Real
San Diego, CA 92130
Phone: (858) 794-3400
Fax: (858) 794-3440

Web site: www.collateralthx.com
Business Summary: Collateral Therapeutics Inc. sells nonsurgical gene therapy products used in the treatment of cardiovascular diseases, including coronary artery disease, congestive heart failure, peripheral vascular disease, and heart attack.

Compugen Ltd. (NASDAQ:CGEN)
72 Pinchas Resen Street
Tel Aviv 69512, Israel
Phone: (609) 655-5105
Web site: www.cgen.com
Business Summary: Compugen combines mathematics and computer science with molecular biology to improve the understanding of genomics and proteomics, the study of genes and proteins. The company develops technologies and platforms to enable life scientists to significantly enhance their research efforts in drug discovery, both therapeutic and diagnostic.

COR Therapeutics, Inc. (NASDAQ:CORR)
256 East Grand Avenue
South San Francisco, CA 94080
Phone: (650) 244-6800
Fax: (650) 244-9208
Web site: www.corr.com
Business Summary: COR Therapeutics develops pharmaceuticals for the treatment and prevention of severe cardiovascular diseases, including unstable angina, acute myocardial infarction, venous thrombosis, and re-stenosis.

Corvas International, Inc. (NASDAQ:CVAS)
3030 Science Park Road
San Diego, CA 92121
Phone: (858) 455-9800
Fax: (858) 455-7895
Web site: www.corvas.com

Business Summary: Corvas designs and develops new-generation therapeutic agents for cardiovascular, cancer, stroke, and other major diseases. The company's drug candidates target major cardiovascular diseases, such as heart attack, unstable angina, deep vein thrombosis, and pulmonary embolism, as well as cancer and acute inflammation associated with reperfusion injury in ischemic stroke drug candidates.

CuraGen Corporation (NASDAQ:CRGN)
555 Long Wharf Drive, 11th Floor
New Haven, CT 06511
Phone: (203) 401-3330
Fax: (203) 401-3331
Web site: www.curagen.com
Business Summary: CuraGen discovers and develops genomics-based drugs. The company collaborates with others to accelerate the discovery and development of products to improve human and animal health and the vitality of agriculture. The company's SeqCalling and GeneCalling are proprietary technologies for use in gene sequencing, gene expression analysis, and biological pathways.

Deltagen Inc. (NASDAQ:DGEN)
1003 Hamilton Avenue
Menlo Park, CA 94025
Phone: (650) 752-0200
Fax: (650) 752-0202
Web site: www.deltagen.com
Business Summary: Deltagen Inc. develops technology to convert raw genetic data into mammalian gene function information that in turn helps pharmaceutical and biotechnology companies expedite the drug discovery process. Deltagen's DeltaBase, a proprietary, searchable database, provides immediate access to gene function information and potential targets for drug discovery contained in the database.

Dendreon Corporation (NASDAQ:DNDN)
3005 First Avenue
Seattle, WA 98121
Phone: (206) 256-4545
Fax: (206) 256-0571
Web site: www.dendreon.com
Business Summary: Dendreon develops immunologically based therapeutic products for the treatment of cancer. Its Provenge is a vaccine for treatment of prostate cancer that is in phase 3 clinical trials. The company is conducting phase 2 clinical trials of APC8020, its therapeutic vaccine for B-cell malignancies, including multiple myeloma and amyloidosis.

Diversa Corporation (NASDAQ:DVSA)
10665 Sorrento Valley Road
San Diego, CA 92121
Phone: (858) 623-5106
Fax: (858) 626-3700
Web site: www.diversa.com
Business Summary: Diversa discovers and develops biomolecules, biologically active compounds and enzymes. The company's products have agricultural, chemical processing, industrial, and pharmaceutical applications. Its gene library stores previously unaccessed genetic material from uncultured organisms found in various natural environments.

Dyax Corporation (NASDAQ:DYAX)
One Kendall Square, Building 600
Cambridge, MA 02139
Phone: (617) 225-2500
Fax: (617) 225-2501
Web site: www.dyax.com
Business Summary: Dyax developed and patented a method, known as phage display, used to identify compounds for the

treatment and diagnosis of diseases. The company also uses this method to identify compounds that can be used to purify and manufacture biopharmaceuticals and other chemicals. Dyax develops technologies to purify biopharmaceuticals.

EntreMed, Inc. (NASDAQ:ENMD)
9640 Medical Center Drive, Suite 200
Rockville, MD 20850
Phone: (301) 217-9858
Fax: (301) 217-9594
Web site: www.entremed.com
Business Summary: EntreMed uses antiangiogenic drugs designed to inhibit the abnormal new blood vessel growth associated with a broad range of diseases, such as cancer, certain types of blindness, and atherosclerosis. The company believes that its antiangiogenic drugs may have significant advantages over traditional cancer therapies, including a reduced likelihood of resistance, fewer side effects, and the ability to be administered in conjunction with other therapies.

Enzo Biochem, Inc. (NYSE:ENZ)
60 Executive Boulevard
Farmingdale, NY 11735
Phone: (516) 755-5500
Fax: (516) 755-5569
Web site: www.enzobio.com
Business Summary: Enzo Biochem does research, development, manufacturing, and marketing of diagnostic and research products based on genetic engineering, biotechnology, and molecular biology. Enzo designs products that diagnose and/or screen for infectious diseases, cancers, genetic defects, and other diagnostics. Enzo operates a clinical reference laboratory with diagnostic medical testing services to the health care community.

Enzon, Inc. (NASDAQ:ENZN)
20 Kingsbridge Road
Piscataway, NJ 08854
Phone: (732) 980-4500
Fax: (732) 980-5911
Web site: www.enzon.com
Business Summary: Enzon develops and commercializes enhanced therapeutics through its two proprietary platform technologies: polyethylene glycol (PEG) and single-chain antibody (SCA). Its PEG technology improves delivery, safety, and efficacy of proteins and small molecules. Single-chain antibody technology is used to discover and produce molecules that behave as antibodies that are as beneficial as, but without some of the limitations of, monoclonal antibodies.

Epoch Pharmaceuticals (NASDAQ:EBIO)
12277 134th Court Northeast, Suite 110
Redmond, WA 98052
Phone: (425) 821-7535
Fax: (425) 821-7539
Web site: www.epochpharm.com
Business Summary: The company sells technologies that enhance the study of genes. Epoch designs and synthesizes oligonucleotides (synthetic DNA strands) that are modified to bind more selectively with their target genes. Epoch also develops molecular tools and reagents for improved genetic sequence analysis.

Exelixis, Inc. (NASDAQ:EXEL)
170 Harbor Way
South San Francisco, CA 94083
Phone: (650) 837-7000
Fax: (650) 825-2205
Web site: www.exelixis.com
Business Summary: Exelixis systematically studies simple organisms, such as fruit flies, nematodes, mice, zebrafish, and simple plants, to rapidly and efficiently determine gene function and es-

tablish its commercial utility in humans and other commercially important biological systems. The company has significant opportunities to develop novel products for the life sciences industries that include companies in the pharmaceutical, agrochemical, agricultural, consumer products, and health care businesses.

Genaissance Pharmaceuticals Inc. (NASDAQ:GNSC)
Five Science Park
New Haven, CT 06511
Phone: (203) 773-1450
Fax: (203) 562-9377
Web site: www.genaissance.com
Business Summary: Genaissance Pharmaceuticals develops technology that allows custom drug development through the use of population genomics and informatics. Population genomics are used to find inherited differences, known as markers, that help predict which patients will benefit from a drug. Genaissance sees this technology as a solution for developing clinical trials that are more effective. This technology is sold to pharmaceuticals with a key benefit of increasing sales of drugs that correlate the response with the patient's inherited responses. This improves development, marketing, and prescriptive application of drugs.

Gene Logic, Inc. (NASDAQ:GLGC)
708 Quince Orchard Road
Gaithersburg, MD 20878
Phone: (301) 987-1700
Fax: (301) 987-1701
Web site: www.genelogic.com
Business Summary: Gene Logic provides products and services used in gene expression information, data management and bioinformatics software, and pharmacogenomics.

Genencor International Inc. (NASDAQ:GCOR)
925 Page Mill Road
Palo Alto, CA 94304

Phone: (650) 846-7500
Fax: (650) 845-6500
Web site: www.genencor.com
Business Summary: Genencor develops genetically based biotech products for use in the industrial chemical and agriculture markets using its proprietary technology platforms including gene discovery and functional genomics. The company has about 3,000 patents and patent applications and delivers over 250 products to customers worldwide. In 1999, Genencor had over $300 million in revenues.

Genentech, Inc. (NYSE:DNA)
One DNA Way
South San Francisco, CA 94080
Phone: (650) 225-1000
Fax: (650) 225-6000
Web site: www.gene.com
Business Summary: Genentech uses human genetic information to discover, develop, manufacture, and market human pharmaceuticals. The company has a strong track record, as 13 of the approved products of biotechnology stem from its science. The products include Herceptin, Rituxan, Activase, Protropin, Nutropin, Nutropin AQ, Nutropin Depot, Pulmozyme, and Actimmune.

Genome Therapeutics Corporation (NASDAQ:GENE)
100 Beaver Street
Waltham, MA 02453
Phone: (781) 398-2300
Fax: (781) 893-9535
Web site: www.genomecorp.com
Business Summary: The company identifies and validates drug targets for many serious diseases using its integrated platform technologies, bioinformatics, disease gene identification, and functional genomics. Genome Therapeutics partners with

other companies to develop therapeutic, vaccine, and diagnostic products.

Gemini Genomics plc (NASDAQ:GMNI)
162 Science Park, Milton Road
Cambridge CB4 0GH, UK
Phone: (781) 449-4328
Web site: www.gemini-genomics.com
Business Summary: Gemini Genomics identifies characteristic relationships between human genes and human health and disease. The company is a development-stage company.

Genzyme General Division (NASDAQ:GENZ)
One Kendall Square
Cambridge, MA 02139
Phone: (617) 252-7500
Fax: (617) 494-6561
Web site: www.genzyme.com
Business Summary: Genzyme develops and markets therapeutic and diagnostic products and services for treatment of genetic diseases. Genzyme consists of the Therapeutics and Diagnostics business units. The Therapeutics business unit develops and markets products for genetic diseases. The Diagnostics unit develops, markets, and distributes in vitro diagnostic products and genetic testing services. The company is a division of Genzyme Corporation and has its own common stock that is a tracking stock intended to reflect its value and financial performance.

Genzyme Molecular Oncology (NASDAQ:GZMO)
One Kendall Square
Cambridge, MA 02139
Phone: (617) 252-7500
Fax: (617) 494-6561
Web site: www.genzyme.com

Business Summary: Genzyme Molecular Oncology is a division of Genzyme Corporation that develops cancer products. Its principal products are in three therapeutic classes: vaccines, angiogenesis inhibitors that treat cancer by preventing the formation and development of blood vessels that tumors require for growth, and pathway regulators that treat cancer by regulating the metabolic processes in cancer cells necessary for tumor cells to grow and survive.

Genzyme Transgenics Corporation (NASDAQ:GZTC)
175 Crossing Boulevard
Framingham, MA 01702
Phone: (508) 620-9700
Fax: (508) 872-9080
Web site: www.transgenics.com
Business Summary: Genzyme Transgenics develops recombinant proteins for therapeutic and other biomedical uses. It has produced over 60 proteins, including many monoclonal antibodies/Ig fusion proteins. Its products are useful in treatment of heparin resistance in patients undergoing cardiopulmonary bypass procedures. The company does preclinical testing for effectiveness and safety and in vitro testing and formulation for other biotechnology companies.

Gilead Sciences, Inc. (NASDAQ:GILD)
333 Lakeside Drive
Foster City, CA 94404
Phone: (650) 574-3000
Fax: (650) 578-9264
Web site: www.gilead.com
Business Summary: Gilead Sciences provides accelerated solutions for patients and the people who care for them. The company's four products that have been approved by the FDA are AmbiSome, a drug for treating and preventing life-threatening fungal infections; Tamiflu, a drug for treating influenza; Vis-

tide, a drug for treating CMV retinitis in AIDS patients; and DaunoXome, a drug for treating AIDS-related Kaposi's sarcoma.

Human Genome Sciences (NASDAQ:HGSI)
9410 Key West Avenue
Rockville, MD 20850
Phone: (301) 309-8504
Fax: (301) 309-8512
Web site: www.hgsi.com
Business Summary: Human Genome Sciences develops proteins for treatment and diagnosis of human genetic diseases. Its gene-sequencing library is one of the largest databases of human genes and microbes.

Hyseq, Inc. (NASDAQ:HYSQ)
670 Almanor Avenue
Sunnyvale, CA 94086
Phone: (408) 524-8100
Fax: (408) 524-8106
Web site: sbh.com
Business Summary: Hyseq researches and develops anti-inflammatory and anticlotting drugs. The company uses its proprietary technology for therapeutic and diagnostic target discovery, in pharmacogenomics and polymorphism analysis, and with its DNA analysis tools.

ICOS Corporation (NASDAQ:ICOS)
22021 20th Avenue Southeast
Bothell, WA 98021
Phone: (425) 485-1900
Fax: (425) 485-1911
Web site: www.icos.com
Business Summary: The company develops pharmaceuticals by seeking intervention points in acute and chronic disease processes that may lead to more specific and efficacious drugs. Its drugs

include Pafase, a recombinant form of a naturally occurring human serum enzyme, and IC14, a monoclonal antibody. ICOS has collaborations that help offset the financial risk of development while retaining product rights.

IDEC Pharmaceuticals Corporation (NASDAQ:IDPH)
3030 Callan Road
San Diego, CA 92121
Phone: (858) 431-8500
Fax: (858) 431-8750
Web site: www.idecpharm.com
Business Summary: IDEC researches, develops, and commercializes therapies for the treatment of cancer and autoimmune and inflammatory diseases such as B-cell non-Hodgkin's lymphomas, psoriasis, rheumatoid arthritis, and lupus.

IGEN International Inc. (NASDAQ:IGEN)
16020 Industrial Drive
Gaithersburg, MD 20877
Phone: (301) 869-9800
Fax: (301) 230-0158
Web site: www.igen.com
Business Summary: IGEN develops and markets products using its ORIGEN technology, which permits detection and measurement of biological substances. The company offers assay development and other services in the performance of analytical testing in the life science, clinical diagnostic, and industrial markets.

Illumina, Inc. (NASDAQ:ILMN)
9390 Towne Centre Drive, Suite 200
San Diego, CA 92121
Phone: (858) 587-4290
Fax: (858) 587-4297
Web site: www.illumina.com

Business Summary: Illumina develops tools for the large-scale analysis of genetic variation and function. These tools enable the development of personalized medicine, a key goal of genomics. Its BeadArray cassettes are reagent kits for analyzing variation in genetic sequences and instruments that automatically read data from the BeadArray cassettes.

Imclone Systems, Inc. (NASDAQ:IMCL)
180 Varick Street
New York, NY 10014
Phone: (212) 645-1405
Fax: (212) 645-2054
Web site: www.imclone.com
Business Summary: Imclone Systems develops cancer treatments, specifically focused on growth factor inhibitors, therapeutic cancer vaccines, and angiogenesis inhibitors. Its drugs include a therapeutic monoclonal antibody that inhibits stimulation of a receptor for growth factors on which certain solid tumors depend in order to grow and angiogenesis inhibitors for the treatment of various kinds of cancer.

Immtech International (NASDAQ:IMMT)
150 Fairway Drive, Suite 150
Vernon Hills, IL 60061
Phone: (847) 573-0033
Fax: (847) 573-8288
Web site: www.informagen.com
Business Summary: Immtech develops therapeutic products for the treatment of opportunistic diseases and cancer in patients with compromised immune responses.

Immunex Corporation (NASDAQ:IMNX)
51 University Street
Seattle, WA 98101

Phone: (206) 587-0430
Fax: (206) 587-0606
Web site: www.immunex.com
Business Summary: Immunex discovers, develops, manufactures, and markets therapeutic products for the treatment of human diseases, including cancer, infectious diseases, and immunological disorders, such as rheumatoid arthritis, cancer, multiple sclerosis, heart disease, and asthma.

Immunomedics, Inc. (NASDAQ:IMMU)
300 American Road
Morris Plains, NJ 07950
Phone: (973) 605-8200
Fax: (973) 605-8282
Web site: www.immunomedics.com
Business Summary: Immunomedics uses proprietary technology in antibody selection, modification, and chemistry to develop products that detect and treat cancers and other diseases. Immunomedics is focused on highly specific monoclonal antibodies designed to deliver radioisotopes, chemotherapeutic agents, toxins, dyes, or other substances to a specific disease site or organ system.

Incyte Genomics, Inc. (NASDAQ:INCY)
3160 Porter Drive
Palo Alto, CA 94304
Phone: (650) 855-0555
Fax: (650) 855-0572
Web site: www.incyte.com
Business Summary: Incyte provides genomic information–based products and services. The company's products and services include database products, genomic data management software tools, microarray-based gene expression services, genomic reagents, and related services. Incyte assists pharmaceutical and biotechnology companies and academic researchers in the

understanding of disease and the discovery and development of new drugs.

Insmed Incorporated (NASDAQ:INSM)
800 East Leigh Street
Richmond, VA 23219
Phone: (804) 828-6893
Fax: (804) 828-6894
Web site: www.insmed.com
Business Summary: Insmed develops products to treat metabolic and endocrine-related conditions. One of the company's products is INS-1, a naturally occurring and orally active insulin sensitizer. It is being developed for type II diabetes and polycystic ovary syndrome (PCOS). SomatoKine is Insmed's human recombinant equivalent to complex of the hormone, insulin-like growth factor-I (IGF-I) and its primary binding protein (IGFBP3) for use in bone repair following hip fracture.

Integra LifeSciences Corp (NASDAQ:IART)
105 Morgan Lane
Plainsboro, NJ 08536
Phone: (609) 275-0500
Fax: (609) 799-3297
Web site: www.integra-ls.com
Business Summary: Integra develops, manufactures, and markets medical devices, implants, and biomaterials used in neurosurgery, neurotrauma, and related critical care. The company's tissue regeneration technology is used to treat soft tissue and orthopedic conditions.

InterMune Pharmaceuticals (NASDAQ:ITMN)
1710 Gilbreth Road, Suite 301
Burlingame, CA 94010
Phone: (650) 409-2020
Fax: (650) 259-0774

Web site: www.intermune.com

Business Summary: InterMune develops products used in the treatment of serious pulmonary and infectious diseases and congenital disorders. The company has the exclusive U.S. license rights to ActImmune for a range of diseases, including life-threatening congenital disorders of the immune system, such as chronic granulomatous disease, osteopetrosis (a bone overgrowth disorder), and pulmonary fibrosis. InterMune also sells products for infections such as tuberculosis and various systemic fungal infections.

Introgen Therapeutics Inc. (NASDAQ:INGN)
301 Congress Avenue, Suite 1850
Austin, TX 78701
Phone: (512) 708-9310
Fax: (512) 708-9311
Web site: www.introgen.com

Business Summary: Introgen is a world leader in the development of gene-based therapeutics with more than 115 pending and issued patents for a variety of viral and nonviral delivery systems, vector constructs, and targeting systems. The company has treated hundreds of cancer patients in advanced clinical trials being conducted throughout the United States, Canada, and Europe. With the poor efficacy and debilitating side effects of current treatments, Introgen's low-toxicity approach to cancer treatment has drawn global interest from oncologists.

ISIS Pharmaceuticals, Inc. (NASDAQ:ISIP)
2292 Faraday Avenue
Carlsbad, CA 92008
Phone: (760) 931-9200
Fax: (760) 931-9639
Web site: www.isisph.com

Business Summary: ISIS's genomics-based drug discovery is focused on RNA and has established a dominant position in RNA research. RNA is a novel target for drug discovery. The company has created two technologies through its expertise in molecular and cellular biology, medicinal chemistry, RNA biochemistry, bioinformatics, pharmacology, and clinical development. In addition to its antisense and Ibis technologies, ISIS has several drugs in the development pipeline.

Keryx Biopharmaceuticals (NASDAQ:KERX)
Kiryat Mada 5, Har Hotzvim
Jerusalem 91326, Israel
Phone: (617) 512-6883
Fax: (978) 689-4267
Web site: www.keryxbiopharm.com
Business Summary: Keryx uses data derived from the mapping of the human genome to derive drug candidates that target the regulation of protein kinases. Keryx is licensed to develop sulodexide for the treatment of diabetic nephropathy.

Large Scale Biology Corporation (NASDAQ:LSBC)
3333 Vaca Valley Parkway, Suite 1000
Vacaville, CA 95688
Phone: (707) 446-5501
Fax: (707) 446-3917
Web site: www.lsbc.com
Business Summary: Large Scale Biology uses its proteomics and functional genomics technologies to develop products and establish commercial collaborations with pharmaceutical, biotechnology, chemical, and other life sciences companies. The company's opportunities for other commercial products include drug targets, therapeutics, diagnostics, and the evaluation of drug effectiveness and toxicity.

Lexicon Genetics, Inc. (NASDAQ:LEXG)
4000 Research Forest Drive
The Woodlands, TX 77381

Phone: (281) 364-0100
Fax: (281) 296-0749
Web site: www.lexgen.com
Business Summary: Lexicon uses gene-trapping technology to discover thousands of genes and to expand its OmniBank library of
tens of thousands of knockout mouse clones for drug discovery.
Its Internet exchange, Lexgen.com, allows researchers to access
the company's OmniBank library and to form collaborations
with the company. Lexicon generates fees and royalties and milestone payments from the commercialization of pharmaceutical
products developed using its genomics technologies.

Ligand Pharmaceuticals (NASDAQ:LGND)
10275 Science Center Drive
San Diego, CA 92121
Phone: (858) 550-7500
Fax: (858) 550-1826
Web site: www.ligand.com
Business Summary: Ligand develops and markets new drugs for
patients with cancer, men's and women's health and skin diseases,
as well as osteoporosis, metabolic, cardiovascular, and inflammatory diseases. The company strives to develop drugs that are more
effective and/or safer than existing therapies and that are more
convenient and cost effective.

Lynx Therapeutics, Inc. (NASDAQ:LYNX)
25861 Industrial Blvd.
Hayward, CA 94545
Phone: (510) 670-9300
Fax: (510) 670-9302
Web site: www.lynxcalif.com
Business Summary: Lynx develops technologies for the discovery
of gene expression patterns and genomic variations important to
the pharmaceutical, biotechnology, and agricultural industries.

The company's Megaclone is a unique and proprietary cloning procedure that transforms a sample containing millions of DNA molecules into one made up of millions of microbeads, each of which carries approximately 100,000 copies of one of the DNA molecules in the sample. With this technology, Lynx gains gene sequence and expression information that provides disease or trait association information.

Martek Biosciences Corporation (NASDAQ:MATK)
6480 Dobbin Road
Columbia, MD 21045
Phone: (410) 740-0081
Fax: (410) 740-2985
Web site: www.martekbio.com
Business Summary: Martek develops products derived from microalgae that are nutritional oils used as ingredients in infant formula and foods and as ingredients in, and encapsulated for use as, dietary supplements.

Maxygen, Inc. (NASDAQ:MAXY)
515 Galveston Drive
Redwood City, CA 94063
Phone: (650) 298-5300
Fax: (650) 364-2715
Web site: www.maxygen.com
Business Summary: Maxygen directs molecular evolution to produce new, modified genes for specific commercial uses. The company has strategic alliances with government agencies and companies to develop vaccines, industrial enzymes, agricultural enzymes, antibiotics, and chemical bioprocessing.

Maxim Pharmaceuticals (NASDAQ:MAXM)
8899 University Center Lane, Suite 400
San Diego, CA 92122

Phone: (858) 453-4040
Fax: (858) 453-5005
Web site: www.maxim.com
Business Summary: Maxim acquires a new generation of drugs, therapies, and vaccines for cancer, infectious diseases, and topical disorders. Its lead product, Maxamine, is in three phase 3 cancer clinical trials in 12 countries around the world. A market launch of Maxamine is planned for early 2001 in the United States and late 2001 in certain foreign countries.

Medarex, Inc. (NASDAQ:MEDX)
707 State Road #206
Princeton, NJ 08854
Phone: (609) 430-2880
Fax: (908) 713-6002
Web site: www.medarex.com
Business Summary: Medarex develops therapeutic products for cancer, autoimmune disease, secondary cataracts, and other life-threatening and debilitating diseases based on proprietary technology in the field of immunology. The company's therapeutic products are currently under development and will need the approval of the FDA prior to commercial distribution. The company's human antibody discovery technology includes the Hu-MAb-Mouse and Kirin's Tc Mouse technologies, which use genetically engineered mice to produce fully human monoclonal antibodies.

Medicines Company (NASDAQ:MDCO)
One Cambridge Center
Cambridge, MA 02142
Phone: (617) 225-9099
Fax: (617) 225-2329
Web site: www.themedco.com
Business Summary: The company acquires, develops, and commercializes late-stage-development biopharmaceutical products.

Its primary product is Angiomax and is used in the treatment of patients with unstable angina undergoing coronary balloon angioplasty. The company received notification from the FDA indicating early approval with a target for marketing by mid-2001.

MedImmune, Inc. (NASDAQ:MEDI)
35 West Watkins Mill Road
Gaithersburg, MD 20878
Phone: (301) 417-0770
Fax: (301) 527-4200
Web site: www.medimmune.com
Business Summary: Medimmune has six products on the market that address significant medical needs in areas such as infectious diseases, immune regulation, and oncology. Synagis, a monoclonal antibody for prevention of lower respiratory disease caused by syncytial virus, accounted for 82 percent of 1999 sales. CytoGam, which accounted for 10 percent of 1999 sales, is an immune globulin product enriched in antibodies against cytomegalovirus and is marketed for prophylaxis against cytomegalovirus disease associated with transplantation of kidney, lung, liver, pancreas, and heart.

Millennium Pharmaceutical (NASDAQ:MLNM)
75 Sidney Street
Cambridge, MA 02139
Phone: (617) 679-7000
Fax: (617) 374-9379
Web site: www.mlnm.com
Business Summary: The company develops breakthrough drugs and predictive medicine products using an integrated approach that the company calls "gene to patient." Millenium has strategic alliances with major pharmaceutical and biotechnology companies to discover, develop, and commercialize a broad range of therapeutic and predictive medicine products. Its three major fields of emphasis are cancer, metabolic diseases, and inflammation. Other

products are developed in the treatment of infectious diseases, cardiovascular diseases, and diseases of the central nervous system.

Myriad Genetics, Inc. (NASDAQ:MYGN)
320 Wakara Way
Salt Lake City, UT 84108
Phone: (801) 584-3600
Fax: (801) 584-3640
Web site: www.myriad.com
Business Summary: The company develops therapeutic and diagnostic products based on the biological pathways of major common disease genes. Its ProNet identifies protein-protein interactions. Myriad has three significant commercial opportunities: the development and marketing of molecular diagnostic and information services, the marketing of subscriptions to the ProNet database of protein interactions, and the development of therapeutic products for the treatment and prevention of major diseases associated with these genes and their biochemical pathways.

Nanogen, Inc. (NASDAQ:NGEN)
10398 Pacific Center Court
San Diego, CA 92121
Phone: (858) 410-4600
Fax: (858) 410-7718
Web site: www.nanogen.com
Business Summary: Nanogen's products integrate advanced microelectronics and molecular biology into a platform technology with broad commercial applications. The NanoChip molecular biology workstation, comprised of two automated instruments and a consumable cartridge, is an integrated bioassay system. The NanoChip is a useful tool for rapid identification and precision analysis of biological test samples containing charged molecules.

NeoRx Corporation (NASDAQ:NERX)
410 West Harrison Street
Seattle, WA 98119

Phone: (206) 281-7001
Fax: (206) 298-9442
Web site: www.neorx.com
Business Summary: NeoRx develops drugs for treatment of cancer. The company improves the effect of and reduces the toxicity of competitors' drugs. Using its Pretarget technology, NeoRx products deliver the therapeutic product to the tumor sites, sparing normal tissue. NeoRx is currently making other fusion proteins that may be used to treat cancers other than lymphoma.

Neurogen Corporation (NASDAQ:NRGN)
35 Northeast Industrial Road
Branford, CT 06405
Phone: (203) 488-8201
Fax: (203) 481-8683
Web site: www.nrgn.com
Business Summary: Neurogen discovers and develops drugs that are designed to selectively regulate the communication between cells in order to influence cell function associated with a given disorder.

Novavax, Inc. (AMEX:NOX)
8320 Guilford Road
Columbia, MD 21046
Phone: (301) 854-3900
Fax: (301) 854-3901
Web site: www.novavax.com
Business Summary: Novavax researches and develops proprietary delivery and vaccine technologies for drugs. The company uses nonphospholipid structures to deliver a wide variety of therapeutic products, including hormones, antibacterial and antiviral products, and vaccines. Novovax does contract research and development and phase 1 and phase 2 vaccine manufacturing of human vaccines for the company's own use, for government laboratories, and for other vaccine companies.

Northfield Laboratories (NASDAQ:NFLD)
1560 Sherman Avenue, Suite 1000
Evanston, IL 60201
Phone: (847) 864-3500
Fax: (847) 864-3577
Web site: www.frb.bsmg.com
Business Summary: Northfield Laboratories develops safe and effective alternatives to transfused blood for use in the treatment of acute blood loss. The company's blood substitute product, Poly-Heme, is a solution of chemically modified hemoglobin derived from human blood. PolyHeme is universally compatible and, accordingly, should not require blood typing prior to infusion. It also has a longer shelf life than blood.

Orchid Biosciences, Inc. (NASDAQ:ORCH)
303 College Road East
Princeton, NJ 08540
Phone: (609) 750-2200
Fax: (617) 542-2241
Web site: www.orchid.com
Business Summary: Orchid Biosciences provides products, services, and technologies for single nucleotide polymorphism (SNP) scoring and genetic diversity analyses. SNP-IT, its proprietary SNP analysis technology, generates highly accurate, cost-effective SNP information. Orchid provides DNA testing through its GeneScreen facilities that conduct paternity, forensics, and transplantation testing.

Ortec International Inc. (NASDAQ:ORTC)
3960 Broadway
New York, NY 10032
Phone: (212) 740-6999
Fax: (212) 740-6963
Web site: www.ortecinternational.com

Business Summary: Ortec develops Composite Cultered Skin, which acts as a dressing that simulates the repair, replacement, and regeneration of human skin. Composite Cultered Skin is intended to be utilized for the treatment of numerous skin wounds, including venous stasis ulcers, autograft donor sites, diabetic ulcers, and damage from some diseases with small patient populations. The product helps stimulate wound closure.

OSI Pharmaceuticals, Inc. (NASDAQ:OSIP)
106 Charles Lindbergh Boulevard
Uniondale, NY 11553
Phone: (516) 222-0023
Fax: (516) 222-0114
Web site: www.osip.com
Business Summary: The company researches and develops pharmaceuticals that are novel, small-molecule drug candidates for commercialization by major pharmaceutical companies. OSI is focused primarily in the areas of cancer, diabetes, and cosmeceuticals and G-protein coupled receptor (GPCR) directed drug discovery.

Paradigm Genetics, Inc. (NASDAQ:PDGM)
104 Alexander Drive
Research Triangle Park, NC 27709
Phone: (919) 425-3000
Fax: (919) 544-8094
Web site: www.paragen.com
Business Summary: Paradigm Genetics, Inc., industrializes gene function determination in an assembly-line manner that generates information used to develop products. Products are developed in four sectors of the global economy: crop production, nutrition, human health, and industrial products. Its GeneFunction Factory studies the functions of genes in selected plants and fungi. This industrial-scale laboratory helps in the discovery and modification

of genes and the understanding of the consequences and reliability of the functions of modified genes.

PE Corporation-Celera Genomics (NYSE:CRA)
761 Main Avenue
Norwalk, CT 06859
Phone: (203) 762-1000
Fax: (203) 762-6000
Web site: www.celera.com
Business Summary: Celera Genomics generates, sells, and supports genomic information and data management and analysis software. The company's customers apply this information in pharmaceutical and life sciences industries to the specific drugs they are developing. Celera has emerged as a leader in functional genomics, particularly proteomics and personalized health/medicine.

Progenics Pharmaceuticals (NASDAQ:PGNX)
777 Old Saw Mill River Road
Tarrytown, NY 10591
Phone: (914) 789-2800
Fax: (914) 789-2817
Web site: www.progenics.com
Business Summary: Progenics develops and commercializes products for the treatment and prevention of cancer and viral and other life-threatening diseases. It uses its immunology expertise to develop biopharmaceuticals that induce an immune response or that mimic natural immunity in order to fight cancers, such as malignant melanoma, and viral diseases, such as HIV infection.

Protein Design Labs, Inc. (NASDAQ:PDLI)
34801 Campus Drive
Fremont, CA 94555
Phone: (510) 574-1400
Web site: www.pdl.com

Business Summary: Protein Design Labs develops monoclonal antibodies for the prevention and treatment of disease. The company's first humanized antibody product, Zenapax (daclizumab), which is designed to prevent kidney transplant rejection, has been licensed to Hoffmann-La Roche Inc.

Qiagen N.V. (NASDAQ:QGENF)
Spoorstraat 50
5911 KJ Venlo, Netherlands
Phone: (212) 696-4455
Fax: (212) 696-9180
Web site: www.noonanrusso.com
Business Summary: Qiagen produces and distributes biotechnology products for the separation and purification of nucleic acids (DNA/RNA). The company also sells robotic equipment to be used with their products.

Quidel Corporation (NASDAQ:QDEL)
10165 McKeller Court
San Diego, CA 92121
Phone: (858) 552-1100
Fax: (858) 453-4338
Web site: www.quidel.com
Business Summary: Quidel develops, manufactures, and markets point-of-care rapid diagnostic tests for the detection and management of a variety of medical conditions and illnesses. These products provide accurate, rapid, and cost-effective diagnosis so that treatment can be determined before the patient leaves the doctor's office.

Quintiles Transnational (NASDAQ:QTRN)
4709 Creekstone Drive, Suite 200
Durham, NC 27703
Phone: (919) 998-2000

Fax: (919) 941-9113
Web site: www.quintiles.com
Business Summary: Quintiles Transnational is a full-service contract research, sales, marketing, and health care policy consulting and health information management services company to the global pharmaceutical, biotechnology, medical device, and health care industries. The company provides a broad range of contract services to help its clients reduce the length of time from the beginning of development to peak sales of a new drug or medical device.

Regeneration Technologies, Inc. (NASDAQ:RTIX)
One Innovation Drive
Alachua, FL 32615
Phone: (904) 418-8888
Fax: (904) 462-1548
Web site: www.regenerationtechnologies.com
Business Summary: Regeneration uses natural human tissue and innovative technologies to repair and promote the healing of human bone and other human tissues. The company provides a wide range of healing and natural tissue products to a broad market. The company distributes and processes allografts in the United States designed for specific surgical purposes. Its BioCleanse system is the only safe, single-system multiple-donor processing system.

Regeneron Pharmaceuticals (NASDAQ:REGN)
777 Old Saw Mill River Road
Tarrytown, NY 10591
Phone: (914) 347-7000
Fax: (914) 347-2113
Web site: www.regpha.com
Business Summary: Regeneron discovers and develops therapeutic drugs for the treatment of degenerative neurologic diseases, obesity, rheumatoid arthritis, cancer, allergies, asthma, ischemia, and other diseases and disorders of serious medical conditions.

Ribozyme Pharmaceuticals (NASDAQ:RZYM)
2950 Wilderness Place
Boulder, CO 80301
Phone: (303) 449-6500
Fax: (303) 449-6995
Web site: www.rpi.com
Business Summary: Ribozyme develops products and services based on the potential of ribozymes. Ribozymes are engineered molecules that have the ability to cleave RNA, including mRNA, and thereby selectively inhibit protein production. Its products are used in the treatment of solid tumor cancers.

Rosetta Inpharmatics, Inc. (NASDAQ:RSTA)
12040 115th Avenue Northeast
Kirkland, WA 98034
Phone: (425) 820-8900
Fax: (425) 821-5354
Web site: www.rii.com
Business Summary: Rosetta has DNA technologies that obtain extensive knowledge of compound and drug target activities in any cell type. The company sells tools and consulting services, including analysis of their proprietary DNA microarrays and advanced molecular biology techniques that support pharmaceutical, biotech, and agriculture companies. Revenue is produced through its technologies as separate components or as an integrated informational genomics system and through professional consulting services.

Sangamo Biosciences, Inc. (NASDAQ:SGMO)
501 Canal Boulevard, Suite A100
Richmond, CA 94804
Phone: (510) 970-6000
Fax: (510) 236-8951
Web site: www.sangamo.com

Business Summary: The company develops novel transcription factors for the regulation of gene expression. Sangamo's Universal Gene Recognition technology platform enables the engineering of a class of transcription factors known as zinc finger DNA-binding proteins that can control gene expression and, consequently, cell function.

SangStat Medical Corporation (NASDAQ:SANG)
6300 Dumbarton Circle
Fremont, CA 94555
Phone: (510) 789-4300
Fax: (510) 789-4209
Web site: www.sangstat.com
Business Summary: SangStat develops products in the transplantation, immunology, and hematology/oncology areas. The company's products improve the outcome of organ and bone marrow transplantation. SangStat has broadened its product development to include therapies for inflammation, hematology, and oncology.

Sequenom, Inc. (NASDAQ:SQNM)
11555 Sorrento Valley Road
San Diego, CA 92121
Phone: (858) 350-0345
Fax: (858) 350-3044
Web site: www.sequenom.com
Business Summary: The company develops technology for use in the field of industrial genomics. Sequenom has developed a highly accurate, high-throughput, and cost-effective technology that addresses the demand for large-scale SNP analysis using mass spectrometry. The technology represents significant potential for cost control.

Scios Inc. (NASDAQ:SCIO)
820 West Maude Avenue
Sunnyvale, CA 94086

Phone: (408) 616-8200
Fax: (408) 616-8257
Web site: www.sciosinc.com
Business Summary: Scios develops and sells human therapeutics based on its capabilities in both protein-based and small-molecule drug discovery and development. The company's primary interests are the areas of cardiorenal and inflammatory disorders and Alzheimer's disease.

Synaptic Pharmaceutical (NASDAQ:SNAP)
215 College Road
Paramus, NJ 07652
Phone: (201) 261-1331
Fax: (201) 261-0623
Web site: www.synapticcorp.com
Business Summary: Synaptic develops enabling technology called "human receptor-targeted drug design technology." The company is utilizing this technology in its genomics program to discover and clone the genes that code for human receptors. Synaptic uses its technology to discover the function of these receptors in the body and thus specific physiological disorders with which they may be associated. The company uses the cloned receptor genes to design compounds that can potentially be developed as drugs for treating these disorders.

Tanox, Inc. (NASDAQ:TNOX)
10301 Stella Link, Suite 110
Houston, TX 77025
Phone: (713) 578-4000
Fax: (713) 578-5002
Web site: www.tanox.com
Business Summary: Tanox identifies and develops therapeutic monoclonal antibodies for use in unmet medical needs in the areas of immunology, infectious diseases, and cancer. The company pioneered the use of monoclonal antibodies in the treatment

of allergies and asthma. Tanox collaborates with Novartis and Genentech in the development of treatments for allergic rhinitis (hay fever) and allergic asthma.

Telik, Inc. (NASDAQ:TELK)
750 Gateway Boulevard
South San Francisco, CA 94080
Phone: (650) 244-9303
Fax: (650) 244-9388
Web site: www.telik.com
Business Summary: Telik is focused on the discovery and development of small-molecule biopharmaceuticals for itself and its partners. Its principal areas of product development are oncology and diabetes. Telik's proprietary chemo informatics technology (TRAP) supplements existing drug discovery and optimization techniques, utilizing a probability-based approach for chemical classification and screening.

Teva Pharmaceutical Industries Limited (NASDAQ:TEVA)
5 Basel Street, P.O. Box 3190
Petach Tikva 49131, Israel
Phone: (212) 850-5600
Fax: (212) 850-5601
Web site: www.tevapharmusa.com
Business Summary: Teva Pharmaceutical produces drugs in all major therapeutic categories. The company produces branded and generic human pharmaceuticals in Israel and has an international impact through its Teva Pharmaceuticals USA and in Europe through the Pharmachemie group of companies it has acquired.

Texas BioTechnology Corporation (AMEX:TXB)
7000 Fannin, 20th Floor
Houston, TX 77030
Phone: (713) 796-8822

Fax: (713) 796-8232
Web site: www.tbc.com
Business Summary: Texas BioTechnology develops synthetic, small-molecule compounds for use in the treatment of vascular and related inflammatory diseases. Its research and development programs are focused on inhibitors that interrupt disease processes.

Titan Pharmaceuticals (AMEX:TTP)
400 Oyster Point Boulevard, Suite 505
South San Francisco, CA 94080
Phone: (650) 244-4990
Fax: (650) 244-4956
Web site: www.titanpharm.com
Business Summary: Titan is a biopharmaceutical company that develops proprietary therapeutics for the treatment of central nervous system disorders, cancer, and other serious and life-threatening diseases. Titan's products include an antipsychotic agent, Zomaril, for treatment of schizophrenia and related disorders; immunotherapeutic products for the treatment of cancer, such as CeaVac, TriAb, and TriGem; Pivanex, for the treatment of cancer by cellular differentiation; cell-based therapeutics intended for use in the treatment of neurologic diseases; and RB94, a gene therapy product for the treatment of cancer.

Transkaryotic Therapies (NASDAQ:TKTX)
195 Albany Street
Cambridge, MA 02139
Phone: (617) 349-0200
Fax: (617) 491-7903
Web site: www.tktx.com
Business Summary: Transkaryotic Therapies has three proprietary development platforms: Gene-Activated proteins, Niche Protein products, and Gene Therapy. Its products are for the treatment of anemia, Fabry disease, and hemophilia A.

Trimeris, Inc. (NASDAQ:TRMS)
4727 University Drive, Suite 100
Durham, NC 27707
Phone: (919) 419-6050
Fax: (919) 419-6051
Web site: www.trimeris.com
Business Summary: Trimeris develops therapeutic agents that block viral infection by inhibiting viral fusion with host cells. The company produces potential drug candidates for production by other companies.

Valentis, Inc. (NASDAQ:VLTS)
863A Mitten Road
Burlingame, CA 94010
Phone: (650) 697-1900
Fax: (650) 652-1990
Web site: www.valentis.com
Business Summary: Valentis develops methodologies for biopharmaceutical delivery. It has proprietary gene delivery and gene expression systems and PEGylation technologies. The company has a broad array of technologies and intellectual property for the delivery of biopharmaceuticals, including genes, proteins, peptides, peptidomimetics, antibodies, and replicating and nonreplicating viruses.

Variagenics, Inc. (NASDAQ:VGNX)
60 Hampshire Street
Cambridge, MA 02139
Phone: (617) 588-5300
Fax: (617) 588-5399
Web site: www.variagenics.com
Business Summary: Variagenics develops and commercializes technologies related to pharmacogenomics.

Versicor Inc. (NASDAQ:VERS)
34790 Ardentech Court
Fremont, CA 94555

Phone: (510) 739-3000
Fax: (510) 739-3003
Web site: www.versicor.com
Business Summary: Versicor focuses on the development of drugs for the treatment of serious bacterial and fungal infections. Versicor looks for products with greater potency, improved effectiveness against resistant strains, and reduced toxicity than existing drugs.

Vertex Pharmaceuticals (NASDAQ:VRTX)
130 Waverly Street
Cambridge, MA 02139
Phone: (617) 577-6000
Fax: (617) 576-2109
Web site: www.vpharm.com
Business Summary: Vertex designs, develops, and sells small-molecule drugs for the treatment of viral diseases, cancer, auto-immune and inflammatory diseases, and neurological disorders. The company has significant collaborations with Glaxo Wellcome, Aventis, Schering AG (Germany), Eli Lilly, Kissei, and Taisho and has a large number of drug candidates in the pipeline.

Vical Incorporated (NASDAQ:VICL)
9373 Towne Centre Drive, Suite 100
San Diego, CA 92121
Phone: (858) 646-1100
Fax: (858) 646-1157
Web site: www.vical.com
Business Summary: Vical's products are based on the company's patented naked DNA gene transfer technologies for the prevention and treatment of life-threatening diseases. Products in phase 2 and phase 3 trials include the anticancer drug Allovectin-7 for use with the aggressive metastatic melanoma. The company has additional products in trials for patients with persistent or recurrent cancer of the head and neck and metastatic kidney cancer and for high-risk patients with locally confined prostate cancer.

Vion Pharmaceuticals, Inc. (NASDAQ:VION)
4 Science Park
New Haven, CT 06511
Phone: (203) 498-4210
Fax: (203) 498-4211
Web site: www.vionpharm.com
Business Summary: Vion Pharmaceuticals is engaged in research, development, and commercial development of drugs for the treatment of cancer. Promycin, Triapine, and Sulfonyl hydrazine are its three cancer therapeutics. Vion's unique drug delivery technology answers the challenge of effectively delivering cancer treatment drugs to tumors while sparing normal cells.

ViroLogic, Inc. (NASDAQ:VLGC)
270 East Grand Avenue
South San Francisco, CA 94080
Phone: (650) 635-1100
Fax: (650) 635-1111
Web site: www.virologic.com
Business Summary: ViroLogic develops and markets products with improved treatment of viral diseases. The company has developed a method to measure the impact of genetic mutations on drug resistance. Its proprietary PhenoSense technology tests drug resistance in viruses causing diseases like AIDS and hepatitis B and C. PhenoSense HIV tests the resistance of a patient's HIV to antiviral drugs, resulting in more effective treatment strategies.

Visible Genetics Inc. (NASDAQ:VGIN)
700 Bay Street, Suite 1000
Toronto, ON, Canada
Phone: (416) 813-3240
Fax: (416) 813-3250
Web site: www.visgen.com
Business Summary: The company manufactures and sells DNA sequencing systems that analyze genetic information. These sys-

tems employ DNA sequencing that enables the analysis in the clinical diagnostic laboratory of individual genetic variations with the result of improved treatment of selected diseases.

Vysis, Inc. (NASDAQ:VYSI)
3100 Woodcreek Drive
Downers Grove, IL 60515
Phone: (630) 271-7000
Fax: (630) 271-7008
Web site: www.vysis.com
Business Summary: Vysis, Inc., is a genomic disease management company that develops, commercializes, and markets clinical products that provide information critical to the evaluation and management of cancer, prenatal disorders, and other genetic diseases. The company distributes over 275 analyte-specific reagent and research products through its direct sales operations in the United States and a worldwide distribution network covering 59 countries.

XOMA Limited (NASDAQ:XOMA)
2910 Seventh Street
Berkeley, CA 94710
Phone: (510) 644-1170
Fax: (510) 644-0539
Web site: www.xoma.com
Business Summary: XOMA develops products to treat infectious diseases, immunologic and inflammatory disorders, and cancer. It works in collaboration with Genentech, Inc., and Allergan, Inc.

D

Glossary of Biotechnical Terms

This glossary is not meant to be all-inclusive. For further sources, see the bibliography.

A

adenine—One of the bases or building blocks in DNA. It is always paired with thymine.

amino acid—The building blocks of protein. There are 20 amino acids, and a group of them is known as a peptide. Groups of peptides form proteins. Amino acids pass through the cell membrane and are available for protein synthesis in this manner.

antibiotics—Drugs that kill or inhibit the growth of bacteria or fungi. Some antibiotics are effective against a broad spectrum of organisms, while others are specific. Penicillin was the first antibiotic isolated.

antibody—Protein molecule produced by special cells called lymphocytes in response to invasion by foreign substances, called antigens. Antibodies are specific for a single invader and attach to it, forming an antigen-antibody complex.

antigen—A substance that causes the production of antibodies by the immune system of an organism.

B

base—In the context of a DNA molecule, it is a compound that provides the connectivity necessary to hold the molecule together in the double helix. There are four bases: adenine, cytosine, guanine, and thymine. Specific base sequences make up genes.

biochemistry—The study of the processes involved in the chemical reactions of living organisms and their application. The study of structure and reactions of proteins, nucleic acids, carbohydrates, and lipids.

biology—The study of life, including all the life sciences: anatomy, biochemistry, cytology, zoology, botany, ecology, animal behavior, embryology, taxonomy, and plant breeding.

bioreactor—An instrument in which microorganisms are placed and given an artificial, usually sterile, environment with optimal conditions of temperature, humidity, and acidity. The organisms are fed a substrate and use it to produce the desired product. Bioreactors are the basic unit of production in biotechnology.

C

catalyst—A substance that speeds up a reaction but remains unchanged once the reaction is finished. An enzyme is the most commonly used catalyst in science.

cell—The basic unit of life. A membrane-bound unit capable of processes associated with life.

cell biology—The study of the processes inside a cell.

cell culture—Special preparations used to grow isolated cells in a test tube in the hopes of maintaining their specific characteristics alive for research or therapy.

codon—A group of three nitrogen bases in DNA, which is the functional unit of genes.

cystic fibrosis—An inherited condition in which a missing enzyme does not allow the lungs to clear mucus.

cytology—The study of cells, including function, appearance, and behavior.

cytosine—A DNA base that is always paired with guanine.

D

DNA—Deoxyribonucleic acid, a double-helix tridimensional structure composed of sugars, phosphates, and nitrogen bases that resides in the nucleus of all cells. DNA contains the genetic code of all organisms, with the exception of certain viruses.

double helix—The pattern of a DNA molecule. It resembles two entwined circular staircases.

E

endoplasmic reticulum—A membranous system of tubes and sacs found in eukaryotic cells. Its function is to store proteins made by ribosomes. *See* ribosome; eukaryote.

EST—The expressed sequence tag, the hallmark of genomics. ESTs are fragments of genes that can be sequenced and extrapolated in order to discover the gene's functions. The process was developed by J. Craig Venter, founder of the Institute for Genomics Research *(www.tigr.org)*.

eukaryote—Every organism that is not a bacteria or a cyanobacteria (blue-green algae) is a eukaryote. Eukaryotes have a clearly defined nucleus that contains DNA. Also present are organelles. *See* organelle; prokaryotes.

F

fermentation—A scientific process commonly known as brewing. In the context of biotechnology, it refers to the placement of organisms and nutrients in large vats with an optimized environment. The organisms then produce material that is filtered in order to obtain the desired product, which could be a medication or even protein used to make food.

G

gene—Unit of inherited material, carried in a strand of DNA and transcribed by RNA.

gene amplification—Laboratory technique in which selected portions of DNA from a single cell can be duplicated indefinitely until there is a large enough quantity to analyze. This is made possible by a process called polymerase chain reaction.

gene therapy—Proposed medical technique in which genetic defects are repaired by removing affected cells from the affected body and repairing them in the lab, to be reintroduced after repair. Of the over 500 people who have undergone gene therapy, none have been cured.

genetic disease—A disorder caused by a defective or partially defective gene or chromosome. There are 3,000 known genetic diseases in humans, including cystic fibrosis and Down's syndrome.

genetic engineering—The deliberate manipulation of genetic material by biochemical techniques. It is used in the creation of transgenic organisms, which carry genetic material from more than one species.

genetics—The study of heredity. Geneticists try to explain how characteristics get passed on from one generation to the next.

genome—The full complement of genes in one single chromosome. Also describes the genetic information in a single individual or the range of genes found in a given species.

genomics—The study of DNA with the hope of separating useful from nonuseful strands. The useful strands are those that contain genes or gene fragments that can be further studied, cataloged, and used.

guanine—A DNA base that is always paired with cytosine.

H

hybridoma—A highly specific antibody derived from a single clone. Hybridomas are used to produce highly reliable monoclonal antibodies, thus reducing the amount of contaminants in the desired product.

I

(the) ice maiden—A South American mummy whose DNA was studied, revealing that her tribe was related to North American natives.

immunology—The study of the immune system. The immune system makes up the body's defenses against foreign bodies, whether microscopic or not. Its main defenses are in the form of proteins called antibodies. The immune system can also make antibodies against itself and cause diseases classified as autoimmune.

M

microbiology—The study of microorganisms, including bacteria, viruses, fungi, protozoa, and yeasts.

microorganisms—Also known as microbes. Living organisms invisible to the naked eye but visible under a microscope.

mitochondria—Cell organelles that produce energy for the cell. Mitochondria also have their own DNA. This DNA is the basis for the theory for mitochondrial origin, which states that the organelles were derived from bacteria that took up residence in living cells in early evolutionary time. New mitochondria arise from division of existing mitochondria inside of cells.

molecular biology—A branch of biology that deals with molecules, such as proteins and DNA.

N

nucleic acids—Molecules found in the nucleus of a cell. DNA is a nucleic acid.

nucleus—The area of the cell that contains DNA. It is found only in eukaryotic cells, which are the type of cells found in humans.

O

organelle—A component of a cell. These "small organs" produce the cell's energy, function in the cell's metabolism, and are involved in protein synthesis. Some commonly known organelles are the mitochondria, the ribosomes, and the Golgi apparatus. Organelles are found only in eukaryotic cells, which are the type of cells found in humans.

P

physiology—The study of the function of cells or organisms.

plasmid—A naturally occurring form of genetic material found in bacteria. Plasmids are small circles of DNA that bacteria exchange with each other freely. They are thought to be the method through which bacteria become resistant to antibiotics. By making changes in plasmids, scientists create recombinant DNA.

prokaryotes—Another name for bacteria and blue-green algae. Compared to eukaryotes, prokaryotes do not have a well-defined nucleus and do not possess organelles. *See* eukaryote; organelle.

R

recombinant DNA—Refers to the creation of a new DNA molecule that results from the placement of a gene from another organism into the genome of the host in the hopes that the new genome will produce a specific compound. It is the basis for the production stage of biotechnology.

ribosome—A cell organelle where protein synthesis is carried out. Ribosomes are attached to an area of the cell called the endoplasmic reticulum. Ribosomes contain their own kind of RNA. *See* endoplasmic reticulum.

T

thymine—A DNA base that is always paired with adenine.

TIGR—The Institute for Genomics Research, a nonprofit research organization dedicated to studying genomics.

Z

zoology—The study of animals.

Bibliography

Beckner, Steven K. *Back from the Brink: The Greenspan Years.* New York: John Wiley & Sons, 1996.

Duarte, Joe. "Combining Sentiment Indicators for Timing Mutual Funds." *Stocks and Commodities,* January 1992.

Duarte, Joe, and Roland Burke. *After-Hours Trading Made Easy.* Roseville, California: Prima Publishing, 2000.

Elder, Alexander. *Trading for a Living.* New York: John Wiley & Sons, 1993.

Galbraith, John K. *A Short History of Financial Euphoria.* Whittle Books, 1990.

Greider, William. *Secrets of the Temple.* New York: Simon & Schuster, 1987.

Lindley, David, and Harvey Moore. *Webster's New World Dictionary of Science.* New York: Macmillan, 1998.

O'Neil, William J. *24 Essential Lessons for Investment Success.* New York: McGraw-Hill, 2000.

Smith, John E. *Biotechnology.* 3rd ed. Cambridge: Cambridge University Press, 1996.

Sperandeo, Victor, with T.S. Brown. *Trader Vic: Methods of a Wall Street Master.* New York: John Wiley & Sons, 1991.

Woodward, Bob. *The Agenda.* New York: Simon & Schuster, 1994.

Zweig, Martin E. *Martin Zweig's Winning on Wall Street.* New York: Warner Books, 1986.

Index